PUSHKIN
VERTIGO

The Mystery of the Crooked Man

'With a prickly protagonist and a plot that's twistier than a bag
full of corkscrews, this one will keep you guessing until the end'

FIONA LEITCH, AUTHOR OF *A CORNISH SEASIDE MURDER*

'As fresh and pithy as a ripe tangerine—a hoot from start
to finish. Tom Spencer has created a riotously funny crime
caper that Agatha Christie would have loved'

M.H. ECCLESTON, AUTHOR OF *THE TRUST*

The Mystery of the Crooked Man

TOM SPENCER

PUSHKIN
VERTIGO

Pushkin Vertigo
An imprint of Pushkin Press
Somerset House, Strand
London WC2R 1LA

First published by Pushkin Press in 2024

1 3 5 7 9 8 6 4 2

ISBN 13: 978-1-80533-510-8

Designed and typeset by Tetragon, London
Printed and bound in the United Kingdom by Clays Ltd, Elcograf S.p.A.

www.pushkinpress.com

To Elizabeth, Alistair and Linus

PART ONE

PART ONE

1

The call is coming from inside the house. As per bally usual.

The guttural voice promising to sever my thus-and-such and rip off my what-have-you. And, as always, describing the scene in minute detail—the white tiles on the kitchen wall with the scarlet trim. My disastrous brown dress with the puff sleeves and the smocking at the neck.

I'm here. You can't see me, but I'm here. I'm in the room.

It is 1980. Being eight years old, I am not at all sanguine about the whole thing; not like nowadays. There are no mobiles, no caller display. I need help, but no one is here. Heri, my brother, is in his room, nursing his wounds from his most recent playground beating. He is the kind of child who elects to go by the German 'Heribert' when his given name is 'Herbert', so you can see why he gets bullied. My mother Clara is off plundering one of the various bottles stashed around the house about which she thinks we do not know. When she finally hears my howls and arrives in the kitchen, I sob that the murderer must be phoning from right here, from the next room. She harrumphs and tells me there is no way to call your own phone number. (Which is true. I don't know how the killer is supposed to have managed it in those seventies horror films.) She takes the phone from me and holds it to her ear. As always, nothing, only the dial tone. I am entirely hysterical, but Clara has dealt with my nonsense too many times. 'Why must you always lie and lie?' she yells. 'Normal children do not lie and lie and lie!' She cuffs me on the back of the head with the handset, which is hefty and made of hard plastic, and tells me she does not want to see me again until the morning. No dinner for Agatha again.

I'm right here with you.

I don't have a name for the Crooked Man yet, but I am already becoming intimately familiar with his ways.

I was in my small office, the smallest one at the Neele Archive, thirty-seven years later. I was trying to placate a headache that had been coming on all morning, while waiting for Ian, my boss, to telephone with the good news. Agatha Dorn, Curator of Prose! That was what I was about to become.

What's the Neele Archive? I hear you ask. And what's a Curator of Prose, for that matter? Well, I suppose I shall educate you if I must. The Neele is like a fancy library in the heart of the City of London, housed in the remaining part of a row of terraced Georgian houses that the German bombs managed to miss during the Blitz. Only, where your ordinary library has large-print editions of romance novels, we have first editions, holograph manuscripts, and other rare items of scholarly interest. Where your ordinary library has old ladies checking out lurid thrillers, we have celebrated academics from around the world visiting our collections. And we don't let them check out anything. They have to work in our reading rooms, under the beady eyes of our curators.

The curators! It has, you see, to be somebody's job to look after the collections—to handle donations—to search out and purchase new items—to create coherent collections around which we can structure exhibitions and on which we can build our reputation. And that was what I was waiting to hear that I had become.

If I were to look over at the door, I would catch my reflection in the little window that looks out onto the Neele's main hallway. When I've had a couple of gins-and-water, I like to think I resemble a taller, bonier Fiona Shaw. When I'm hideously sober, which I am now, I have a less flattering opinion of my appearance.

I hate the little window in my door; it lets any old hawker snoop on me in my own sanctum, which is frankly unconscionable. I tried taping paper over it when I first started working here, but Ian said the paper looked disreputable and made me take it down.

Next to the door is a hatstand, on which is arranged my usual drag—a big grey tweed greatcoat and a red hunting hat with ear flaps. I wear them winter or summer. Though climate change is making that less tenable these days.

Instead of looking at the window then, I tried looking at the back of the anglepoise lamp that cannot be restrained from swinging directly into the path from the door to the desk. The desk itself only fits because it is wedged so close to the wall that eking my way to my chair feels like getting into the middle seat on an aeroplane.

But looking at the lamp was making my head worse, so I closed my eyes. I get these headaches that start as a little dry sensation in my left eye. One can hardly tell if it is a headache or if one's just dehydrated or something, but one has to get good at noticing the exact quality of the sensation. If one doesn't start taking ibuprofen the very second one feels it, one is essentially finished. Today, I had missed the window. I hoped no one would look in, or they might think I was sleeping on the job, which would be unfortunate today of all days.

Vera, the bed-blocking former Curator, had retired six months previously, and I had been serving as what everyone assumed was a *faute-de-mieux* interim while we did a search. When I had asked Ian if my new position would be made permanent, he said that I was welcome to apply for it—meaning that there wasn't a chance in hell. The Neele was where I had ended up when I dropped out of university, and I had spent the last twenty-five years being ignored, passed over, and generally made to feel like a waste of space.

But all that was about to change. I had called Ian's bluff and applied. More than that, I had been a first-rate interim. I had always excelled in small, unnoticed ways. So, I simply ensured that people noticed. For example: I saw that the catalogue still had a subject heading, 'Indians of North America', and I altered it to 'Native Americans'. Before, that would have been that: just me, muggins, silently making our place of work better, with no hope of reward. Now, I circulated an email assertively but compassionately chiding the staff for having let a racial slur stand in our catalogue, and noted that, incidentally, I had now taken the initiative to change it. I could just imagine them reading the email and respecting the heck out of me for it.

Now that they could see what a great colleague I was, the job was basically in the bag.

And yesterday, Bunner, the ovine granny who does accessions, and whom I pretend to like, had told me that Ian had told *her* he was going to announce it today.

The phone rang. At last!

'Miss Dorn,' said a voice that was not Ian's. 'Are you the daughter of a Mrs Clara Dorn?' Christ. Now? *Now?* I suppressed the urge to tell him it was none of his business. Instead I said that I was.

'I am the manager of the Sunshine Garden Centre in Palmers Green. We have your mother here in the security office.'

'Why is she in the security office?'

'One of our loss-prevention operatives found her outside the premises with a bar of Kendal Mint Cake she had not paid for.' I wondered how many loss-prevention operatives one garden centre needed. 'Ordinarily we refer such matters directly to the authorities but your mother appearing to be a little—well, a little *confused*—not to mention, ah, the question of her advanced age, we chose to detain her on site until further arrangements could be made.' He seemed to expect me to say something at this point, but I let an uncomfortable silence drag on instead.

'We asked her if there was someone we could contact and she gave us a card that had your name on it,' he said at last. Another pause. I think he thought I would have been speeding to rescue her at the first mention of *the authorities*. 'Do you think you could—come and get her?'

God's teeth! Where the h— was Murgatroyd?

There was nothing for it, though. What was one supposed to say? *No, I'm too busy waiting to be promoted to come and bail my hateful mother out of garden-centre pokey?* 'I'll be there as soon as I can,' I said. It was more than she deserved.

Clara's long-standing and harmlessly eccentric lapses— the occasional finding herself in Tesco without her skirt or serving the chicken without having cooked it and so forth—had recently been anointed *dementia*. When he had told me, Clara's GP had seemed surprised that I did not immediately leap up, grab my things, and move back to my childhood bedroom in Palmers Green in order to wipe Clara's bottom for her until she died. Instead, I was making do with a system where she gave a next-of-kin card to whomever came across her in difficulties. Murgatroyd was the top name on the list, but she had been falling down on the job. Murgatroyd's being my—what? best friend? ex-girlfriend? Ugh, I don't know, whatever she was—being *that*, Murgatroyd was admittedly not next of kin, or even kin at all. But she had been happy to do it, and I had not. At least, that was what I had thought.

I looked at my watch. It was just before ten. We had a staff meeting at one. Perhaps Ian was going to announce the promotion then. And if he wanted to reach me in the meantime, he could always ring my mobile. I could get Clara home, pray to God I could reach Murg, and get back in time for the meeting. I decided to go for it. It was not as if I had much of a choice, in any case.

Having extricated Clara from the garden centre and got her back to her house without too much trouble, I succeeded in raising Murgatroyd. It wasn't hard. You just had to keep ringing over and over until she picked up. I made a mental note to put an addendum to that effect on Clara's senility card. I told Murgatroyd she needed to come over.

When I got off the phone, Clara was standing over the stove, making an omelette, and at the same time, smoking a cigarette. She was wearing her nicotine-stained dressing gown and her slippers that looked like she had walked through a puddle of diarrhoea.

'It's good to see you again, Agatha,' she said, without turning round.

'Yes, you too, Clara.'

'Agatha, I forget how you take your tea.'

I liked my tea poured directly down the sink, like all right-thinking people, but I didn't want to start a fight. 'Milk and two sugars,' I said.

'And how is your mother?'

'She's suffering a little bit at the moment.'

'Aren't we all? And you're doing a degree, aren't you? Something to do with libraries?'

'That's sort of right.'

'And your mother's paying for that, I suppose? That seems to be how it is nowadays, children just stay at university forever, don't they? Well, it's better than working.' I said nothing. 'It takes all sorts, doesn't it? Everyone finds their little niche. Be it ever so humble.' She turned and placed in front of me a perfectly cooked French omelette, larded with cigarette ash.

I heard the front door; Murgatroyd had arrived. I gratefully fled the kitchen.

Murgatroyd's short, round body, wrapped in a swath of tie-dyed material that one supposed was a dress, ambled into the room. 'Murgatroyd, what on earth are you playing at,' I said. 'You're supposed to be first call! This is the third one I've had to do in two weeks!'

I expected Murgatroyd to be apologetic, or defensive, or angry, but instead she just seemed solemn and headed into the sitting room.

'Agatha, are you going to be strange if I try to talk to you about something serious?' she said.

'I can't think what you mean,' I said. 'I shall be as appropriate as always.'

'Well—' Murg said. 'Maybe you'd better sit down. That's what people say in these situations, isn't it?'

'What situations?' I said, remaining standing.

'Look,' she said, 'when you phoned for the fourth time in a row, I was in the doctor's waiting room. That's why I didn't answer.'

'Thank you for picking up then,' I said. 'I kept ringing because it was important.'

'Agh!' said Murgatroyd. 'I *knew* you'd be like this! Look! Whatever it is that makes you incapable of caring for your mother, you need to deal with it. Agatha, I don't know how to tell you. I have cancer. That's why I haven't been available lately.'

I had a whole retort lined up, but, thanks to Murgatroyd's irritating announcement, it would be in poor taste to say it now.

'Is it bad?' I said, like an idiot.

'I'm afraid so. They think I have a few months. You'll have to make other arrangements fairly fast.' Her voice cracked a little bit, whether because she was laughing at her witticism or because she was starting to cry, I wasn't sure.

'Agatha,' she said. 'I need to tell you something else.'

'Yes?' I said. I was still cross about the cancer.

The irritation must have come through in my voice, because Murg made a face as if she had thought better of whatever she had been going to say. 'Well, no,' she said instead. 'It's not a good idea—yet. When I'm gone, look in the Secrets Book. It's important. You know where to find it.'

Honestly! Why she couldn't just spit it out! In the old days, Murgatroyd used to make a great performance of writing in a purple journal made for tweenage girls, with SECRETS BOOK embossed on the front and a heart-shaped padlock. If I annoyed her, she would say 'That's going in the Secrets Book' or 'When they read the Secrets Book, they'll see all the s— you put me through, Agatha Dorn.' I never really knew what she wrote in there. But I knew she kept it in her bedside table.

'OK,' I said. I have never been good in this kind of situation. I hate it when people are ill or unhappy—it sort of spoils everything for me. I did nothing for a moment, then I awkwardly put my hand on top of Murgatroyd's. She seemed to take this as a sign that I couldn't find the right way to express the profound sympathy I was feeling, and gave me a disgusting, sentimental hug, sniffling as she did so. She had always cried easily. I hugged her stiffly in return for what I hoped was an appropriate amount of time. How did one tell? Then I gave her a release-me pat on the back and said I was sorry, I had to go back to work, I had a migraine coming on, which might or might not have been a lie, I couldn't really tell. I would telephone her the next day with a plan about Clara, I said. *That* was definitely a lie. I had no idea what I was going to do. Then I speed-walked down the street to the bus stop to begin the trek back to the Neele.

2

I made it to the office with mere minutes to spare. On my way to the meeting room, I walked past Nancy's office and glanced inside. Now I thought about it, it looked roughly the same size as mine, but somehow hers felt serene and uncluttered. Nancy waved at me and trotted towards the door so we could walk to the meeting together. I pretended not to have seen and sped up.

Did I tell you about Nancy? Nancy is twenty-four years old. Archive people are typically a motley crew, all weird hairlines and undiagnosed spectrum disorders, but Nancy has sharp eyes and bright little teeth. She is English, but she did her postgrad at Yale, as you do, where she got herself named co-director of her adviser's extremely high-rolling project digitizing Emily Dickinson's manuscripts. Just after she started, they had her on Radio 4, talking about Emily Dickinson. I tried to avoid listening, but the interview came on while I was in a taxi one day, causing me to have a panic attack. I had to tell the driver I was carsick and get out. It was like those T-shirts: *My girlfriend went to Tenerife and all I got was this lousy T-shirt.* Nancy had created 'a landmark in public digital humanities', and all I had was this lousy assistant curator's job. Did I say I hated her?

The meeting started with no announcement about my new job, but I was cheered by the fact that Nancy immediately put her foot in it. We were talking about the summer exhibition, and she came out with something like 'What if we showed the Poe material?' There were two reasons why this was a stupid thing to have said. First, our unrivalled collection of early Edgar Allan Poe papers—purchased for a song by Woodward Neele III, on a trip to New York in the early 1840s, when Poe was still a nobody—they were kind of our thing. We had the holographs of 'The Purloined Letter' and 'The Murders in the Rue Morgue'. Everybody knew it: we had shown them about ten trillion times. Nancy's suggesting we display them for the summer exhibition was a bit like the new hire turning up at the Disney board meeting and saying, 'Hey, I really think we might be able to make something of this "Mickey Mouse" character!'

Second: last time we did a Poe show, a few years back, Ian had tried to augment our collection by purchasing what was supposed to be a rare private pressing of *The Raven*. The Neele had ended up with a good deal of egg on its face. Not only had the chapbook turned out to be a fake, but it had been printed on paper whose watermark, on closer inspection, featured an image of Mr Poe doing something unspeakable to a grinning cartoon character. Ian valiantly suggested that Poe, who was after all something of a literary hoaxer, might have engineered the scandalous device himself. However, Bunner—of all people!—pointed out that the gentleman being violated in the image was an Internet meme known as Trollface, whose creation post-dated that of *The Raven* by more than a century and a half. In any case, the matter was settled a couple of days after the discovery when a masked 'YouTuber' named art-brute posted a video of himself wiping his bare posterior with a second copy of the fake chapbook before burning it, along with our exhibition catalogue. Attempts were made to identify him from the video, but all we could tell was that he was a tough-looking gentleman wearing a dog mask. I suppose it was meant to be funny, but we all just looked stupid. Even though the *Sun* published a still from the YouTube video with the headline 'EDGAR ALLAN POO', no one at the Neele was laughing.

But Nancy was sharper than I thought. It turned out she had a whole spiel about how, in this age of fake news, Poe was the troll-as-performance-artist way ahead of his time—didn't he fool doctors all over Europe with his story about how a terminally ill patient had been kept alive with hypnosis? Didn't crowds take to the streets in celebration when he wrote a story claiming that an aeronaut had crossed the Atlantic in a balloon? We could put it on display next to a selection of Flat-Earther tweets from this year. And so (she said) when you looked at it like that, even though Poe hadn't himself made the obscene *Raven* chapbook, hadn't it been created precisely in his spirit? We should show it again—show the video next to it—reclaim it—show it with pride!

There was a disturbing quantity of nodding around the table. I had to act fast. 'Nancy dear,' I announced, 'I'm sure it's a tremendously clever idea. But Poe wasn't a member of the Yale Performance Studies faculty. He was a hack journalist who needed the money.'

Ian gave me a brief, enigmatic look. He would certainly have grinned except for the fear of upsetting Nancy.

'Plus,' I declaimed, 'he was a paedo who married his thirteen-year-old cousin and then wrote creepy stories about it before dying drunk in the street.' I was getting into the swing of it. 'And this place parades his doodles and laundry lists around like the Tablets of the Law. Shall we go and dig him up and sell bits of his bones in the gift shop? Great horn spoon!' That was the end of that. Nancy looked as if she was going to have a good sob in the ladies' loo as soon as the meeting was over. Like I said, I was on fire.

You will note from the above, by the way, that since my early educational failures, I have become quite well read under my own steam. I am unembarrassedly an autodidact, although this is a fact about which I do not like to brag.

Mid-afternoon. The meeting had ended with no announcement having been forthcoming. I was back in my office with a damp flannel on my face.

There was a knock on my door. I cracked it open and took up a defensive position. It was Ian. This was the first bad sign. People who are in charge of you only come to your office if a) they have bad news, or b) they are just passing and suddenly remember something they wanted to ask you. When they want to give you good news, they make you go to them.

'Hi, Agatha,' he began. 'Can I come in? I can, of course, or then again maybe not. Depends on whether or not I could overpower you. Oh dear, that's highly inappropriate, why am I envisaging that, even as a joke? Don't call HR, ha ha. *May* I come in—is the word—*may* I?'

I forget what I said, but somehow he was in my office. His big body took up most of the space in the room. He looked like he had been a ruggedly handsome prop forward once, in some long-ago public school, but had since gone to seed. He was dressed, as usual, in a shapeless vaguely military style jumper and a worn-out pair of slacks that no doubt originally cost half what I made in a month. Despite appearances, there was nothing careless about how Ian presented himself. Everything about him, down to his Boris Johnson haircut, was as meticulously calibrated as a jeweller's scale.

'How's the Gladden Green stuff?'

This was a box of junk that had been donated by the Cadigan family of Harrogate, Yorkshire. Mrs Cadigan's father had recently passed away but had paused long enough to extract a deathbed promise from his family that they would donate the papers of his own father, an amateur writer named Alexander Cust, to a literary archive, where some future researcher would discover their overlooked genius.

I would not have countenanced accepting it, except that this Cust had been, for a period that included the year 1926, a porter at the Pale Horse, outside Harrogate. This was, as I am sure you know, the year in which Gladden Green, the empress of Golden Age mystery (for those of you who have never been to a bookshop or turned on the television), famously disappeared and was after ten days discovered at the Horse. There was just a possibility that there was something good in there—a previously unknown photo of Gladden, a check-in slip with her autograph, some bonbon or other.

'Haven't seen it yet,' I said. 'Bunner has it in the freezer.' Old papers have to go in quarantine before we process them, to kill the microbes that might otherwise get out and eat our whole collection.

'I'd have thought you'd have wanted to get your hands on it,' he said.

'I asked Bunner if I could have it early, and she looked as if she was going to cry,' I said.

'There's gold there, I know it. You have the magic touch.' Ian had this schtick where he said things in a tone that sounded ironic, but one was supposed to understand that he was serious really. The truth was, though, that Ian didn't give two hoots about Gladden Green. But he had done his homework Re: on what I was working. He always went the extra mile. 'I'm so excited; it's so exciting.' Was it? Wasn't it? I couldn't tell.

Ian was directing the Neele as a second career, having made a good deal of money in fund management. This was just as well, since the Neele paid peanuts. It was anyone's guess what he was doing here, instead of raking it in keeping gentleman's hours at a think tank. Did someone, somewhere, have some terrible dirt on him? Or did he just really love old books?

'Listen,' he went on. 'I shan't beat around the bush. It's about the curator position.' He took a pen from the holder on my desk—my favourite Montblanc fountain pen, but I didn't say anything—and twiddled it awkwardly between his fingers. I ran through some possible outcomes in my head. They were going to do an external search. They were going to give it to me, but there would be no raise. They were going, god forbid, to make me share it with Bunner. What else?

'We're going to go with Nancy,' said Ian.

I said nothing, as oceans of time seemed to pass. But Ian did not, on examination, appear disturbed, so I supposed it had been only a second or so. The Crooked Man! Ian had been the Crooked Man all along!

'Nancy's only been here six months,' I said, in what I hoped was a neutral voice.

'I know. It's probably an idiotic move, god knows. She's a child. There are a couple of things I'd like to say, though.' He had practised this before he came. 'You really mustn't think this has anything to do with your ability as an archivist. Nothing at all. You've been absolutely exemplary here.' He twiddled the pen some more.

Eff him.

'These senior positions, they're all PR jobs nowadays, no matter what the job description says. Nancy's not going to be looking after collections. Not really. She's going to be schmoozing the bluehairs, glad-handing, raising filthy lucre. She does have a truly unique—they call it *handshakefulness*, rather horribly.' That was what they called it, was it? I thought of the way she touched the forearms of male donors and laughed at their jokes while they fantasized about setting her up in a West End sex flat.

'You don't want to be doing all that, not really,' said Ian. 'You wouldn't be able to tell everyone off about liking Edgar Allan Poe.' He smirked ruefully.

So that was it. Had they mistaken my plain-spokenness for a lack of tact? Had they found me—*annoying*? It seemed hardly possible.

'This is balls, Ian, you know that,' I said.

'I know, dear. If you'd rather take the opportunity to move on, we would quite understand.' Smug fool. 'You can punch me in the face if you like.' He smiled again.

Quite so. What was there left to do? It was done. Even though a hasty cost/benefit analysis of hitting him in the face yielded a negative recommendation, I considered it for a good few seconds. But no. 'OK,' I said. 'OK, OK.'

For some reason, Ian didn't leave. 'I'm sorry,' he said, 'this is awkward, but are you saying you are or are not going to punch me?'

'God, no,' I said. 'I'm telling you to eff off.' My headache had become really quite acute. Only after he had left did I notice that he had taken my Montblanc pen away with him.

3

The next morning before work, the reality of the situation in which I was about to find myself vis-à-vis Clara began to hit home. My mother needed full-time care. The help-card arrangement barely worked as it was. And now there would be no Murgatroyd either? If I wasn't careful, I would find myself back in Palmers Green permanently.

I decided to telephone my brother Heri and try to bully him into paying to put Clara in a home.

Once I made it past his assistant, which was no small feat, I tried to take him to task. I told him that the time was past for his lazy estrangement. I told him that I had it on good authority that he was one of Britain's Richest Doctors, and that doctors were renowned in the first place for the healthy size of their salaries, to wit, this wasn't some kind of 'tallest dwarf'-type accolade. And, I told him, he had Responsibilities towards his family.

He put on his extra-calm and reasonable manner, so I would know that he was Handling Me, and said oilily that, while he was indeed fairly well off on paper, like many well-off people he in fact had very little cash on hand, and that if he were to attempt to raise funds for our mother's care, he would be obliged to liquidate certain assets that were currently held in the form of property.

He meant my fancy flat in the Gatehouse. The Gatehouse, the brutalist wonderland the Corporation of London had created in the 1970s to fill one of the swaths the Blitz had cut across the City. Home of the Museum of London, the Gatehouse theatre, and the great high-rise towers: Chesterton, Conan Doyle, and Sayers. Plus, the Neele Archive. I could walk to work.

'It's in my name, Heri!' I said.

'A technicality,' he said. That bull's pizzle! I had always hoped—assumed, even—that he, like me, saw the money he had paid for the flat as a loan in name only. I would certainly never be able to pay it back without selling up. Nowadays, everyone wanted to live in the Gatehouse, and flats sometimes went for more than £2,000,000.

When I moved in, in 1997, everyone hated it. Today the complex had a gift shop selling socks with pictures of the towers on them, and the flats' weird square vertical sinks are considered Design Classics. People who got rid of them in the eighties now spend large amounts of money to retrofit them. I myself, who has excellent taste, had always loved the sink. Sometimes I would stare at it for minutes at a time of an evening. This is all to say that I was jealous of my flat. It was a fetish onto which, in the light of the failure of every other aspect of my life, I had projected significant portions of my self-esteem. Heri knew I would do anything rather than let him sell it.

'Heri, you are a bull's pizzle,' I said to him, and hung up. I consoled myself with the knowledge that I had done something in the service of finding help for my mother, but I was no closer to solving my problem.

I had to go to work. In a foul mood, I headed out onto the access deck, where I nodded at Mrs Hernandez, my next-door neighbour of a decade's standing (I did not actually know if she *was* called Mrs Hernandez, but in my mind I had so designated her.) 'You look as if you have been sucking on a lemon, Miss Dorn,' she said cheerily. I gave her the least offensive gurn I could muster. Then I took the lift down and made for the Neele.

At work, we had our monthly meeting with Arise.

You'll remember that Arise was at that time trying mightily to turn the entire Gatehouse complex into their London base of operations. The Neele sat in the middle of the Gatehouse. Everything on the original site had been obliterated. All except the Neele.

Both the British government and the Corporation of London, which owns the rest of the Gatehouse, had been really quite keen to make Sir Ed Ratchett's London 'campus' happen.

In the early nineties, when Ed (without the 'sir') had looked a little more like a computer nerd and a little less like a Hollywood beau, he and his business partner Aristide Leonides had founded Arise (AR for Aristide/Ratchett, plus Rise, you see), the first viable online bookshop of the Internet era. Then in—when?—ninety-seven? ninety-eight?—Aristide Leonides had died—young. I remembered that there had been perhaps something unseemly about his death, but I couldn't remember the details. Anyway, after that, the whole thing had exploded into an unstoppable retail behemoth and—more importantly—an emphatic marker of Britain's membership of the world's economic Premier League. It was no wonder the government didn't want the likes of us standing in their way.

Plus, Sir Ed had proposed the creation of a series of free schools, to be built in low-income areas, the salaries of whose teachers, and the standards of whose buildings, would be far higher than could otherwise be afforded. All the company asked in return was the exclusive right to manufacture and sell to these schools all the books and equipment they would need. It felt churlish to point out that the government could build the schools itself if Arise would simply pay its taxes.

We were all that was standing in the way. The Neele led a charmed life. The land on which it was built had been given outright to some ancient Neele, or Neil, or McNeill, by William the Conqueror himself, and so it was extraordinarily difficult to get rid of it. Not even Hitler had been able to do it.

This kind of thing happened to us all the time, and the proper way to deal with it was to pretend to consider the proposal for a few months until it went away.

To that end, I would need my best pen back, in order to take pretend notes. I stopped by Ian's office on my way, in order to fetch it. Ian was just coming out, but, oddly, hurried to shut the door as he saw me coming.

'I was hoping to retrieve my fountain pen,' I said. 'You walked off with it yesterday.'

'Did I?' said Ian. He looked appalled.

'Could I fetch it from your office?' I said, gesturing at the hastily closed door.

'What?' said Ian. 'No! I mean, I'll bring it with me to the meeting.' I stood awkwardly for a moment, until it became clear that Ian wanted me to leave before he would reopen his office door, so I did. That was curious. I wondered what Ian had in there that he didn't want me to see.

Especially since, once he did arrive at the conference room, he did not have my pen with him.

When I got to the table, there was a cup of tea waiting at my spot. As I went to sit down, Bunner appeared at my elbow with the expression of a bellboy waiting for a tip. 'I thought you might need a pick-me-up, Agatha,' she said, too loudly. I wished she wouldn't do things like this. Quite apart from the fact that I am sure I have told her I hate tea, it was a pitiful attempt to buy my affection. I cheers-ed her with the tea and tried to look appreciative.

Oliver from Arise kicked things off as always with one of those overhead-projector presentations he called a *slide deck*. The first one read 'Now' and featured a group of sad waifs and strays huddled around a harried young female teacher with a dog-eared textbook. Oliver tended to make the slides more melodramatic each month. This time, one of the waif-and-strays was actually crying. On the right-hand side was a picture of the Neele, in which the lighting had been adjusted to make it look sad and depressing.

The next slide read: 'The Arise Future!' In this one, the children all had shiny new books. The teacher, who had acquired the happy-idiot look of a woman in an advert for sanitary products or yoghurt, was sketching inspirationally on a tablet whose screen was mirrored at the front of the class on a cinema-sized monitor.

The other half of that slide was a picture of me in a crimson convertible, pulling up to a shiny new glass-and-steel building surrounded by nature. The caption here read: 'The Neele Sunningdale'.

The old hat I typically wear while travelling to and from work is scarlet, but in this month's picture they had recoloured it crimson to match the car. Sometimes I text Bunner during these meetings. I tried it now: 'They've tinted my hat to match the car LOL.'

It seemed to me that Arise was on the verge of giving up.

That picture of the sad children reeked of desperation. I texted Bunner so, but again got no response.

But instead, at about the point where these meetings usually wrapped up, Oliver paused, with the air of a girlfriend about to announce that we needed to talk.

'So look,' said Oliver, 'I should let you know that our new GC has recommended that we change course and pursue compulsory purchase.' He sounded sad that we were going to have to give up our little get-togethers.

'Oh, I shouldn't think so,' said Ian, as if it were a matter of opinion. 'We're really going to go back down that road? I don't think I see that what made it a bad idea last time doesn't still make it a bad idea this time. The Neele is a national treasure. You'll get crucified in the media, won't you?'

'Well, OK,' continued Oliver, 'but here's the thing. Our new GC doesn't think the Neele *is* a national treasure. He thinks no one has heard of you, except for that Edgar Allan Poo nonsense a few years back. And you know I like all of you very much, so maybe this is just my bad mood speaking, tell me to shut up or whatever, but I'm inclined to agree. I think no one cares about the Neele Archive at all.

'And you know what else? I think if it goes to the Supreme Court, we'll win. It's in the public interest, a large majority of the landowners want to sell, there's a substantial contribution to the local community. I think we'll edge it.'

'Well,' said Ian, whose poker face was intact, 'we'll prepare a response for next month's meeting.'

'Oh, this is awkward,' said Oliver. 'I was hoping we might be able to come to terms without getting to this. We've actually already filed the motion for compulsory purchase. I was rather soft-pedalling it, to give you a chance to save face. So we shan't be meeting next month, I'm afraid. As I say, we're taking a different course.'

'I don't see Bill going for that,' pressed Ian. A little flush had emerged above his collar.

'In fact,' said Oliver, 'Sir William has assured us that the Home Office will endorse our motion.'

'We'll see,' growled Ian, but Oliver cut him off.

'We'll still move you out to the sticks if you like,' said Oliver. 'As long as you don't misbehave about the compulsory purchase—and, as we've said many times of course, the new building we're proposing for you is a really wonderful facility, far superior to this one in all sorts of regards. But let's say we essentially have the decision: Arise will be buying the Gatehouse.

'In any case,' he continued after a pause, 'it's been absolutely delightful working with you all. Maybe the book world will bring us all back together one of these days?'

As Oliver was packing up his things, I finally got a text back from Bunner. 'Is this a disaster?' it read. When I looked up at her, she was all stunned and sad; everyone was. It was indeed a disaster.

4

I mentioned the Crooked Man before. Let me tell you what that is all about. Reading about Gladden's idea of the Crooked Man at university is how I became a Green enthusiast in the first place. Is it embarrassing if I show you a passage from a book?

You would be having a lovely dream—you might be at a picnic in the park or a boat party. Suddenly, you would get a queer feeling. Somebody at the party was not who he said he was. Somebody at the party was the Crooked Man. You could not tell just by looking. The Crooked Man would reveal himself in his own time. Until then, though, you were terrified. All the joy went out of the day.

Anybody to whom you talked could be the Crooked Man. Mummy. Auntie. Daddy. Your best friend. You couldn't relax and play.

Then you were talking to Mummy. You realized that all along you had known it was Mummy. Her back began to hunch over. She looked down at you and you saw her terrible steely blue eyes from beneath the brim of her black hat. Did Mummy wear a hat? Strange how one had never noticed before. And then, from the sleeve of the long black coat in which she was suddenly wrapped—out came the horrid stump! It wasn't Mummy! It was the Crooked Man! And you woke up, knowing, always having known, that nothing was what it seemed to be.

I mean, I don't know what to say about it. I just think it is the truth. This was how the world had felt to me for as long as I could remember. Nothing was what it seemed. The Crooked Man. Of course.

It's funny. There are no supernatural characters in Gladden Green novels. Even this one, the Crooked Man, is merely a figure from a recurring dream one of her protagonists has. But this weird character epitomizes the appeal of Gladden's work for me. The world of her novels looks benign at first glance. But never believe it, no matter how much you might want to! The secret to life is never to be lulled into thinking things are OK. Always be on the lookout for the spectre, because he's always there. That's Crooked Man thinking.

Do you remember the television adaptations they made of the Père Flambeau stories in the 1980s? The title sequence had things just right. It featured a series of sketches of Steeple Aston, the village where Flambeau lives. Each one would at first glance depict a bucolic scene—a cricket match, a country house—and then the camera would zoom in and reveal some hidden horror. Behind the wicket lay a mangled corpse. The face of the woman standing in the window of the manor bore an expression of such vitriol that it made one gasp. This vision—not merely that the world is riddled with evil, but that its evil is both always present and always lurking just out of view—well, I stand in awe thereof.

And so I became a Gladden Green enthusiast and then, once I arrived at the Neele, a Gladden Green expert—though on the sly, since I do not really like the idea of anyone knowing that anything matters to me very much. I especially did not want them knowing about my love of what they might wrongly consider the subliterary corpus of a conceited old sow.

For I should say, even now, people mostly do not take Gladden Green seriously. But then, people are idiots. And Green herself did not help matters. The Pale Horse scandal made her an unsympathetic figure after 1926, and she did little to repair her public image. Instead, she seemed to cultivate the aspect of a petty-minded Little-Englander. In later life, many of her public pronouncements concerned the twin disgraces of how much tax her father had had to pay while she was growing up, and how much she now had to pay as the world's most successful novelist. She dressed like an embarrassing maiden aunt, wearing cat's-eye glasses and fake-fur hats with polyester bows. The only thing anybody liked about her was Flambeau, but Green would go on television and tell everyone how much she had grown to hate her detective. In a letter to *The Times Literary Supplement* in 1972, she made fun of the name of an up-and-coming Indian novelist. She proclaimed her admiration for Enoch Powell. Feminist publishing houses and graduate students did not find it congenial to reclaim her as a lost genius, and, besides, she was far too successful ever to have been 'lost'.

But I bought us many things, somewhat *sub rosa*, so that the Neele now had amongst its holdings one of the finest collections of Green first editions, holograph manuscripts, and other materials, in the world. (Fun fact: I purchased the aforementioned 1980s sketches from the Flambeau title sequence for the Neele ten years ago; I superstitiously keep them in a portfolio with a lock on it, in particular to stop the vitriolic lady from getting out and murdering me in my sleep.) Ian and the others knew that I bought Green stuff, but the full scope and value of the collection was something of which only I was aware.

If you have been sufficiently careful not to allow yourself to hope for something too much—a promotion, for instance— it is easy enough to manage when you do not get it. I had, I admit, been caught off guard by the news about Nancy, but two days later, I was fairly well along in the task of stuffing my disappointment into the memory hole. I was almost all set to hunker down into my bitterness and channel what fury I could not repress into creating a five-year plan for getting even with Nancy and the rest of them.

But my fortunes were about to change with astonishing speed.

When I got to my office, I found that Ian was there.

'Hello, Agatha,' he said. 'I hope you don't mind my barging in.' I did rather, but it didn't seem like the moment to say so. 'I realized,' he said, 'that we didn't make much headway on the subject of the summer exhibition in the end. I got a good idea of what you didn't think we should do, ha ha, but I wondered if you had any sense of what we might do instead?'

This was an odd subject for him to bring up, especially with the threat of eviction hanging over our heads. I wondered if Ian was trying to make amends for the whole promotion situation by making a point of valuing my opinion. In fact, however, he had merely succeeded in putting me on the spot.

'Well,' I said, casting around for an idea and finding that only one immediately came to mind. 'We've never shown any of our Gladden Green material. I wonder if that might be popular. I've been acquiring in that area for some time now, as you know.'

'Gladden Green,' he said, musing on the idea. 'That's a thought. She is popular. Is she a little *too* popular for a Neele exhibition, if you see what I mean?'

If Ian was trying to placate me, he was making a mess of it, for my hackles went up immediately.

'I think she is very much underrated as a serious author,' I said.

'Of course, of course,' he said. 'I know she is a particular passion of yours. Well, it's certainly an idea to give some thought. And you have these new papers coming in.'

As if on cue, there was a knock at the door.

It was Bunner, carrying the very papers Ian had mentioned. 'Agatha!' she cried in delight. 'I have the box from Harrogate. And Ian has had the most wonderful idea.'

Ian looked slightly shamefaced, as if he suspected that I would not find his idea to be wonderful. 'It's just,' he said, 'I wonder if you would share processing the box with Nancy?' I looked at him with a deadpan expression. So that was what he had been here for. 'I want to get her more familiar with our protocols,' he said. 'And besides,' he went on in a stage whisper, 'she's rather terrified of you. She just wants to be friends.' This was an obvious lie. I had been justifiably stern with her at the staff meeting, and now she was going to interfere with my project as revenge. It was just the kind of petty viciousness in which she would engage. 'I'll tell her to come down when she's got a minute then, shall I?' he concluded—then he swept out.

'Thank you *so* much for waiting for the box, Agatha,' said Bunner. 'I'm sorry the accession protocols take such a long time.' Bunner could be quite passive aggressive when she wanted to be.

I looked down at the box. I had not had high hopes for its contents and had been planning to procrastinate, but between Ian's dismissal of Gladden Green and the news that I was going to be sharing the project with Nancy, it suddenly became a matter of urgency. How dare Ian suggest that I wait for Nancy to lollygag all day?

I lifted the lid, then the first couple of leaves. Two stanzas of pious doggerel, *eheu*, inscribed on the verso of a hotel-wide memorandum about the prompt laundering of linens. The next was similar. Resentful tetrameters backed with receipts and reminders from the Receptionist and the Clerks of this and that, written in what was only-too-recognizable as the universal language of workplace passive-aggression. 'Per our several previous conversations…' 'The Bell Captain wishes to remind the Porters…' 'Your cooperation in this most significant matter is greatly appreciated…'

In 1911, there seemed to have been much to-do over a visit from Harry Houdini and his entourage. Cust wrote in paranoid fashion about his suspicion that the Bell Captain, one Mr Scaife, had deliberately attempted to withhold from him the opportunity of meeting Houdini out of spite, in order to thwart the blossoming of his literary career. Nevertheless, apparently Cust had triumphed in the end by managing to obtain Houdini's autograph, along with a written endorsement (neither of which could be found in the box). Although I remained unsure of how meeting Houdini was supposed to be of help with one's literary career.

Next, a handwritten letter: 'Dear Mr Cust—for I am told that this is your name—For the services my requesting of which you have graciously humoured, much, indeed, incalculable, thanks'.

This sounded more interesting.

I have stayed in many hotels that fancy themselves firstrate, but never have I come across such dedication to duty. I connfess I was slightly dissappointed on my arrival to have been given a room on the first floor, since I do prefer the ground floor, but from the moment you hauled my extremely heavy trunk across the threshhold and heaved it onto the rack, I was imppressed by your attentiveness. You somehow intuited precisely when I prefer my tea and my turn-down service and never failed to appear (or disappear) at the perfect moment. Such solicitousness!

As it is possible you will have discovered, though I did not give to the hotel my real name, I am by occupation a writer, and have spent the bulk of my time in Yorkshire composing the attached, which I had hoped would form the skeleton of a novel. For reasons that will become apparent after you read it, however, I find that it will be immpossible to make use of it in the way that I had intended. Indeed, I hesitate not to throw it immediately into the fire. I risk something by letting it out of my travelling bag at all and would certainly have to disclaim its creation in the strongest terms were it ever by some axident to see the light of day. Yet it seems so fitting that I should entrust it to you, my partner of these strange ten days, that I will undertake the risk, and enclose it here. I hope you enjoy it.

Yours sincerely,
G. GREEN (MRS)

At this point, as you might be able to imagine, I had to put the letter down, because my hand was literally trembling. I took a couple of deep breaths and pulled myself together. Was the enclosure present? *Was the enclosure present?* I moved ahead until I found another manuscript page, and read on:

> 'Mon ami,' said Père Flambeau, as Captain Brown inched the Lagonda around yet annother cramped bend in the lane—

I was trying to comprehend what I might have discovered. Captain Brown driving his classic headlights-on-stalks roadster round the English countryside, Flambeau in tow. The 'skelleton' of a lost Gladden Green novel—judging by the number of pages in the pile under my hand, more than a skeleton—a draft! And perhaps only the late Mr Cust, I, and, of course, Gladden herself, had ever read any part of it.

Suddenly, I heard dainty little Nancy-steps in the corridor outside the office. I realized that I had to think fast.

What I held in my hand was very likely a Big Deal. If Nancy got hold of it, it would quickly become her Big Deal, not mine. I'd be listening to her gushing on Radio 4 for a second time, and about my personal darling, my own Gladden!

I should explain that at the Neele, as in all archives, there are extremely strict rules about how and under what circumstances materials may be taken out of the collection, especially if the materials are rare and/or valuable. Once something has been accessioned, you need a committee meeting and a form with five signatures before it can leave the building. We take this extremely seriously.

With that in mind, I slid the manuscript and the accompanying letter under the table and into my big handbag. And when, a moment later, Nancy came into the room, I enthusiastically announced that I had an urgent appointment and left her to sort through the now-worthless box of assorted doggerel and miscellanea I had obtained from Harrogate.

I suppose I ought to have spent the rest of the day wringing my hands about my mother's and Murgatroyd's situations. But I did not. Instead, I read the manuscript. Well, what would you have done?

I devoured it. I ate it up. It was the best of all possible manuscripts. Green's referring to it as a skeleton was false modesty, to say the least. 'The Dog's Ball', as it was entitled, was a fully formed Flambeau novella as good as anything she ever wrote. It glowed with her eldritch power.

The cherry on the cake, from my point of view, was that the villain was none other than the Crooked Man! Or, rather, the woman writer who turns out to be the murderer dresses as a hunchbacked bogeyman in a black hat and coat in order to commit a series of killings that appear supernatural. The Crooked Man! It was as if the thing had been written just for me.

It was obvious why she could not have published it. Green had checked in to the Pale Horse under a false name, Andromeda Vane. People think she did so in order to humiliate her husband Archie, who had recently run off with a much younger woman named Ariadne Vane. She seemed to have imagined that Archie, finding that she had disappeared, would panic, swiftly locate her, and then feel so grateful and chastened that he might even return to her. In fact what happened, as most people know, is that Archie did indeed panic, but then failed to find her, launched a nationwide manhunt that lasted for ten days during which time questions about the disappearance were asked in Parliament, and Green, when she finally turned up hiding at a luxury hotel under a false name, got vilified as a selfish, calculating time-waster.

At this point, she took one of the few paths open to her: she claimed to have gone temporarily insane and to have no memory of the disappearance whatsoever. No one much believed her, but it gave people an excuse to forgive her, which they eventually did because they liked buying her books.

'The Dog's Ball' basically blew all of that up. Its protagonist is a mystery writer named, oops, Andromeda Vane, who lures a variety of people, connected with one another only through the fact that each has at one time or another wronged her, to an overnight party at an inn named the Dog and Bear. The party is naturally entitled 'The Dog's Ball', a name that, cleverly, has a different significance for each of them—one was a member of a regiment nicknamed 'The Bloodhounds', another went to a school named St Bernard's, and so forth. Once they arrive, Andromeda, dressed as the Crooked Man in order to muddy the waters, begins to murder them in turn, until Flambeau, who has inconveniently turned up at the inn after Captain Brown's car breaks down, puts a stop to the whole thing and unmasks her.

The chief problem for Green would have been the fact that the first victim—and the primary one, judging by her impassioned confession at the book's end—is Andromeda's cheating former husband. There could have been little question that it was a fictionalized version of Green's own situation. Were it to have been published, no one could, even in theory, have bought the memory-loss story. The press's initial view of her as a vengeful narcissist would have been confirmed. Who knew what would have happened to her career then?

It felt like a miracle. I hardly slept at all. I would doze off, and fantasies of Flambeau triumphing in a library full of suspects turned themselves inside out and became images of myself addressing a rapt lecture hall filled with Green fans.

5

By the morning, it had occurred to me that 'The Dog's Ball' could not only advance my career but also take care of my Clara problem.

I would have to engage in a little skulduggery.

And I would have to be sure 'The Dog's Ball' was the real McCoy. I didn't want to find it besmeared with excrement in a YouTube video a few months from now.

Thankfully, a careful page-through on the light box revealed no pornographic watermarks.

Additionally, all sorts of things about the Cust papers strongly argued against the possibility of the manuscript's being a forgery. There was the accompanying letter, both it and the manuscript itself written in Green's familiar scrawl, which I knew well. Then there were Cust's papers, which corroborated the encounter with Green, all in the same hand. The chances of someone faking up all that were next to zero.

Then, within the manuscript, were the characteristic tics of Green's writing—'paper back' for 'paperback', a general lack of attention to apostrophes—'cant' for 'can't', 'were' for 'we're', and examples of the notoriously poor spelling I'd seen elsewhere in her writing—'sentance', 'sincerly', and some others.

There was one thing: the names were odd. Or, rather, what she did with them was. Most of the characters in 'The Dog's Ball' had names that popped up elsewhere in later Green novels: there was an heiress named Tara Finch, for instance, who reappeared in *An Egyptian Mystery*. There was a Major Macmillan, whose name was recycled for *Murder on Montserrat*. And of course the Crooked Man, who was recycled from the early novel *Death of a Ghost*, where I had first encountered him. The plot, however, was all new—Green had never gone back and retooled it for another book. This was the exact opposite of her usual approach. In other cases, when she had expanded a story into a novel or novella—'The Cruel Orchid', for example, which became *Effervescent Arsenic*, or 'Delicious Death', which had become *The Adventure of the Chocolate Cake*—she had reused the plot and changed all the names. She never did it this way.

But that all added up to not very much. I was persuaded. There was nothing about which to worry. I was a professional; I did this sort of thing for a living.

So I put my plan into action.

A couple of days later, I called in ill at work and headed to an appointment with Fraser Green at Whitehaven Tower, which housed his Marylebone flat. You may remember that Fraser is Gladden Green's grandson and the Chairman of Gladden Green, Ltd. His job is to ensure that his late grandmother remains a national treasure and that her book sales thus continue to keep him in the manner to which he is accustomed. 'Come to the flat,' he had said to me on the phone. 'I shall be in town, reviewing Flambeau scripts.'

Fraser's word is the law when it comes to anything related to his grandmother. He signs off on every script of every adaptation of her work and every new edition of a book. He had, for instance, all traces of Green's pre-war social prejudice scrubbed from the modern reprints. He would threaten to sue postgrads for quoting tiny snippets of her work if he thought they were not toeing the party line. He probably couldn't win such a suit, but so far no penniless student had bet against his expensive lawyers. If Fraser approved of 'The Dog's Ball', it would happen. If he didn't, it wouldn't. I had spent two nights sleeplessly typing up the manuscript and had biked him a photocopy of it the day before. I had left off the ending.

Luckily, Fraser liked me. Some years ago, Channel Four had produced a muck-raking exposé of Green's anti-Semitism. Fraser reached out to me—we had encountered one another over email a number of times during the course of my collecting career—and asked me to write a rebuttal in the *Spectator*. I did a fine job, if I say so myself. Did Green ever feature a Jewish villain? No. In fact, on one occasion she admiringly referred to a Jewish character as 'a decent one'. Who knew to whom she was referring with the phrase 'yellow-faced bankers'? Not I. Perhaps the well-known outbreak of jaundice among the financial community that occurred in 1913. And so on. I had my eyes on the brief, appreciative postcard that would, and did, arrive from Fraser in due course. It was a check for the quo I was due in payment for my quid. I was coming to cash it in.

Whitehaven Tower turned out to be a pedestrian address for a man who regularly appeared on lists of The UK's Wealthiest. Fraser was even out of Heri's league. But the block I was approaching was an ex-council, redbrick stack with none of the dash of the Gatehouse. Last week Fraser had featured in a TV documentary about top summer reads, in the kitchen of the family's Devon pile, with an Aga and a Labrador. Did the same man really live here? It was very strange.

He buzzed me in and opened the grimy door of flat 403. 'Come,' he said by way of acknowledgement.

The flat was almost completely bare and painted white, with an unpleasant grey shag carpet that must have been thirty years old. A small framed photograph of Gladden Green was the only conceivably personal possession in sight, except for a pair of expensive-looking brogues under the console table.

I had heard that Fraser had to be coached extensively in order to make his TV appearances, such was his lack of charisma, but in person his gracelessness was truly striking. It was as if, when he looked at me, he was looking down a long tunnel at a blurred shape. His white silk shirt and navy-blue moleskin slacks looked like a poorly chosen costume. The greasy polyester socks that protruded from the bottoms of the trousers were the only authentic part.

We headed to the kitchen, which had been badly painted neon-yellow. 'Daughter broke up with her boyfriend. I'll have it painted over when she's finished expressing herself,' he said. I supposed that I knew he had a daughter, but seeing him in the flesh, it was impossible to imagine it. How had he got her?

'I haven't anything to drink, unless you want a glass of champagne,' he continued.

He opened the white, vinyl-sided fridge to reveal a bottle of Taittinger, a box of leftovers from a restaurant, and nothing else. He did something with his mouth that was supposed to be a smile.

'I always say that no pied-à-terre should be without a bottle of champagne. And, oh! You can have some of these!' He pulled out the leftovers box, which turned out, improbably, to be half a serving of pressed duck from a restaurant in Paris. The liverish smell of the blood and mashed innards drifted up between us. After an awkward pause, I picked up a piece with my fingers and masticated it joylessly. Fraser did the same.

'I read this typescript you sent,' he said, mid-chew. 'It's quite good. Very characteristic of her, which is good. Exciting. Potentially big.' Based on his manner, a casual eavesdropper might have thought we were discussing shades of paint. His eyes had developed a kind of ferocity behind the blankness though, like a great white shark.

'And she did it on the trip to Harrogate, you say?' he continued. He did the smiling thing with his mouth again. I had thought he might like that. Fraser's one variance with the official Green family story was his disdain for the memory-loss part. He supposedly hated his grandfather bitterly for having left his grandmother, and much preferred the version in which Gladden acted out of a desire for revenge. My prediction that this would predispose him in favour of the novella seemed to be working out.

'Have some more duck.' He gestured at the box, then at the typescript. 'I want to do it.'

'That's wonderful!' I said, through a bloody mouthful. It was, though the hard part was still to come.

'Now, what we'll do, we'll get the lawyers on it.' He was getting into his stride now. 'Tell me again about the provenance? Some family from Harrogate? Are they going to be any trouble? They're not on the make?'

'They gifted the papers to us outright. They can't come and ask for it back just because they find out it's valuable.'

'I trust there is an ending, by the way,' he said, his tone altering. 'Why did you not send it to me?'

48

It was time to make my move. 'I want royalties. On retail basis,' I said. 'One per cent.'

'No, no, no,' said Fraser. He was right. It was an absurd demand. 'What would I pay you royalties for?'

'Writing an introduction.' No one got royalties for writing introductions. 'And also because otherwise I'll shred the whole thing. You won't have the end, and you won't have the holograph manuscript, which is how I authenticated the text.'

If we sold hardbacks at £15, which we would, I was asking for 15 pence from each sale. If we sold a million copies in pre-orders alone, which we would, I would get £150,000, and that was just for starters. I could pay someone enough to take care of Clara and never even have to talk to them. It was nothing to what Fraser would make—but that was on what I was banking. It would cost him more to try to force me to give him the manuscript than it would to pay me.

'I don't believe it for a second. Are you honestly attempting to blackmail me?' he said.

'You don't have to believe me,' I said. 'You just have to take a chance.' I was absolutely terrified. I had planned out what I was going to say in advance. My palms were sweating and my hands had gone all pin-and-needles. My voice, in my head, sounded as if it were coming from far away. 'It's loose change to you. It would cost you more to fight me. I could destroy the manuscript as soon as I get back to work.'

His shark eyes retreated further inward for a moment. I felt lucky the flat was so under-furnished. There was nothing within reaching distance with which he might club me to death. His eyes came back, his brain having completed whatever calculations with which they had been engaged.

Suddenly, it was as if I hadn't mentioned money at all. 'You've had it authenticated, then?' he said. 'Paper composition, age of the ink, all that? We don't want to be made a fool of.' I wondered whether he cared about what happened to me, or whether he was employing the majestic plural.

I had run through the standard authentication procedures, but I hadn't gone as far as chemical analyses. Hardly anyone ever did, and I had assumed Fraser wouldn't ask for it. 'It's done,' I lied. 'With something of this magnitude, there was no sense in wasting time. The paper has no whitening agents. No synthetic resin in the ink. It doesn't give us a precise date, but it's consistent.' I had no idea if any of this was true.

'You're satisfied?' he said, after a pause.

'I've only had a verbal précis of the report, but I am.'

'Send it to me as soon as you get it,' he said. 'Very well. I'll issue a statement endorsing this major discovery.' He turned back to his horrid duck. My head was throbbing from all the lying and the playing of hardball.

'Um—' I said, more feebly than I had intended.

'You can have half a per cent,' he said, without looking up.

I still didn't move. He looked up. 'What?' he asked.

'I want a whole per cent,' I said.

He looked at me slowly, then made his smiling face one last time. There was a hint of something I could not make out in his expression. Was it respect, for having stood up to him? All these money men secretly want to be defied. 'All right,' he said, after a pause. And just like that, I had won. Easy Street was just around the corner.

*

After the meeting with Fraser Green, things moved fast. Fraser announced the existence of the novella and sent me a contract that awarded me the royalties for which I had asked, on the basis of my introduction, which I wrote and he approved. Green's regular publishing house, Aeolian, was going to put it out—they did whatever Fraser told them to, as far as she was concerned. There was immediate and considerable media interest. Newspapers went to Harrogate to interview Lily and Tom Cadigan. Tom was Alexander Cust's grandson-in-law, and excitedly told the press that he had had no idea that his wife's grandfather had met Gladden Green, let alone been given a lost novel. Cust had a daughter-in-law too, but she proved impossible to find. The neighbours said she had sold up and disappeared the moment her husband died. No one minded much, though. There was plenty of story to go around—even though Tom's wife Lily, née Cust, seemed overwhelmed by the whole business, and gave diffident replies. She smiled in all the photographs, though, which was all that was required.

These were the first of my days of favour. A little picture of me appeared in the *Daily Mail*, next to a tiny image of Tom Cadigan—was that really the best shot they could get?—and alongside that an obsequious article detailing how 'The Dog's Ball' had come to light. I developed a set of stock phrases to say to reporters. 'I like to think Gladden's ghost is happy it will see the light of day at last.' 'I really do think the Neele is such a national treasure.' Agents set up meetings and talked airily for a while about things I might do: a popular biography of Gladden; a memoir; who knew? who cared? One of them, a woman named Nora Blackborow, even signed a contract with me.

Murgatroyd made the expected telephone call to tell me that she could no longer serve as Clara's emergency carer. I said, 'How are you?' and she replied that she was bearing up, and thanks for asking.

Then she said, 'This manuscript, Agatha,' and left a pregnant pause. This was just like when we were talking at my mother's house. I wished to god she would just spit it out!

'It's everything I've ever wanted, Murg,' I said defiantly.

'That's what I was afraid of. Just—well, just be careful,' she said. 'And look in the Secrets Book when I'm dead, all right?'

Be careful! Was she worried that my fifteen minutes of fame was corrupting my soul? 'I never thought you were such a prig, Murgatroyd,' I said. There was a hurt silence on the other end.

To cheer her up, I asked her if she wanted to have dinner with me at Luxembourg, a much-hyped fish restaurant near me where one ordered an expensive twenty-course tasting menu. I was spending the money I had not yet received. I thought treating Murgatroyd was the least I could do after all she had done for Clara, and plus, there was, you know, the cancer. But she said, 'For Christ's sake, Agatha,' and hung up. The call was a win on balance, I felt.

I engaged an extremely expensive private nurse to deal with Clara. I needed that problem to disappear as quickly as possible. The lady on the phone seemed surprised by my lack of willingness to show up in person to manage things but, like Clara's GP, this person did not understand the nature of my situation at all.

I purchased a pair of expensive saddle shoes that I had wanted forever, with a navy-blue suède panel and bovver-boy soles. I felt as if I was finally getting on with life.

Generally, nothing seemed quite real. The City felt enchanted. I would take a pointless detour through Postman's Park on my walk home, and the hedge-fund yahoos on the other side of the fence seemed not a hellish mob but picturesque fauns.

We got our million pre-orders and then some. I fielded calls from Green scholars who wanted to look at the manuscript and blew them off.

Ian, who had initially, like most of the other Neele folks, been livid with me for pilfering the manuscript, was forced to climb down when some months into our publicity campaign, Oliver phoned and informed him that Arise was going to 'walk back' the timetable on the compulsory purchase. After that I was a hero, at least when anybody was watching, though privately Ian avoided speaking to me whenever possible.

One December day in the middle of it all, I received a phone call. 'Is this Agatha Dorn?' said the voice on the other end. I said that it was. 'This is the Metropolitan Police. I'm calling because Amy Murgatroyd has you listed as a close contact, is that right?'

'Is she there?' I said. I did say some stupid things these days.

'I'm afraid not,' said the voice, which had a heavy estuary accent and the calming, authoritative intonation of a satnav. 'I'm sorry to have to tell you that she's dead.' The PC, whose name turned out to be Dorothy, asked some questions about Murgatroyd: was it her house, where they had found her? Was I her next of kin? (*Was* I?) That kind of thing. I was going to have to go to the mortuary at North Mid in a couple of days formally to identify the body.

Murgatroyd had pinned a note to her neighbour's door shortly before turning on something called a suicide kit, which she had apparently bought off the Internet. Thus, happily, she was found before she began to smell. She had told no one what she was going to do, not even her current partner Dimitra (Greek, since you ask). It was discovered that I was her chief beneficiary as well as her executor, which must have driven Dimitra into one of her rages. I did not undertake the executoring very thoroughly.

There was a funeral, which Dimitra organized. I told myself that I might not go, but I found I was unable to stay away. Murgatroyd had elected to be buried in a special woodland cemetery in Epping Forest. Or maybe Dimitra had elected it for her. Lord knew from where the money for that came.

I drove my hire car up a leafy lane towards the car park, intending to find the whole thing beneath me. But the day was clean and bright, and there was something horribly poignant about the forest setting. Murgatroyd was determined to make me mourn for her.

There must have been thirty cars in the car park. I didn't know Murgatroyd knew thirty people. Who on earth were they? Shoppers at Gee-Haw? As I pulled up, I felt a guilty tension in my chest. Murgatroyd knew all these people well enough that they had come to her funeral, and I had no idea who any of them were. Some must have dated from the days Murg and I lived together, just as a matter of probability. But I had never bothered to find out who Murg's friends were.

There was a sizable, stylish wooden hut that served as a chapel, and I made my way there. Two women walking slightly ahead of me started a conversation; they knew one another. I had no one with whom to talk.

I went into the chapel. There's that Philip Larkin poem where he won't go into the church until he's sure there's nothing going on 'up at the holy end'. That would have been me. Except for the fact that I couldn't really avoid what was going on at the holy end of the wooden chapel. There, on trestles, stood a wicker coffin, surprisingly large. Murgatroyd. Horrors! Was she really in there? I wondered. Well, where else would she be? It would be wicker, I thought. That was perfect for Murgatroyd. If anywhere in Camden Market sold coffins, they would surely be wicker ones. I sat down.

Neither Murg nor, as far as I was aware, Dimitra had any truck with churches of any kind, but, after a time, a woman in a stole stood up and announced that we were celebrating the life of Amy Murgatroyd. I wondered where Dimitra had found her. Did she come with the funeral package? Probably. A projector hooked up to a laptop was shining photographs of Murgatroyd onto a screen. Murgatroyd as a child. Murgatroyd and Dimitra. Nothing from the Agatha Dorn era. Dimitra hadn't asked me for pictures, and I don't know that I would have had any if she had.

Were we celebrating the life of Amy Murgatroyd? To me, everything just felt terribly sad. Not that I begrudged the stole lady the euphemism. Maybe, in the moment, it's too painful to name what people are really doing at a funeral.

People were going up in turn to a lectern at the front of the chapel to say things about Murgatroyd. I had no intention of going up myself, but I found myself getting angry with everyone who did. All of these people getting up and talking about Murgatroyd, and none of them, with the exception of Dimitra, of whom I was all of a sudden madly jealous, knew her like I had. I began to cry like a child. Tears were rolling down my cheeks. I had to grit my teeth to prevent myself from emitting loud sobs. Ordinary images from Murg's and my life together flashed into my head, each one feeling suddenly unbearably moving. Murgatroyd's cleaning the house in Palmers Green in an old T-shirt, singing 'Sweet Home Alabama' in the world's least Alabamian accent. Murgatroyd's attempting to do the washing up one-handed while dangling an awful Silk Cut out of the window with the other. Murgatroyd's sitting on the garden furniture after midnight in summer, drinking a Ribena and white wine and finding everything hilarious.

When everyone who wanted to speak seemed to have spoken, Dimitra got up and delivered a longish remembrance, from notes, that included thanking everyone for coming and that sort of thing. Six people who had apparently known Murgatroyd well enough to be pall-bearers, none of whom was me, grasped the wicker coffin and headed outside, with the rest of us following. I hung back at a distance, not wanting to embarrass anyone with my inability to control myself. The grave had a small carved wooden Green Man in place of a headstone. The pall-bearers, who must, I thought, have somehow practised this, produced canvas straps and began to lower the coffin into the hole. *What on earth are you doing?* I suddenly wanted to shout. *Don't put her in the ground! How will she ever get out again?*

6

The first weird thing happened on the day I couldn't find the Secrets Book. In common with all sensible people, I avoided visiting the North London suburbs as much as possible and had thus largely stayed away from Murgatroyd's house—which was now my house. However, it turned out that Murgatroyd's estate consisted primarily of debt, and I was having to fob off creditors over the phone with a degree of regularity that was becoming irritating.

This was because Murgatroyd and Dimitra had—well, let me tell you about my history with Murgatroyd. My 'relationship' with Murgatroyd was the longest one I ever had. The only one, really. Her personality was a unique mixture of the waspish and the bovine that was, to me, irresistible. She gave the impression of being a dim bulb but was in fact dangerously sly. Almost twenty years ago, at the start of my (till now) undistinguished career, we had met on a course for archive types. A group of us formed one of those holiday friendships that plummet to the ground the moment the trip is over. On the last day, in the grip of it, I said something like 'I can't bear the idea that we might not see each other again! We should have a monthly tea or something!'

'Agatha, what a wonderful idea!' said Murgatroyd sweetly. 'Let's definitely pretend that we will.' I thought that was brilliant. When she called to ask me out two days later, the memory of it was the reason I accepted. I cannot stand people with no cruelty to them. For one thing, people who aren't cruel aren't funny, and who can abide the unfunny?

I used scare quotes around the word *relationship* just now (although scare quotes are a loathsome form of imprecision I generally do my best to avoid). Here is why. When I dropped out of university, I had a new job, and was desperate to escape the clutches of Clara. After a series of trips to restaurants and pubs that some might have called dates, Murgatroyd said I could come and live with her. Of course, she happened to live in the next street from Clara—literally the last place I wanted to be—but I liked Murg, and it was cheap, so I said yes. We became like an old married couple: she amassed possessions in a manner that suggested some concerning level of unhappiness; I pretended not to notice.

One night she made what used to be called a pass at me, which I rebuffed. It's not that I don't like sex. I just don't like having to talk about it or think about it or have it. Otherwise I have no problem with it. I told Murgatroyd I enjoyed being in a kind-of couple with her, but there wouldn't be any funny business. Murgatroyd asked how I would feel about sleeping in the same bed as her. I said I'd sooner not; she said that was fine. She would get her funny business elsewhere. I understood that she did.

For Murgatroyd, so she told me, the human body was a kind of miracle in the pleasure it was capable of giving and receiving. For me, it is an incontinent traitor whose oozing crevices and quisling urges are best kept out of sight and out of mind, especially at bedtime.

Whatever could have brought to an end this highly satisfactory arrangement, you ask? Murgatroyd was fundamentally extremely passive. We were 'together' for five years. She never asked me when my birthday was, and I never told her. She just bought me a present on hers.

I came to believe on a deep level that she would never leave me. I had dropped my guard. That was when I knew I had to get rid of *her*. Otherwise I might never see it coming when she decided to dump *me*. No matter how low one sets one's expectations, one has constantly to be on the alert for failure on the horizon, and foul up preëmptively in order to get out ahead of it. That's good Crooked Man thinking.

Plus, the fact that she got on with my mother so well was pretty galling. It got so that if Murg and I wanted to go out somewhere, I would have to make a point of asking her not to invite Clara. Murgatroyd was forever running to the shops for Clara on her way home from work or popping round at the weekend to do a bit of cleaning, dusting the red-leather Reader's Digest collection of abridged classics, and whatnot. Just the sort of things a dutiful daughter might have done. When I visited my mother (something I tried to do as little as possible), I would almost invariably find them sitting on the rattan-effect furniture in the conservatory, smoking their beastly Silk Cut. Well, better she than I.

And so when, five years in, Heri uncharacteristically offered to buy for me a flat in the Gatehouse, I leapt at the chance. Bye-bye, suburbs! The idea of continuing my cohabitation with Murgatroyd when I had the opportunity to live in a concrete space station was unthinkable.

And yet. The relationship having fizzled out at my instigation, I found myself wistfully remembering the house in Palmers Green with surprising frequency. I found myself staring at my phone of an evening, wondering if Murgatroyd would call. Had I been too hasty with my preëmptive ending of our arrangement? Had I been *in love* with Murgatroyd all that time? It hardly seemed possible.

Who knows what would have happened had Murgatroyd not started a new relationship with a woman named Dimitra Leonard, who did not like me one little bit? It was sufficiently serious that Murg gave up archiving, and the two of them opened a shop in Murg's beloved Camden Market. The shop, which was called Gee-Haw, sold what are popularly known as *novelties*. With its peeing Santa soda dispensers and hen-night ticklers, it was my Room 101. I went there once, just to show willing. When I arrived, Murgatroyd was nowhere in sight, and Dimitra, discovered in the act of restocking a spinner of edible underwear, brandished a candy G-string in my face and told me to buzz off.

Gee-Haw, as anyone might have predicted, was a money pit, and was the reason why I was now having to field telephone calls from banks and debt-collection agencies, when I would rather have been fielding calls from journalists asking to interview me about my astonishing literary find.

It was clear that the house in Palmers Green would have to be sold, but I couldn't sell it until it had been cleared. This was easier said than done. Murgatroyd's attitude to stuff was much like my attitude to guilt: accrue it, little by little but unceasingly, until you have a problem. My flat was tidier, but Murg did not have deep-seated neuroses concerning her mother, so who was the real winner?

I had used some of my new-found wealth to hire a house-clearing company. They had got rid of anything perishable, but I had to go through the other stuff and remove anything I wanted to keep or sell, before they would deal with the rest of it. It was, as Murgatroyd used to say of her ability to move one eyeball independently of the other, both a blessing and a curse, since it meant I had to go to Palmers Green.

As I opened the front door, it raked a pile of post into an arc across the hall carpet. But, besides the post, the house was deceptively serene. Murgatroyd hid her hoarding like alcoholics hide their bottles. There were no yellowing piles of newspaper or doomsday stacks of tinned food. When I had first moved in though, I had disturbed what had appeared to be an ordinary guest bed, only to find three irons, two extra duvets, and a pile of tea towels stacked up roughly in the shape of the absent mattress. Seemingly innocent cupboards held complete sets of dinnerware from three decades ago, long replaced, but never disposed of.

I headed to the kitchen and pulled at the first cabinet at head height that I reached. It opened a centimetre and stuck. We fought, the cabinet door and I, until the entire thing came away in my hand and smacked me in the forehead. The cabinet vomited forth a stack of what looked like bank statements. The one on top was dated September 1986.

I really didn't think I wanted any of Murg's awful sandalwood knick-knacks and Camden Market tat, though. It struck me that the only thing about which I was even curious was the Secrets Book, which I now remembered that Murgatroyd had several times told me to read after she died. On what mawkish nonsense it would contain, I hardly dared to speculate. But I had come all this way, so.

I headed for the bedroom to ransack the bedside table, where the book had always been kept, and was brought up short. Improbably, the bubblegum-pink helium canister from Murgatroyd's suicide kit still stood by the bed. I supposed it too belonged to me now.

In order to do away with herself, Murgatroyd had, the police said, bought something called a helium hood from the Internet, where you put a special plastic bag over your head, twist a valve, and pump the fatal gas into it from a canister. A ghoulish fun fact is that, since most people who buy helium canisters do so in order to blow up birthday balloons, the canisters typically come in candy-floss colours, even when you buy them as part of a suicide kit. I had not known that suicide kits even existed. You learn something new every day.

Except for the hoarding, Murgatroyd seemed a model of sanguinity in everything she did, even her suicide note. 'To whom it may concern,' she had written. 'Upon recently being apprised that my existence was shortly to be terminated due to pancreatic cancer, I was generously awarded a three-month notice period. I regret to inform you, however, that it will not be possible for me to serve out my notice in full.' It went on to say how sorry she was, and where her will could be found. It was all very matter-of-fact. Even if she had put 'due to' where she clearly meant 'owing to'.

I started shaking but averted my eyes and returned to my task. On top of the table was Murgatroyd's grimy pink mobile phone, plugged into the wall. There was a James Patterson paperback in the drawer—Murgatroyd had shocking taste in mysteries. Next to it was an ultraviolet lava lamp and a container of sand-coloured powder whose label was entirely in Chinese, except for the words *asparagus root*. Then there was a sentimental Catholic card with a picture of a saint and an icky prayer about cancer, a neck massager, and half a block of hashish.

But no Secrets Book. Which was both disappointing and curious. If Murgatroyd had wanted me to read the darned thing so badly, she could at least have left it where I knew it lived.

I was about to walk away, when I glanced down and saw two pieces of paper sticking out from under the bedside table. I pulled them out. One was large, one small. Both looked some years old, one older than the other. The first was covered with text that began: 'Well, the Dog and Bear it is!' On the second scrap, in very similar handwriting: '997 IHR, Aris–'.

My heart shuddered. I knew what the first piece of paper was, or at least appeared to be. It was a piece of a page from 'The Dog's Ball' manuscript. What on God's green earth had Murgatroyd been thinking? Why on earth did she have it? And how? You didn't just pilfer something like this for a souvenir. This was sacrilege. My colleagues would turn in their graves if they knew the manuscript had been compromised, and they weren't even dead, technically speaking.

The first piece of paper being what it was, the second was surely some kind of reference to my boss Ian Harcourt-Reilly and what—a word? It could have been *Arise*. Well, that made sense. The Neele had been talking to Arise a good deal of late. But I had the beginning of a bad feeling about this, one I wasn't prepared to give room to turn into a thought, just yet. I emptied out the contents of an ancient envelope from another drawer, replacing them with the papers, and pocketed it.

I moved on to the bathroom and opened the cabinet. It was crammed with pill bottles—not old ones, but new, each one a little totem of the cancer gods. There was one of those daily pill organizers ill and old people have. Closing the door, I saw the edge of a smear on the mirror. Murgatroyd always wrote inspirational twaddle to herself on the mirror, like someone in a self-help book. I breathed on the smear and revealed a word: *Floreat!* So she was still doing that rubbish then, right up until the end.

I found myself feeling nauseated. Seeing the suicide kit and finding the unexplained papers had been a bit of a one-two punch. I knew I was supposed to be finding things to save from the clearance company. Suddenly, I wanted to tell them, *Just burn it all, and bulldoze the house while you're at it.*

I hadn't found the Secrets Book though; something told me that there I would find the explanation for the theft of the manuscript page. But at the same time, I had no energy left to look for it now. Where would I even start, in this archive of the useless, where every drawer was a junk drawer, every cupboard a gallimaufry of nothing? The only thing to do was leave, put off calling the house company, and wait for my head to stop spinning and tell me what to do. Probably going home for a couple of gins and sleeping on it would be a good start.

7

Murgatroyd continued to nag at me. If I had one too many gins, I would start to get weepy again, like I had at the funeral. If I had insufficient gin, by contrast, I would worry about what I had found in her house. Why did she have a piece from 'The Dog's Ball'? What about the reference to Ian? Did she know Ian? I hadn't thought so. Why would she? I remembered her telling me to 'be careful' about the manuscript, or some nonsense. Did she know something I didn't? Did Ian?

Frankly, though, I didn't like where such wool-gathering was leading. I was well on my way to becoming a literary mini-celebrity, and I was not inclined to pull too hard at any threads that could disturb that.

My ego began to swell. The BBC approached us about a documentary on 'The Dog's Ball', to be entitled *The Lost Green*, and production began. I was to be the main talking head in the talking-head bits. They spent the best part of a morning shooting footage at the Neele. I beau-ed them around like Rhett Butler. I learned new terminology and casually threw it about. I barged into offices with the cameraman, whether they liked it or not. 'We're just getting some B-roll for the BBC special, I do hope that's OK,' I said. 'Would you mind *very* much being quiet while we get a couple of seconds of room tone?'

I behaved badly, without really meaning to. Ian and Nancy had been cultivating a long-term bluehair who had suggested that she had a *lot* of money to give us. When people give very large gifts to an institution, they don't just type their credit-card number into the website and click 'donate'. There are preliminary emails, then conversations over the phone, then someone writes a proposal, explaining precisely for what the money will be used. There are sometimes preliminary meetings. But before anybody signs a gift agreement, there is almost always a ritualistic meeting, often at the donor's home, in which somebody important actually asks for the money in person, and the donor agrees. Ian is the one who does this, since he is the boss. (This is the kind of thing that Ian meant when he said senior positions were all about PR, if you remember my not getting promoted.) But this lady, who was a big Green fan, wanted to meet me in particular; in fact, I was to give her a private tour of the Green collection before the big ask. But—wouldn't you know it?—on the day of the tour I had to shoot some new, last-minute interview segments for the documentary, and I had to cancel. The whole thing with the donor had to be rescheduled; Ian rather melodramatically told her my mother had died. He was livid. I really couldn't understand why. 'It's the BBC!' I said to him. What was more important? Showing an old lady round some old books, or being on the television? Surely even he could see there was no contest!

And so I tried not to allow myself time to brood on Murgatroyd.

And so arrived the evening of the *Dog's Ball* launch. Once again, I had one of my headaches, worse luck.

I needed to be at the event, but I holed up in my dark office and tried to get myself together. The show had to go on. I had to get in gear. I unearthed the bottle of gin from my desk drawer, poured some into the grimy glass on my desk, topped it off with water, and drank it fast.

What would Nancy have done in my situation? Put her face on and strolled out in her best heels like her only wish in the world was to talk about how wonderful Gladden Green was—and incidentally, how wonderful she, Nancy, also was. That was what I had to do, too.

There was a knock on my door. I had not thought anyone had known I was in here. 'Yes?' I said. A grey-haired, pudgy gentleman sidled in, wearing the weather-worn black get-up of techies everywhere.

'Is it Miss Dorn?' he said diffidently. I grunted. 'Yeah, I'm really glad. I'm sorry for bothering you in your office. I saw you come in. I'm one of the technicians. I really like Gladden Green. I've read all her books. I was just wondering if you…' He trailed off, proffering a copy of *The Dog's Ball* in my general direction.

'Oh, wonderful,' I said. 'Listen, I need some help. Could you run to the little Tesco down the road and get me some of that super-ultra Nurofen? I have a terrible headache.' I gave a little *away* motion with my hand.

'Well, uh, I just work for the event company, and we're not really supposed to leave the site for anyone,' he mumbled. 'I was just hoping you could sign my book. I can come back later…'

'Christ's wounds!' I said. I was enraged. The Crooked Man was not going to get me at my own book launch! 'You are the help. Can you not help? I am not "anyone". I am the talent. If I cannot go out there, there will not be an event for you to manage.' He made an abject, helpless face and did not move, except to wave the book again. 'Give me that thing,' I said. 'What is your name?'

'Eric,' he said.

'To Eric, who needs to learn some manners,' I wrote, signed my autograph, and thrust the book back at him. He read the inscription and looked down-hearted. 'Now buzz off, if you can't be useful,' I said. Eric reverse-sidled whence he had come. I felt slightly bad about having snapped, but one thing I was learning in my new-found mini-celebrity: you had to act as if people owed you their deference, or you would not get it. And I had had enough years of not being deferred to by anyone, in anything.

Cursing Eric, I staggered down the road to the Tesco Express and got a packet of the strongest painkillers they had, which I washed down with a gin miniature. Belt and braces.

In the loo by my office, I tried to tidy myself up. I peeled off my aged red hunting hat and my ancient tweed coat. I splashed water on the front of my face, shook my head from side to side, then dried it with a paper towel. I mussed my hair with my hands. Would I do? I would do. I did not have any heels, but I had the natty saddle shoes with the navy-blue panel.

When I got to the better of the Neele's two function rooms, Ian was already giving his little introduction, which meant I had almost missed the start of my own speech. In the gratifyingly healthy crowd, I saw that the Cadigans, Tom and his wife Lily, were there. There was Fraser Green, unescorted as always. My agent—what a thrill, to say those words!—*my agent*. Felicity, our ancient administrator, was there. Felicity had been an avant-garde artist and an It Girl *avant la lettre* in the Soho scene of the 1950s. She was ninety years old, but still had a Louise Brooks bob, dyed an obsidian black. Clara was there with her nurse, whose name was Mabel Palmer, as well as my brother

Heri. Heri's paying attention to Clara was new—to the best of my knowledge, he had hardly seen her since he was eighteen, though he had remained her favourite despite this. My theory was that Heri was auditioning the comely Miss Palmer for the rôle of his third wife.

Bunner span round when she heard the door and made an exaggerated grimace in my direction. 'Thank goodness you're here, Agatha! I was so worried!' she stage-whispered. But Bunner needed to calm down. What would they have done? Had the event without me?

Nancy appeared not to have bothered to come. I couldn't believe it! Anger began to boil inside me, but then I got annoyed with myself for being angry, because it suggested I cared whether or not Nancy was there, which I certainly Did Not.

The room had been got up very nicely. Artefacts from my Green collection, now organized in our summer exhibition, *Gladden Green: A Life of Crime*, filled the glass cases that lined the walls. My discovery had driven Nancy's old idea, 'Edgar Allan Poe: FAKE NEWS!', into next year, although it had not, I thought sadly, nuked it completely. There were waiters with high-class *hors d'œuvres* and booze, and at least one man who, judging by the large size of his camera rig, appeared to have come from one of the real newspapers. I continued to feel a little unsteady, so I grabbed a flute of champagne from a passing tray and necked it. The cyclorama behind Ian showed the enlarged and glowing image of the front cover of *The Dog's Ball*. I looked for my name, directly underneath Gladden's—'edited and with an introduction by Agatha Dorn'. Somehow, though, it was being obscured by a shadow from a microphone stand or something. Well, no matter.

'… extremely proud,' Ian was saying, with a fine mixture of restraint and sincerity. As I approached the daïs, he looked at me blankly, noting that I had arrived without catching my eye. After everything that had happened, I was looking forward to hearing the glowing testimonial to me that the circumstances would oblige him to make. 'While this discovery might have come to light in any number of ways, it seems only fitting that it has been unearthed under the auspices of the Neele Archive, one of our country's preëminent literary institutions, through the diligence of our world-class team of archivists.'

Our world-class team? How about the world-class Agatha Dorn! Well, perhaps he was saving up his tribute to me for the end. 'Their work really demonstrates that the Neele is truly a national treasure,' he continued, grinning.

This was a sound bite for the benefit of Oliver Manders at Arise. As score-settling went, I thought, it seemed unlikely that it would get back to him—but then I noticed out of the corner of my eye that he was here. That was a weird choice for an invitation, our erstwhile mortal enemy. And he, like Ian, seemed to have a smile on his face. Very odd.

Now, Ian was thanking people. '—Nancy Miller, Dora Bunner, and our other wonderful staff, and Mr and Mrs Tom Cadigan, who made the historic decision to donate the papers of Alexander Cust to the archive, thus making it possible for *The Dog's Ball* to be discovered. And finally'—at last, it was going to be my turn—'there is one special thank-you I need to make—without whose unimpeachable work this evening would not have been possible.' I began to blush. 'I refer, of course, to the waiting staff, who have done such a wonderful job with the food and drink this evening. Please, a round of applause for the staff.' The audience obliged. 'And now,' he concluded, 'it is my duty to deliver you into the hands of a member of our top-notch team, Miss Agatha Dorn.'

So this was how it was. Ian continued to hold his petty grudge. Never mind. Neither he nor anyone could take my moment from me. Ian vacated the microphone with a courtly gesture in my direction, and I took up my place, to scattered applause.

'Thank you all,' I began. Strangely, though, the microphone did not seem to be working. I peered into the dark, but my view was obscured by a spotlight that seemed suddenly to have ended up directly in my eyes. I tapped the microphone. 'Hello?' I said. Nothing. I called out to the audience: 'There seems to be a slight problem with the microphone. Hang on.'

I gripped the microphone with both hands. A massive blast of static electricity sent me stumbling backwards into the speaker, from which came a howl of feedback. 'Gah! God's teeth!' I said. It came out as a boom: evidently the microphone was now operational and linked to a sound system that had been turned up to rock-concert volume. Laughter rippled through the crowd. I wanted to bite off their heads, but, with the spotlight on me, all I could do was acquiesce with a smile that I hoped came across as charmingly self-deprecating. Knowing me, though, I doubted it. As I rose again to the microphone, I saw my techie friend Eric at the control desk, grinning widely, and making a little *away* motion in my direction. Righto.

8

Rattled as I was, my speech went from an inauspicious beginning to an uninspired middle, before limping to a lacklustre conclusion. The applause was quite generous, though more in honour of the occasion than of me, I suspected. I looked out at the crowd. Clara was beaming at Heri, which was a little on the nose, I thought, even for her. Heri was ogling the nurse. Fraser Green was staring in my general direction with his vacant expression—one never could tell if he was actually looking *at* one or ten yards further on. Tom Cadigan's wife Lily was scrutinizing him with steely eyes. Murgatroyd's girlfriend Dimitra Leonard, who hated my guts, had apparently turned up at some point during the event, and was looking daggers at me. Well, of course. Ian was whispering with Oliver Manders.

I wanted nothing more than to leave and try to collect my thoughts, but I couldn't very well disappear immediately from my own reception. I made a beeline for the bar instead.

Then Tom and Lily appeared by my side. 'Congratulations!' said Tom, full of beans. Though the manuscript had arguably belonged more to Lily than to her husband, having been written by her grandfather, it was Tom who had taken the lead in the whole business, visiting me at the Neele to work out the deed of gift, and dropping the papers off. He was some kind of media freelancer, who had meetings in the City on occasion, so it made sense for him to have done so, but it was also clear that he was the one with the enthusiasm for publishing the novella.

Tom Cadigan was getting a paunch and had grey hair at his temples but wore a skinny suit and thin black plimsolls designed for someone fifteen years younger. He had the air of a disappointed up-and-comer. The book was supposed to have shone the glory on Tom that he had for years believed was his due, and who cared if it was reflected?

'Thanks,' I said.

'I heard Zadie Smith might be here,' he said, 'but I haven't seen her. Do you know if she is?'

'I haven't heard anything like that,' I said.

'Oh,' he said. There was awkward silence for a moment.

Then there was a bustling, and the gentleman with the big camera appeared. I turned to face him and turned up the corners of my mouth as best I could manage. I felt an arm around my waist. Tom Cadigan was sure to want to get himself in the *Standard*, or wherever this shot might turn up. But when I turned to look, it was Heri, my brother, muscling in next to me with a faeces-eating grin for the camera, and Tom was nowhere to be seen! The camera flashed.

Having been silent all this time, Lily seemed as surprised by her husband's sudden departure as I was. She looked around for him in the crowd.

'You found this book, then, did you?' Her North Yorkshire accent was clipped, not broad. There was something compelling about her cheekbones. I found myself imagining scenarios wherein I might have to see her again.

'Yes,' I said. 'We're all so grateful to your grandfather for preserving it. You must be very proud.'

'Why?' she said. It was a fair question. Was it really a source of pride to be related to someone who happened to have been given something valuable? I had just been saying the sort of things people say. Lily Cadigan had made the mistake of actually listening.

'Yes,' I said, 'I suppose so. Why?' I laughed awkwardly. 'Why? Well, I like to think Gladden's ghost is happy the book is seeing the light of day at last.'

'Do you?' she said pointedly. She seemed determined not to settle for my hogwash. I should have made my excuses and left, but for some reason I wanted this woman to know I wasn't what she seemed to have concluded I was—*what*? A sell-out? But then, I was one. I'd been longing to sell out for twenty years; the chance had come along, and here I was, yukking it up and raking it in. In addition to her compelling cheekbones, she had a glittering eye, like the Ancient Mariner. There was something about her. I decided to tell the truth.

'No,' I said. 'I think Gladden's ghost is probably furious with me. I expect she wishes she'd burned the manuscript, just as she wrote to your grandfather. But if you tell anyone I said that, I'll deny it.' I went for a winning smile, but I just knew it had come out as a grimace.

Lily Cadigan looked at me with sharp eyes that seemed to be trying to read me, to figure out what kind of person I was. 'Would you, though?' she said. And then, for a moment, I thought she was about to tell me something else. But instead she plunged back into the throng, either in search of her husband or to get as far away as possible from him. It was impossible to tell.

I turned to my brother.

'Hello, Heri,' I said. 'Glad you could make it.'

Heri had a face reminiscent of that of a sheep. He had made the best of this, however, by developing a resting expression that implied he had chosen such a visage deliberately, in order to make fun of you.

I mentioned before that Heri is an extremely wealthy doctor—a surgeon, in fact. He does not do any actual surgery, though. He has a team of minions, who, for a very great deal of cash, carry out proprietary kinds of neurectomies, inguinal hernia repairs, and adductor tenotomies on professional sportspeople. I'm quoting his website here. I myself have no idea what these terms even mean, much less the capacity to recall them from memory. There were rumours of some kind of scandal, back in the late nineties or thereabouts, which Heri, they say, had to use chunks of his cash to hush up. Now it would be unfair to leave out the fact that my brother worked hard for many years. He has two former wives and two children he sees on their birthdays and Christmas who can testify to that. But he was never motivated by the love of healing, or whatever. Rather, he worked out up front what subspeciality of which branch of medicine would yield him the most massive amount of money and pursued it with all his might.

'Hello, Agatha!' he said. 'Moving up in the world, eh? I couldn't miss my sister's hour of triumph, now could I?'

No, I thought, *nor the opportunity to be associated with any kind of media bunfight.*

'Bit of trouble with the speech there, though?' I wanted to punch him in the mouth.

'Eff off,' I said. 'What are you doing in the same room as Clara, in any case?'

'Well,' he said, 'I'm getting interested in some drug therapies for dementia—very new, very unusual. Could be terribly lucrative. Thought I'd spend some time around Mum, get a feel for the condition.'

'I hope you're not using her as some kind of guinea pig,' I said.

'What do you care? You hate her more than I do,' he said. 'But no—nothing of the sort.' I didn't trust him as far as I could throw him, though.

Clara appeared, with Mabel Palmer at her elbow. 'Well now, this evening has been very interesting,' she said. 'I do love a good Gladden Green. I'm so glad you brought me.' She smiled at Heri. 'Did I read something about a new one coming out, that someone found?'

'That's this, Mrs Dorn,' said Mabel. 'That's the book that's being launched here tonight.' Under normal circumstances I would have added that I, her daughter, had discovered it, had edited it, but I was trying to keep it together, and anyway, why give her the satisfaction?

'Ah, I see,' said Clara. 'That makes sense.' She went on. 'I *thought* I read something, but Murgatroyd took it away. She said I wasn't to bother myself reading about *that* book. And then I never saw anything about it till this evening. I think that's what happened. You know I'm having a little trouble with my memory at the moment, dear.' Curious. If I believed that such an odd exchange had in fact occurred. Why would Murgatroyd have wanted to stop Clara reading about *The Dog's Ball*?

'Mr Dorn, we should get Mrs Dorn home before she gets too tired,' said Mabel Palmer to Heri, ignoring me.

'Hm,' said Heri, shrugging at me. 'Well, nurse's orders, I suppose. See you later, Sis.' And off they went. Heri had got his photograph taken; he had what he came for. Why stay longer?

They hove out of view, revealing Murgatroyd's girlfriend Dimitra behind them. She didn't spot me, thank god. Not wanting to get yelled at, I shuffled away, keeping one eye on her…

… and crashed directly into Ian and Oliver, still together. Oliver was muttering to Ian about how something had 'gone to her head'. The envious toad.

'What's gone to my head?' I said, calling his bluff.

'Agatha, congrats,' said Ian, in his dry way. 'Shake your hand.' He made a pantomime of doing so. 'Very nice. Well done to you.'

'You might have said so in your speech,' I said.

'Oh, rubbish,' he said affably. 'I said you were world class. What more does she want, eh, Ollie?' I didn't feel like chopping logic, so I said nothing. He was being nice now—so was I, since anything else felt like too much trouble—but he had known exactly what he was doing.

'Agatha, good to see you,' said Oliver. 'Number two on the Arise fiction chart. Not too shabby.'

'I didn't know you two knew each other,' I said. 'Outside our business from last year.'

'Oh, we don't,' said Ian. 'I think this is the first conversation we've ever had outside the Neele conference room, isn't it, Oliver?'

'I think it is, yes,' said Oliver.

'Really?' I said. 'You two have been very cosy all evening.' I smiled, to show it was a joke.

'Oh, well,' said Oliver. 'I suppose it turns out we get on quite well now we're not adversaries, is that fair to say?'

'I suppose it is,' said Ian.

'Agatha, you're empty,' said Oliver. 'Might I get you another?'

'Thanks,' I said. 'I'll have a gin.'

'Anything with it?'

'Water,' I said.

'Gin and water,' he said with a smirk. 'Very austere of you. I'll be right back.'

What with Ian acting so oddly about knowing or not knowing Oliver, the fact that I had found Ian's initials on that paper in Murgatroyd's house sprang to mind. Had he known her, too, after all? I decided to test a theory. 'I still haven't been able to bring myself to finish clearing Amy's house,' I said. I thought, *If he doesn't ask whom that is, I'll know he and Murgatroyd knew one another.*

'Amy?' he said. Curses.

'My friend who died. About four months ago—I thought I told you. She had cancer, but then she killed herself so as not to die of it.'

'She killed herself so as not to die of cancer?' said Ian. 'That's absolutely extraordinary. I wish you had told me about it. I don't think you can have. I would have remembered. I suppose it must have been right when all this *Dog's Ball* business kicked off, mustn't it?'

'It was, yes,' I said. 'I suppose that's why. You might remember, though, I used to live with her in Palmers Green, right when I first worked here. That's the house. She left it to me.'

Ian got a strange look in his eyes, as if he were beginning to realize something. Then he snapped back to his usual self. 'I *do* remember you commuting from Palmers Green,' he said. 'God, those were the days, eh? Palmers Green! That would have been a fate worse even than Sunningdale!'

An eminent bluehair from whom we had a chance of extracting some money hailed Ian from across the room. 'I'll be right back, Agatha,' he said, and disappeared, leaving me stranded in a cocktail party's official worst situation: waiting for someone you don't really know to reappear with the drink they've gone to get you.

Bunner appeared unctuously at my elbow. 'It's not, you know,' she said.

'What, Bunner?' I said. 'Do you have to be cryptic?'

'It's not the first time they've talked to each other, Ian and Oliver,' she said.

This was potentially significant information, but I couldn't abide Bunner's tattletale-ing manner. 'Were you eavesdropping on me?' I asked, irritated.

'I'm sorry, Agatha.' She made a hangdog face. 'I couldn't help overhearing.'

Now I felt bad. 'What of it, then?' I said.

'I saw them, a couple of months ago. After one of the Arise meetings. Oliver came out of Ian's office. They were thick as thieves.'

I was irked by the way she seemed to expect me to be so pleased with her. Plus, I realized I had an opportunity to make headway with another mystery. 'Bunner,' I said, 'did you let my friend Murgatroyd have access to the *Dog's Ball* manuscript by any chance?'

'Was that your assistant who came in a few months ago?'

'My assistant? You'll have to explain,' I said.

'Well, about five months ago it must have been, a larger lady in a flowery dress — would that have been her?' I said that it would. 'This larger lady came in and said she was just back from Harrogate, that you had been very interested in where *The Dog's Ball* had been written, and that she wanted to check something on a page.'

'Wait—' I said. 'Murgatroyd told you she had *been* to Harrogate?'

'Yes,' said Bunner. 'She said you were very interested in the place where *The Dog's Ball* had been written, and that she had just come back from there.'

This was extraordinary. Not only had Murgatroyd got hold of a page from the manuscript, but she had also travelled to Harrogate to visit the Pale Horse? What on earth had she been doing?

'And she said she was working for me?' I said.

'Yes. Well, now I think about it, not as such. More implied it. I suppose I assumed she was, because she had mentioned your name. She asked if I would let her take a photograph of a page of the manuscript with her phone.'

'I see,' I said. 'And you let her do that.'

'Oh yes,' said Bunner. 'I know we're not meant to let just anyone have access to the collections, but since it was for you... but—well, oh, I suppose I shouldn't have, should I?'

'Bunner,' I said, 'did you leave her alone with the manuscript, by any chance?'

'Well, I did, as a matter of fact. I know I'm not supposed to. But it was just for a moment. Someone rang the bell at the desk, and I got rather flustered, I'm afraid. But she seemed terribly nice and responsible, and she said she was an archivist as well, and she knew what to do, and she wouldn't touch anything, she would just take the photograph and come out—which she did, just a few seconds later. And when I went back in, everything was just as I had left it. I hope I didn't do the wrong thing.'

I told Bunner that everything was all right and that Murgatroyd had indeed been terribly nice and responsible; I had just wondered. Bunner seemed quite relieved.

So now I knew how Murgatroyd had got hold of the page of the manuscript.

'Let me go and get you a drink,' I said. 'You don't have anything.'

'Oh, would you? Oh, thank you, Agatha. Are you sure? You shouldn't have to, you know. You're the star of the evening. I should be fetching things for you.' At least someone realized it.

'It's really no trouble,' I said. 'What would you like?'

'I'll have a white wine then, if you're sure. Thank you.' She beamed, and I headed to the bar. Halfway there I reëncountered Oliver with my gin and water. With an apology, I redirected him and the drink towards Bunner. Now I wouldn't have to go back. And who wouldn't be pleased to receive a lovely gin in place of some nasty supermarket wine? Bunner would thank me when she got it. I thought about how I could make my escape.

I had made it halfway to the door when I heard a voice. 'You!' it said. Dimitra was bustling my way like an angry prairie dog. 'No one can track you down any more, but I knew you'd be here!'

'Hello, Dimitra,' I said, 'it's nice to see you.' People who wear as much tie-dye as she did are supposed to be at peace with the universe, but Dimitra was a taut ball of bitterness. Her face looked like the wind had changed and it had stayed like that.

'Yes, well,' she said. 'It's all right for some. I've been in touch with a solicitor, I've written to the probate office. Then we'll see.'

'I'm not sure what you think you'll see,' I said.

'You know all too well, Agatha Dorn,' she replied. 'While you've been gadding about, I have been struggling vainly to keep Amy's legacy—which, by the way, she was leaving to *me*—alive. The house needs to be sold. Gee-Haw needs the proceeds.

'Meanwhile,' she continued, 'you've illegally taken possession while you work on your cirrhosis—oh yes, I have my sources around the place! Though, frankly, I get a whiff of the booze from here. Well, I'm putting an end to it. Amy left the estate to me, no matter what nonsense you've pulled. She told me so.'

I wanted to note that I had never, to the best of my knowledge, gadded about, but instead I said, 'Dimitra, there are no proceeds. There are just debts. They'd have turfed you and your vanity shop out months ago if I—' I was going to say, *If I had done my job as executor properly*, but I realized that would rather have undercut the air of superiority I was trying to project. Unfortunately, I was unable to take the sentence in a suitably cutting direction in time, so I ended up trailing off.

'You're very uncharitable, for an old hippie,' I said. 'Aren't you supposed to be all peace and love?' Dimitra was silent. I thought a specific question might help. 'Is that really what she told you was in her will?'

'She used to say, *always*, she'd make sure I was comfortable. When she bought me out, she said, "You can have everything, if you like."'

'Did she say that lately?'

There was a long pause. 'She didn't tell me what she was going to do. She didn't even tell me about the cancer! So I found out she had killed herself when *you* called, which was bad enough, but I didn't even know she was going to die! Why would she trust a—a fishwife like you with that, and not me? She never moved on from you! But she hated you. So no, she didn't say it lately, but that's how I know she meant to leave it all to me. She was furious with you, livid, the last couple of weeks. Furious. She'd phone me up fuming and say "These f—ing Dorns! These f—ing Dorns are going to be the death of me!"'

I shook her off, but the attack had smashed the façade of good humour I had been managing thus far to keep going.

I ran away down the corridor towards my office.

9

I wedged myself into my darkened office and tried to process everything that was now itching at my brain. I couldn't really tell if something truly mysterious was going on, or if I was just in a funny mood. Clearly, I had not managed to banish the papers from Murgatroyd's house from my mind. I got out a notepad and starting jotting things down. That was number 1):

1) Murgatroyd had a scrap of a page from *The Dog's Ball* and a paper with Ian's initials. Why?

I had tried to find out if Ian knew Murgatroyd but had not. On the other hand, I *had* found out (if Bunner was to be believed) that:

2) Ian did know Oliver Manders from Arise better than he had let on.

On the subject of the stolen page, I knew that:

3) Murgatroyd had apparently bamboozled Bunner into letting her steal it, and
4) Murgatroyd had apparently been poking around at the Pale Horse in Harrogate also, *and*
5) Murgatroyd had told Clara not to read *The Dog's Ball*, *AND*

6) Murgatroyd had been fussing at me about the manuscript before she died, too.

And finally, if I was in the business of entertaining questions
of a minor sort:

7) What was Heri doing escorting the hated Clara
around to social events?

and

8) Why was Tom Cadigan, who looked to me like just as
much of a fame-strumpet as my brother, taking pains
to avoid the limelight?

Like I said, it was all very unsettling. Or perhaps I was simply
myself unsettled after my disastrous performance… But perhaps I ought to head back to Murgatroyd's house and see what
else I could discover. Perhaps it was important that I make a
real search for the Secrets Book?…

Before I could get any further though, there was a knock
on the door. Honestly! I was blithely available in my office all
day every day, and no one knocked for weeks at a time. But let
me try to get some privacy for a minute, with the lights off and
the door closed, it's like Piccadilly blooming Circus!

My spirits sank further when I saw Nancy—making her first
appearance of the evening—poke her pleasingly symmetrical
face through the doorway. I thought she was going to gush or
simper or apologize or something, but instead she looked at
me quizzically, then strode into the room, grabbed my arm,
and said, 'You look like you need a drink. Come on.'

'I've had a drink,' I said.

'Well, you look like you need another one,' she said, and more-or-less marched me out of the building.

Nancy steered me out into Silk Street. I was too wired to resist, or even say anything. After a moment, she rang a bell on a door next to the newsagent's. My next-door neighbour, Mrs Hernandez, answered. If I'd known I'd be seeing her this evening, I definitely would have made an effort to learn her name sometime in the last ten years.

'Mrs De Castina!' said Nancy.

'Miss Nancy,' said the woman, who was apparently in fact named Mrs De Castina. At me, she nodded. There was an ancient podium next to her, with a fake-walnut veneer and a thin brass plaque that read: 'Sampson the Gelding: The Heaviest Horse in the World'. I gasped inwardly. My neighbour headed back down the stairs, and Nancy and I followed.

At the bottom was a concrete basement decked out with those white plastic lawn chair-and-table sets. In one corner was a bar. It was built out of red bricks with a thin brass counter-top. An apparatus made of veneered chipboard slats sprouted from the top of it, on which hung large bottles of spirits with optics attached. A teenager in a nylon tracksuit stood behind. Everything was bare concrete except for the back wall, which was completely filled by a mural of an extremely large horse, in bright colours. The heaviest horse in the world, one supposed. Most of the chairs and tables were taken up with vaguely famil-iar-looking people. I had seen them around—at the library, in the laundrette; they were all Gatehouse old-timers from before the money moved in.

Sampson the Gelding was an urban legend: a secret club for certain Gatehouse residents who wanted somewhere to socialize that was not one of the twenty-six All Bar Ones within a half-mile radius of the estate. It was like the illuminati for ageing City residents. One heard that people were members, but how they got to be that way, no one had a clue. Bunner maintained that Sampson didn't really exist.

'How—?' I coughed.

'Oh, I saw the door open one day and was curious, so I rang the bell and asked if I could come in.' Life is very different for the beautiful.

We sat down. Next to us, a gaggle of sixty-year-olds had pulled several of the white lawn tables together and were playing Monopoly, of all things. European folk music was drifting from somewhere. An elderly couple was dancing. There was a small dance floor made out of that spongy parquet-effect plastic they use for portable dance floors at outdoor weddings. The conversation was animated but peaceable. The City never felt peaceable. I walked from Spitalfields to King's Cross the other day and felt like the only grown-up anywhere. Liverpool Street was full of boisterous money children and Clerkenwell was full of romping media children. Where were all the old people who just wanted to sit down for a minute? Apparently they were down here, getting a drink without me.

A man at the Monopoly table next to us called for rent and his friend, a man in a tank top and a flannel shirt, amiably paid up. This was a far cry from how Monopoly had proceeded at my house when I was a child. If I had the misfortune to own a property, and Heri landed on it, he would simply browbeat me until I gave up attempting to make him pay, while Clara praised him for his hard-headed business acumen.

Another teenager, this one seemingly employed as a waiter, though he showed no outward sign of it, arrived at our table with two plates, each bearing a congealing cube of Spanish omelette and a king prawn. We had not asked for them; everyone seemed to have one, though. Both looked like a quick way to get salmonella, but Nancy tucked in. She asked the teenager for two double vodkas, then turned to me and said, 'We've got to take our medicine.' When they arrived, she downed one. So did I. I wasn't sure I wanted to, but I had made a rod for my back by refusing the food. It would have been churlish to not drink as well.

'Did you have plans this evening?' I asked.

'What?' she said.

'Oh, it was the *Dog's Ball* launch!' I said breezily.

'Was it?' she said.

'You know it was,' I said. I felt as if an iron band was contracting around the circumference of my head.

'Yes, I do,' she said. 'Sorry.'

'This place is more cavernous than I expected,' I said.

'I suppose,' she said.

'I expected it to be like a dive bar,' I said, 'like a snug. Like a den. Do you think it's like a den?'

'No,' she said.

'Not even a little bit?' I said. 'On second thoughts, I think it is quite den-like. Just for the elect, you know.'

'Agatha,' she laughed, 'what are you even talking about?'

'It's "About what are you even talking", if we're being correct,' I said. 'So did you have plans? Did you have a better offer? You probably did have a better offer.'

'Agatha, are you angry with me for not coming to the launch?'

'No, no, of course not,' I said. 'I know you're a busy person. Much in demand.'

'This is too funny,' she said. 'Here you are all angry with me for not coming. I didn't know you cared.'

'It's not about caring,' I said without thinking. 'I had to sit through your mumble-crusting Emily Dickinson party while everyone ooh-ed and aah-ed. You think I wanted to go to that? Go and play also-ran to my twenty-four-year-old boss? But I went. It's just what we do. But no—when the shoe's on the other foot, you don't even bother to turn up! What was it, you had to do an interview? Record a television programme? Judge the Booker Prize?'

'Christ, Agatha,' she said. 'You have a very strange idea of what my life is like. Leaving that aside, however: first, I didn't come to the launch because I hate those f—ing things more than anything.' I thought of Nancy at every function at which I had ever seen her, grinning and small talking and drawing people to her like a magnet. But sure, she hated them. 'Second,' she said, 'did I not come to your office to take you out for a drink to congratulate you?—which I would have done sooner if you hadn't been being so f—ing weird this whole time. And third, if you want to know, I never want to hear about Emily Dickinson again in my life. That b— has made my life a nightmare for three years now, so you can f— right off with that one. Here!' She hallooed the wait-boy, who was carrying a trayful of shots, and helped herself to two. She pushed one in my direction. 'Drink that. Congratu-f—ing-lations.'

Well now. This was a surprise. Where did Nancy get off being so unconscionably rude? And yet, I found *myself* wanting to explain, to make amends! I wanted to tell her about Murgatroyd, and the manuscript, and why I was not being nice. But that did seem a bridge too far. 'Why don't you like Emily Dickinson?' I asked in a small voice.

And so Nancy told me.

The original director of the Emily Dickinson project at Yale, for whom Nancy had first worked as a research assistant, was a woman named Anne Beddingfield. Beddingfield was one of those charismatic narcissists the power structures of academia tend to enable, who liked to choose and unchoose selected students. Nancy had been one of her students of the moment. Beddingfield would embarrass her with gifts and undeserved praise in classes she forced Nancy to audit, so that the other 'grad students' came to hate her, Nancy. Once, Beddingfield turned up with what must have been a fantastically expensive, elaborate birthday cake, with 'I Fancy Nancy' in icing curlicues. Nancy had no idea how she even knew it was her birthday.

Then things turned bad. When Nancy refused to schedule meetings at Beddingfield's flat at 2 a.m., 3 a.m. ('I have to meet when my brain is at its best, dear'), she found herself kicked off the project. Her funding got revoked. The Department of Homeland Security turned up on her doorstep out of the blue one day, having got the idea from somewhere that Nancy had fabricated a false identity in order to obtain a student visa.

Luckily for Nancy, Beddingfield had sent her a series of emails nasty enough that an in-house lawyer became convinced that the university was exposed to the possibility of a lawsuit.

And so, at some point, the director of the library, to whom Nancy had barely spoken before, suggested at a reception, as if merely making small talk, that, given the quantity of work Nancy had done on what was sure to be an extremely prestigious and well-publicized project, she really ought to be named a co-director.

He knew all about Nancy's complaint against Beddingfield. But Nancy didn't have to worry, he said. He was more than understanding—proud, even—that she was pursuing it. Everyone in the Humanities knew Beddingfield was a toxic abuser whose day of reckoning was long overdue.

But they did have to think, he mused, apropos of nothing, that if they fired Anne, they would probably lose the entire Dickinson project, much of which was Beddingfield's own intellectual property, and then there would be no career-making showpiece of which Nancy might be named co-director at all. What he really wanted to know was, as the victim in all this, what did *Nancy* think they ought to do? The university's only desire was to ensure that justice was done to her satisfaction.

Nancy had, after a pause, said that, all things being equal, she was certainly attracted to the idea of the co-directorship.

And pretty swiftly, the grubby deal played out precisely as the library director had suggested it might. Almost as if they hadn't merely been having a casual conversation at a library reception at all. Nancy had returned to England and communicated with her new co-director only in scrupulously formal emails. And Beddingfield was destroying some new favourite as we spoke. 'So that's the rather dirty story,' she concluded.

'You—you always seem to be so in your element, though, with the pressing the flesh and so forth,' I said.

'Oh, well,' she said, 'I'm one of those people who has been schooled from birth on how to seem absolutely entranced by anyone.' (I wished I was one of those people.) Nancy smiled winningly, then looked me in the eyes. 'I'd love to be like you and be honest all the time.'

You might believe Nancy and I had had a kind of break-through here. I did. And yet I was aware of a voice saying that this was the essence of her pretence, right here, this knack of making anyone to whom she spoke feel as if they were the only person in the room, the only person worthy of being taken into her special confidence. It was flimflam, but it worked without fail. I recognized it for what it was, and it still worked on me. Who doesn't want to be singled out as the only one to whom it is worth talking? Who does not in their secret heart believe that they *are* the only person with whom it is worth bothering? Really? You filthy liar.

Had I found all this out by any other means, I'd have gleefully told Ian that his star employee was a chiseller as soon as I could. But now I had nothing but sympathy. Anne Beddingfield was a monstrous gargoyle. Nancy was not to blame. Anyone would have done the same. No one, least of all a woman, needed to ruminate on the ethical minutiae of her behaviour in a case where she was so vastly more sinned against than sinning.

When Nancy went to the loo, I wondered why I was so keen to absolve the woman who had until five minutes ago been my nemesis. One does overlook the obvious when one is drunk, though. Because of course I hadn't been thinking about Nancy at all, but about myself. I was an idiot if I thought I was going to go around playing detective in Murgatroyd's death and the rest of it. I had a career that was threatening to burgeon—to burgeon!—for the first time in my life, and I had to nurture it! Nancy's story confirmed it: this was no world for ethical niceties. It was Beddingfield-eat-dog, and I was done, as they say, being the eatee. The Crooked Man wasn't going to get his victim this time.

PART TWO

10

And then, after the launch, *The Dog's Ball* actually came out. You know how old films depict a big media event by having front-page headlines spinning towards the screen from all the newspapers? We were like that, except we were, you know, the lead in the book-review section somewhere towards the back of the weekend magazine. The picture of Heri and me from the launch appeared in a 'Bystander' spread in the *Tatler*, doubtless to his great satisfaction. The literary press was so saturated with coverage that the *Paris Review*'s blog felt 'compelled to declare ourselves a *Dog's Ball*-free zone'.

And people liked the book: it wasn't *literature*, of course, but it was an *event*. 'Up there with the classic Greens,' somebody said, somewhere. 'For Green fans, it's like finding water in the desert.' I loved that one. I got some praise too: 'Agatha Dorn's diligent introduction tells the fantastic story of how this classic was rescued from obscurity.' 'Agatha Dorn is the archivist who found herself caught up in the fairy tale of the lost manuscript, and she tells the story with brio.' *Brio*, if you please! I still have these clippings, by the way, in a drawer. I couldn't bear to throw them away.

My royalties began to flow in. As predicted, I would have enough to ensure I could retain the services of Mabel Palmer for the foreseeable future and more.

I did interviews. I had meetings with Nora. I did podcasts. I made appearances at bookshops. I made appearances at crime bookshops. Crime bookshops smell weird, because of all that cheap paper in one place. The crime-fiction subculture is a world in which, my career in Green notwithstanding, I have never had much interest. There is something vaguely pornographic about it. When one talks to hard-core crime people, one invariably has the impression that they would much rather be listening to a description of the mutilated body of a young girl than whatever one is saying.

I no longer needed Nancy to accompany me in order to gain entry to Sampson the Gelding. There were enough mystery fans among the crowd that I had become a minor celebrity. A table of Sampson regulars invited me to join their mah-jong games, during which we largely discussed the competing merits of the various Gladden Green TV adaptations, and occasionally played mah-jong. I gloated inwardly when I received a call for an interview on Radio 4.

For a while, the circus of it all carried me from one thing to another as if on a conveyor belt. And whilst it was mostly just interviews for little websites and back rooms of bookshops— have you ever been somewhere where everyone is there to see you, to gain your approval? Have you ever felt the centre of gravity in the room shift with you as you move around? Known that everyone in your peripheral vision is waiting for their turn just to say two words to you? It is intoxicating.

I met with Nora about my next project. When it first became clear that I had no clue what I was going to do after *The Dog's Ball* (Stupid Agatha! A rube's mistake!), we had spent some weeks toiling over various bad ideas. A series of detective novels based on my experience. 'Murder in the Mobile Shelving'. I had always wondered what would happen if someone got stuck in between two rolling units as they closed. 'Death in Special Collections'. Ugh, no. A memoir of some kind—wistful? 'An Antiquarian Life'. Funny? 'A Duck in the Stacks!: More Hilarious Anecdotes from Twenty Years in the Archives'. 'Paperworld: An Autofiction'. *Gott in Himmel!* At one point we sunk so low as to conceive of a thriller-themed healthy-eating cookbook ('No, Mr Bond, I Expect you to Diet!').

But eventually we had located what Nora called my *unique selling point*. With *The Dog's Ball*, I had stumbled onto a literary mystery like no other and solved it—the case of the missing Green! There were all sorts of other literary mysteries out there. What killed Edgar Allan Poe? Who killed Christopher Marlowe? Was Shakespeare Shakespeare? Well, not that one. That was the kind of idiocy about which people who said things like *As the Bard tells us* thought. But something. There must be loads! I would try to solve them—and that would be the book!

Some days, I felt as if *everything would be all right*. Nancy and I began to socialize quite regularly, now I was someone worth knowing. I even started bouncing ideas off her for 'Literary Mysteries'—an idea that she *loved*, by the way—and she agreed with me about giving *Was Shakespeare Shakespeare?* the widest of berths, which endeared her to me still further. She had ideas of which I hadn't even thought. Who wrote *Beowulf*? What does the *Voynich Manuscript* say? (That's a weird fifteenth-century tome written in an unbreakable code.) I'd have to remember to give her a plum mention in the acknowledgements.

One night, I had been drinking with Nancy in Manor House, where she lived long term flat sitting for her aunt. I had a large number of gins and water. I got well and truly sozzled. I wasn't even going to be able to make it home, so Nancy said I could stay in her aunt's spare room.

Shortly after going inside the flat, it became clear that my drunkenness would impede further conversation. I refused to remove my hat or coat and sat on Nancy's aunt's blue velvet sofa, clenching my muscles in an effort to remain upright. Nancy must have shown me to the room where I was going to sleep. It was a child's room. The single bedstead was white-enamelled wrought iron, with a tasteful striped duvet cover of the kind parents want their children to want, on which sat a series of dolls and soft toys. It's funny what you remember clearly when you're wasted. I lay on the bed on my back in my hat and coat with the lights on, and then I was asleep.

In my dream, I was in a sea of soft toys. Hands I knew to be Nancy's reached down through the pile and pulled me out. She unloosed my coat, she touched me with an oiled hand. She and I were silhouettes in a blue window of a twilight house, and what she visited upon me was a crime. I writhed and moaned like a murder victim. I was lightning in the sky across the ocean of soft toys in the child's bed.

I couldn't for the life of me imagine what it signified.

For all that everything was going swimmingly, though, Murgatroyd continued to scratch away at some corner of my brain. I started having a recurring dream that I first had had as a child after watching *Flambeau* on television. It would be very late evening, almost night. I would find myself outside a large house with twelve windows arranged in four regular rows of three. Some of the windows were open and some had blinds drawn down, but all radiated the same steely blue light. From time to time the blinds in the covered windows would pop up, revealing a dreadful crime being committed upon Murgatroyd by the Crooked Man, in silhouette. Men murderers, women murderers, shootings, stranglings, stabbings; all of them were some aspect of the Crooked Man, of that there was no doubt. In the logic of the dream, whenever a blind popped open, I would realize with a new surprise every time that crimes were being committed behind every window. And Murgatroyd always the victim. It was like variations on the theme of the murder on the train in Green's *Judas Window*, murder after murder, without consequence. I wanted to scream, but, in character-istic nightmare logic, I found I could not. And in my *Flambeau* dream, Flambeau never arrived.

Nancy be darned! I had to go to Palmers Green and search for the Secrets Book. I just needed to be sure— I just needed to be sure that the Crooked Man had not done for Murgatroyd. I just needed to be sure there was nothing truly strange going on, that was all. Then I would feel fine about everything, I just knew it.

So it was that, that night I found myself back at the house in Palmers Green. I re-entered the bedroom. I had to start somewhere, right? In this one room alone, there was a standing wardrobe, an intimidatingly large built-in closet, and a chest of drawers, all of which were bound to be heaving with junk. I resurveyed the scene from the last time I was here. The obscene suicide kit. The bedside drawer with the prayer card and the Chinese medicine. The inspirational scrawl on the bathroom mirror. Where could one even start? Surely she had thrown the Secrets Book away anyway! I almost decided then and there to go home and leave it to the house-clearance people.

But by 2 a.m., the contents of the wardrobe and the drawers were laid out across the bedroom floor in haphazard piles. The other rooms in the house looked the same. Every time a trunk or a bureau, a tallboy or a chiffonier, failed to yield up the Secrets Book, I would be gripped anew by the epiphany that it was definitely in the next place in which I was going to look. A tattoo throbbed in my head: *In for a penny, in for a pound; in for a penny, in for a pound.*

Three hours later, slumped in the middle of the living room, a pile of decade-old gas bills to my right, a complete run of the 1990s computing magazine *Amiga Format* to my left, I had almost convinced myself she had put the dad-blamed book in the rubbish, when something occurred to me that made me stop dead.

It was all wrong. All those pill bottles in the bathroom. I stumbled back to Murgatroyd's bedside table and did some hasty googling. The asparagus root—it was a traditional Chinese medicine for fighting cancer, because what did Murgatroyd have to lose by trying it? The card with the saint. She must have been desperate if she was calling on Catholic saints, after her upbringing (her parents' church did not approve of *inverts*). The word on the bathroom mirror: *Floreat!* It meant to *flourish*. She had not calmly extinguished her own life, the way her note had suggested. She had been desperate to live! And she would never, never have thrown out the Secrets Book—not the woman who kept twenty-year-old pepper pots as if they contained the ground bones of St Peter!

I looked around the room, trying to calm myself down, but instead everything span around me. This was utter rot, surely? As had happened before, my gaze was caught by the uncanny helium canister next to the bed. I went over to it and took hold of the valve. I wanted to hear the last sound Murgatroyd must have heard—I thought it might work like a defibrillator on my sanity.

I turned the knob, and my stomach hit the floor. The little plastic seal holding the valve in its closed position broke with a click. *The gas flow had never before been turned on! The suicide kit had never been used!*

I sat down on Murgatroyd's tasteless pink chenille bedspread, unable to take it all in. What did it mean? It meant that Murgatroyd had not killed herself with the suicide kit. It implied, instead, that she had been *killed* and that her death had been *made to look like suicide*. It was bad enough that she had apparently killed herself when she was already terminally ill. Now it looked as if someone had done the job for her? And it threw quite a different light on all the strangeness of her behaviour before her death—the stealing of the manuscript scrap and whatever the other paper was and so on. Had she been scared? Had she been poking around in something or other that someone felt very strongly that she shouldn't have?

As I was running over all this in my mind, I was startled out of my reverie by the ringing of a mobile phone. At first I thought it was mine, but the ringtone wasn't right. Then I realized that the buzzing was coming from Murgatroyd's bedside table. It was her greasy old pink Nokia. Its plastic cover was cracked and greying like the equipment in a sad council playground. How did people let their stuff get like this? In common, I imagine, with most sane people, I myself wipe down my phone with an alcohol-soaked towelette every evening.

The display was too damaged to show a number, so I picked it up. Why not? I supposed. I did my best impression of an ordinary person: 'Hello, Agatha Dorn.' There was a pause.

'Hel— Agatha?' said a shocked and frightened voice. There was a fumbling sound, then he hung up. The funny thing was, I knew who it was. I recognized the voice very well. It was Tom Cadigan. Of *Dog's Ball*-donation fame.

But how on earth had Tom Cadigan known Murgatroyd? And what was he doing phoning her up? Had he known she had died? If so, whom was he trying to reach? I tried to access the call log, but the cracked screen just flashed a glitchy pattern—well, what did I expect from Murgatroyd's phone?

My first thought was that I ought to call 999 immediately. The police needed to be involved in all this, and fast! But then I looked at my watch. 5.30 a.m. If I called now, I would get some tired night-shift person unlikely to take me seriously. I decided that I wanted PC Dorothy, who had called me about Murgatroyd's death. She and I had been to North Mid together for me to identify Murg's body. We were practically sisters. I had her card. I'd call her during regular office hours. That would get things moving.

As for right now: I had been awake for almost twenty-four hours. I was rattled, but I had a solution to that. I remembered where Murgatroyd kept her booze. I navigated my way to the kitchen past the various piles of paper, had myself a robust gin and water, headed back to the bedroom, and curled up on Murgatroyd's pink bedspread, waiting for the gin to work its magic and hoping that it would be morning proper when I next opened my eyes.

*

11.15 a.m. The gin had done its work rather too well, perhaps. I'd have some explaining to do at work.

'So you're saying the seal on the gas canister has not been broken,' said PC Dorothy, of whom I had got hold on the phone.

'No, it has,' I said.

'Well, it would be,' said PC Dorothy. 'Miss Murgatroyd would have broken it when she turned on the gas.'

'No, no,' I said, '*I* broke it.'

'I'm sorry,' she said. 'My understanding was that you were not present when the deceased—' She paused, unsure how to proceed—'when she *became* deceased.'

'No,' I said, 'I broke it later. I broke it last night. Nobody had ever turned it on before I turned it on.'

'Except Miss Murgatroyd. When she—when the incident occurred.'

'No! That's what I am saying,' I said. 'I do not think she did—make the incident occur.'

'Right. But my understanding is that you were not present.'

'I wasn't! Christ on a bike! But I'm saying, *someone* was. Someone beside Murgatroyd. I know it sounds ridiculous. I'm saying I think it's possible someone killed her.'

'Miss Dorn. Agatha.' Research shows that if you are on a telephone call with a crazy person, a good way to deëscalate the situation is to use the person's name.

'Could you—' I interrupted—'Do you think you could send someone to look around? Is there—a detective who could come? Instead of a uniformed officer?' I felt utterly ridiculous. What did I want, a maverick gentleman investigator who would turn up and find what the others had missed? But real police detectives bore no resemblance to the figures in my imagination. Did they even call them detectives in the real police? Wasn't it *CID* or something?

'You're saying you need an officer to come and take possession of the unbroken plastic seal?'

'No! No! It is broken!'

'Agatha, I'm afraid I don't think I understand what you're asking for, Agatha.' Twice in one sentence! Was I so unhinged?

'Just someone to come to try to find—something!' God, would I listen to myself!

'Agatha. In the first place, my understanding was that Miss Murgatroyd was terminally ill. Why would someone kill a person who was about to die? In the second place, the premises were thoroughly examined on the night of the discovery of the body, four months ago, and it was determined at that point that no foul play was involved.'

I took a deep breath.

'There's something else. I got a phone call—on Murgatroyd's mobile—from someone I know, but someone she didn't know—I think it might be relevant.'

'Why's that?'

'The person who called—he had donated a manuscript to the archive where I work—a valuable one—and Murgatroyd— she had taken a page of the manuscript—I think he must have been calling about that for some reason—but why?'

There was a silence, longer than I would have liked, on the other end of the line. 'Now, Agatha,' Dorothy eventually replied. 'Grief can affect us in ways that we don't fully understand. What I'd like to do, Agatha, is to put you in touch with a Family Liaison Officer, whose job is to provide a primary point of contact for bereaved next-of-kin. Now, I can find you—'

I hung up. I had a horrible feeling that she was about to offer to send me a leaflet.

So that was that. The police were prepared to do precisely nothing. I had spent the last however many months swanning about promoting *The Dog's Ball* while Murgatroyd had been mouldering away in that ridiculous wicker coffin she had chosen for herself, entirely unavenged. If had just gone back to Palmers Green before now, instead of drinking in speakeasies with Nancy! It seemed to me that I had about one good option: *I could investigate Murgatroyd's death myself.*

That sounded like a good idea for about a second, before I thought, *Would I listen to myself?* As if I were the protagonist of the imbecilic James Patterson book on Murgatroyd's nightstand. Middle-aged archivists with a full-time job and an incipient drinking problem didn't *investigate* things. And probably the people whose job that actually was didn't do anything remotely resembling what people like me imagined they did. Even police detectives probably didn't *find out* exactly *what happened*. They ran through an operational checklist in a manual somewhere and, when they had ticked enough of the boxes on the list, they arrested a person about whose guilt there had really been no mystery all along and then did a lot of paperwork for it.

I didn't have the first idea about where to start. But you know what? I was going to figure it out.

11

As things turned out, having no idea what to do was not a problem.

I had decided that, much as it was the last thing I wanted, I needed to see Dimitra and discuss how to deal with some of Gee-Haw's most persistent creditors. I could have telephoned her, but I feared she might hang up on me. The best strategy, I thought therefore, was to beard the lion in her lair and go to Gee-Haw. And so I headed to Camden Market.

Camden High Street was much the same as I had remembered, which is to say, awful: overgrown toddlers, head shops, and painted brickwork. Looking up at a giant boot affixed to a storefront, I collided with a glossy black mannequin wearing some kind of sexual harness. The mannequin rocked, and the fat-necked proprietor of the shop whose dummy I had discomposed glared at me. I quickly headed for the market.

You're being very rude about my favourite place, Ag, I suddenly heard Murgatroyd saying in my head.

This was an interesting development. I appeared to have acquired an internal Murgatroyd along with my investigation.

Hello, Murg, I thought. *Now just because I'm avenging your death, it doesn't mean I have to change my opinion about Camden.*

When I was a teenager, Camden Market was all trestle tables selling incense and bootleg CDs. Nowadays it was 'housemade' shawarma and twenty-quid aviator hats for babies. It was the same bunch of coddled hippies, but now they had money. It was early, and the morning disinfectant smell was just barely preferable to the afternoon sweat and fry-oil.

Gee-Haw was located in a dank, efflorescence-ridden railway arch next to a club-clothing lair from which leaked ultraviolet rays and thirty-year-old rave music. I lurked in the doorway of the rave shop and worked on summoning up the courage to see Dimitra.

But just then, a curious thing happened. Someone I recognized headed towards Gee-Haw: my boss Ian. I almost didn't realize it was him. He was wearing a blue anorak, despite the hot morning, and a cap, as if he were in disguise, and he had his head hunched down as if he were trying not to be noticed. I thought about emerging and hallooing him, but he looked so much as if he were trying to avoid drawing attention to himself that I decided against it.

I had no idea that Ian knew Dimitra. I wondered what was going on. In the spirit of investigation, I decided to try to listen in on what they were saying. I had to get closer. I sneaked along from my doorway to a row of wind-spinners and crouched down behind them. A wind-spinner is a bejewelled garden pinwheel-thing that spins when the wind blows, on the lawns of people with no self-respect. I don't know why Dimitra stocked them alongside the bawdy novelties. It's a totally different brand of tastelessness. A couple eating curry from plastic boxes sauntered past, pointed at me, and smirked. I gave them my most ferocious look. Whatever Ian and Dimitra were saying was indistinct. I thought I heard Ian say the name *Murgatroyd* and then heard the barking cadence that signified Dimitra getting annoyed.

You knew my boss? I thought, in Murgatroyd's general direction.

Then it was footsteps. Both of them were coming back towards the front of the shop! This was good from one perspective—now I would be able to hear them—but extremely bad from another—now there was every chance they would see me!

My phone chose that moment to buzz in my pocket quite audibly. But thankfully, Ian and Dimitra seemed too wrapped up in their argument to notice. 'If Arise has a guilty conscience,' shouted Dimitra, 'they can pay my rent for me! Otherwise I don't want to hear anything about it!'

'Can you keep it down?' whispered Ian theatrically, backing away, almost as far as the wind-spinners. (Christ!) 'Don't say that, please!'

'What?' said Dimitra. 'ARISE? F—ING ARISE? IS THAT WHAT YOU'D LIKE ME TO NOT SAY? AND WHAT'S MORE, IF MURGATROYD HAD GIVEN TWO SH—TS ABOUT ME, SHE WOULDN'T HAVE BEEN TRYING TO CLOSE THIS PLACE DOWN, SO THINK ON THAT!'

Ian's foot was an inch from my knee, and he was still coming. At the last moment before he would have stepped on me, he veered in a different direction, heading for the exit of the market. Saved! But we weren't done yet. To mark her victory, Dimitra went beyond the doorway, patrolling the borders of her domain. Gah! Once again, I thought she would look in my direction. But she was too pumped up from shouting to notice me, and she headed back into the shop, thank god.

It was over, and what was more, I had learned valuable information. I stood up.

The flap of my hat caught on the rotor of a spinner, and the whole row went down like dominos, with the world's loudest crash. From the corner of the yard, Ian span around and looked back. This time, aghast, he definitely saw me. Then he fled. Inside the shop, Dimitra turned as well. Quickly recovering from her shock at finding me there, she began to shout. 'Dorn! Spying on me, are you? Well, I have nothing to hide! Unlike you! Don't forget, I have spies of my own! Don't forget for a moment!' I tried to ask what she meant by this, but she shouted, 'Now get out!' and flounced back inside. If her shop had had a door, she would have slammed it.

For what it was worth, I appeared to have begun an investigation.

Good girl, said Murgatroyd.

Back at work, Ian reappeared, wearing his normal clothes, but without his normal suave demeanour. To me, he made no acknowledgement that we had seen one another in Camden, and I was too abashed by the episode to bring it up with him. Instead, he oddly asked everyone in turn if they had seen a man resembling a bantamweight boxer hanging around the office. When no one said they had, he retreated to his office, shut the door, and did not emerge again.

I thought about the interchange I had observed. Ian's circle of acquaintances now appeared to include Dimitra Leonard. He seemed to have wanted to warn her about Arise for some reason—he seemed scared of them. But Dimitra did not. She, by contrast, seemed peeved about what Murgatroyd had been going to do to Gee-Haw. What had she meant that Murgatroyd was going to close it down? Had she simply been referring to the fact that Murgatroyd had left her assets to me and that I was unlikely to fight for the continued existence of that horrid establishment? Possibly. But that wasn't what she said. She said Murgatroyd has been *trying to close Gee-Haw down.* Was that—a motive for murder? Surely not! My trouble was, I had spent so much of my adult life reading detective novels that I could not distinguish the way people acted in Gladden Green stories from the way they acted in real life. And yet. The police might think I was crazy, but I was still feeling fairly certain that *someone* had killed Murg. And, well, the partner is always in the frame, right?

Keep at it, Ag! said Murgatroyd's voice in my head. *There are things to find out here,* said the voice. *I can't tell you what, but keep at it.*

Before I could test that hypothesis, my fledgling investigation got overtaken by events involving Ian once again. For the next day, Ian did not show up at work. This in itself was not terribly troubling. But it happened again the day after that.

Nancy needed his signature urgently. She needed quickly to pay a large amount of money for something 'FAKE NEWS'-related in order to stop somebody else from doing so. She was in a foul mood, and even went so far as to instruct Felicity to telephone him at home. Felicity, who was smoking a cigarette in a jade holder at her desk, was quite taken aback (and, furthermore, there was no answer at Ian's house). This may have been the first time anyone had asked Felicity to do any work in thirty years. Although she was nominally our administrator, Felicity's presence was purely ornamental. Her ancient bones would have broken if she had attempted to change a toner cartridge or lift a box of files. She was rather like the ravens at the Tower of London: no one really knew what she did, but we feared the cataclysm that would ensue were she ever to leave.

On the third day, Nancy forged Ian's signature, and a general consensus emerged that he had taken some kind of impromptu holiday.

I was unsettled, given everything, but I told myself there was still no need to bring everything into the open. Anyway, the idea of calling the police still seemed absurd. Someone like Ian taking a spontaneous trip without telling anyone seemed not outside the bounds of possibility. And even if he had disappeared, a grown-up had the right to disappear if he wanted to.

I thought, though, that I might take a little look in his office. So, when the coast was clear, I slipped inside. Maybe there would be a receipt for a plane ticket in his email or something.

I had been in Ian's office from time to time. Where my office was dark and uninviting though, Ian's appeared somehow high, light, and messily genteel, although it had precisely the same basic layout. It smelled of beeswax and dusty sunlight. He had had the paint stripped off the wainscoting, revealing the bare wood. I brushed my hand against it. It was warm. In my office, the walls are mummified by layers of gloss paint that had once been white, like a university seminar room. Where I had boxes of stationery and jars of pens, he had expensive-looking trinkets made of brass. This sort of thing was why he was the boss.

I turned on his computer, but it was, alas, protected by a password. In novels of the kind Murgatroyd would have bought, the absurd protagonist is able to use his ratiocinative abilities to guess passwords of this kind with ease.

Agatha, I heard Murgatroyd say, *I read them to relax.*

Relaxation is not a legitimate reason to read a novel, Murgatroyd, I thought in reply.

As a mere mortal, however, I didn't fancy my chances of guessing his password through some cryptic-crossword logic or other, so I left it alone. I tried the filing cabinet, but it was locked. When I headed for the desk drawers for the key, I found that all of these were likewise unopenable. On closer inspection, even the detritus on the desktop and the tables was scrupulously bland. A copy of the *Spectator*. A pile of flyers for one of our own events. A teacup and saucer. For a room that made such an effort to appear casual, it was locked up tight. Was that in itself suspicious? Ian's being Ian, I was not sure. Our art-brute forgery of *The Raven*—the copy, thankfully, not besmeared by the forger himself—was on the desk; Ian must have been talking 'FAKE NEWS' with Nancy—even in my hour of triumph, they were figuring out what to do next!

I worked through the rest of the day, but I kept thinking about what Ian might have known, what he might have said. The voice of Murgatroyd kept chiding me for not doing anything about it.

You should find Ian, Ag.

I'm sure he's fine, Murg. I'm sure he's just on holiday.

Or someone has hooked him up to a suicide kit.

Stop it, Murg. You know I'm not a woman of action.

Maybe it's time to become one.

So, by clocking-off time I had decided I would swing by his house and make sure everything looked OK.

12

I knew Ian had an address in West London somewhere. In the administrative office, I made sure to ask Felicity if she would mind if *I* looked in Ian's file. She shook her silent-movie-vamp hairdo affectlessly in the direction of a large filing cabinet. In a folder inside, I found a form with an address in Holland Park, plus a landline number—and a mobile number as well, which Felicity had passive-aggressively withheld from Nancy—though dialling achieved nothing. In common with many important people, Ian had neglected to set up the voicemail box on his mobile, in order not to have to receive messages. In the bloodless age of text and email, there was something intrusively intimate about having to deal with a recording of someone's actual voice, and then being faced with the possibility of having to dial their number and, god forbid, actually speaking to them. It was disgusting, somehow. Good on Ian for opting out.

Anyway, I took the tube out to Holland Park and made my way to Ian's street. His building was number 73, a large white terrace; I wondered which floor he had. I made my way up the steps to the front door, looking for the little grey panel of buzzers, but there was only an expensive-looking doorbell. Silly me. He owned the whole building! There were several flyers sticking out of the letter box, which suggested Ian had not been home in more than twenty-four hours at least, I hoped that was what it suggested. The alternative was that he was inside but unable to get to the door. Instinctively, I pulled out the flyers and crumpled them with their whiff of cheap printing into my pocket. Then, since I didn't want Ian to think I was some kind of prowler, I rang the bell. No answer. I shouted through the letter box. I thought I'd try the mobile one more time. This time, I could hear the ringing of the actual phone, not far beyond the door. This was worrisome, because who goes anywhere without their mobile, let alone for *three days*?

The left-behind mobile made me think I should try to get inside. The front door was locked, so I retraced my steps and looked for an entrance into the next lane, where I might be able to find the backs of the houses to this one. Happily, my conjecture was correct, and I found myself in a lane filled with garage doors and gates. Ian's was even labelled with his house number! There was a sign above it reading: 'ONE WAY', and another, a little further on, proclaiming: 'Barbed Wire In Use'. The garden door was not, however, open.

The wall surrounding Ian's yard was not terribly high and, had I been some kind of parkour-doing urban warrior, I probably could have yoinked myself over it. As it was, however, my upper-body strength had peaked at the age of six, when I nearly traversed the entire rack of bars on the climbing frame on my school playground. I looked around, thinking that this was probably the end of my derring-do for the day, until I saw a large orange B&Q bucket lying alongside the wall a little further down. When I got nearer, I realized it stank. It was about a third full of unidentifiable black liquid, in which were floating what looked like a set of old fried-chicken bones and a Coke can. Ugh. I shuddered, then touching it as gingerly as I could, tipped the thing over so the grossness flowed out. Honestly, was it worth all this just to try to get into Ian's d—d house? Surely not! But as before, an image of him wounded by my dastardly adversary, this time stretched out on his kitchen floor like the woman in the old-lady panic-button advert flashed into my head, and I decided to press on. I carried the bucket over to Ian's back door—getting god-knows-what slime on my hands in the process I should add—turned it upside down, and, looking around again to make sure the lane was empty, climbed on it. From this height it was feasible to lever myself over—although I couldn't see all the way down. Hoping desperately that the barbed wire of which I had been forewarned was not In Use at this particular spot, I heaved my weight onto the top of the wall, flinching as my arms headed into the fringe of ivy that topped it.

As my flesh sank into the leaves, no barbed wire shredded my skin. With relief, I hung myself by my arms from the inside face of the wall and dropped down.

The back 'garden' was an urbanely furnished square of concrete with a few hardy-looking shrubs in pots and steps leading up to the back door.

I tried it. Locked, again. I looked under everything under which I could conceive that a key might be hidden—the chairs, the table, the plant pots, the doormat, a couple of likely-looking loose bricks—but there was no spare key to be found.

Was this it, then? I supposed so. But somehow, the abandoned mobile told me that something was wrong.

I walked over to the loose bricks. This was a terrible idea. I picked up a brick. This was the worst idea I had ever had. I returned up the steps to the back door, looking at the sash window abutting it, thinking I could smash a hole with the brick, reach around, and open the door from the inside. Provided it had a Yale lock and not a deadbolt. Which it probably didn't. And provided there was no alarm, which there almost certainly was. This was an incredibly stupid idea and no good could come of it.

I decided to do it. Having decided, though, I realized that I didn't really know how to go about what I was proposing to do. I looked down at my brick-holding hand as if it were a foreign object. Did I *throw* the brick, like some kind of hoodlum? Surely not. I rotated it in my hand, so the short side was facing the pane, and pantomimed sort of ramming a hole into the glass. That seemed like a better idea.

I drew my arm back and brought it forward fast but balked at the last minute. The brick clanked against the glass, which did not break, though it got a bit scuffed. Like a suicide making a hesitation wound, I thought, then felt guilty for thinking that, what with Murgatroyd and everything. I tried again, harder this time, but not quite using my full strength since, I reasoned, I didn't want to make a great, big, smashing noise and alert the neighbours. I just wanted to make a clean, little hole, like a bullet hole, but brick-sized. But, no joy, once again.

After a couple more tries, in frustration, I did what I had told myself I wouldn't, and chucked the dastard thing at the glass as hard as I could. It bounced off, but a crack appeared in the pane from top to bottom. *Oh, eff,* I thought. *Now I've damaged Ian's window.* At this stage, I suddenly decided, the best thing actually was to retreat from the scene as gracefully as I could. There was after all a ninety-nine per cent chance that the outcome of this would be Ian coming back from his surprise holiday to find that some idiot had dumped a bucket of wee and chicken bones outside his back gate and cracked his window. The brick had succeeded in dislodging part of the cracked pane from the wooden frame, though, so that it stuck out precariously. *I should just press it back into place,* I thought. *It won't look so bad then, when Ian discovers it.* I pressed cautiously on the glass. The crack creaked ominously. And then the whole pane fell out and shattered on the ground.

Nice going, Ag, said Murgatroyd in my head.

Oh, eff off, will you? I thought in reply.

Well. Now what to do? My heart was racing, and my stomach was filling with acid. My brain, though, which seemed to have dissociated itself from the panic enveloping the rest of my body, was telling me that this latest turn of events had changed the equation. At this stage, going into the house and looking for Ian couldn't make things any worse, and might in fact make them better, insofar as I might now find him passed out on the floor or what-have-you, and that if I did, that would surely excuse me from the crime I had just committed in order to get in. And so I climbed through the window.

As I entered the kitchen into which the window led, I noticed that the door was indeed locked with a deadbolt, which meant that had I managed to make the discreet little hole I had been imagining, I wouldn't have been able to get in anyway. So, silver lining to having smashed the whole thing. I also saw a white plastic box on the wall with a blinking red light. So, there was an alarm. That meant that in about a minute there was either going to be a deafening noise or an automatic call placed to the police, or both.

I thought that what I would do was sort of jog through the house and stick my head in each room, which would allow me to tell if Ian was lying on the floor hurt or dead or something, and still give me a shot at getting out before the alarm went off. Kitchen—that was already checked off. Hallway. No. Living room. Not that I could see. Awful saggy hessian-covered sofa. Great big picture on the wall, de Kooning imitation. Probably not, actually, knowing Ian. Probably an effing real one. Keep going! Not in the downstairs loo, which was papered with old *New Yorker* covers. Upstairs. Not in the empty bathroom. Not in the bedroom. Hardwood sleigh bed. Very expensive, not very nice. Wait a minute, though. There were clothes all over the bed.

I put my plan on pause and went in. Still no Ian. But clean shirts, trousers, underwear pulled from the open wardrobe and dresser. As if someone had packed to leave in an extreme hurry. I took a closer look, to see what I could see. Nothing immediately. Then I went into the bathroom. It really was almost empty, as in emptied of stuff. And on the floor, drops of what looked like blood—honestly!—leading out into the corridor.

If I had it in me to sprint, I would have sprinted up the next set of stairs to the second floor. As it was, I sweatily jog-walked. The browny-red drips continued to the second-floor landing, where they stopped. Spare room with retrofitted bathroom, dark granitey tiles (god, no imagination at all!). Office. Messy. More expensive-looking paintings on the wall, eighteenth century this time. Still no Ian. Christ on a Bike!

It occurred to me that, what with the discovery of the clothes and the blood, more than a minute had surely gone by. My watch confirmed it. So the alarm was either silent or a decoy. I told myself that if it hadn't gone off by now, it wasn't going to, so I might as well walk down the stairs. After I had a little sit-down on the top step to catch my breath. OK.

After a short but revitalizing break, I arrived back in the kitchen, where the red light was still blinking. The moment I did so, Ian's mobile began to ring. I moved to the hallway, where I thought I had heard it ringing behind the front door and picked it up from the console table.

'Lanham Security, we've had a report of an alarm being triggered at your property?' The voice sounded bored to death, which struck me as odd until it dawned on me that almost every burglar alarm that ever goes off does so by accident. Then I remembered that I was not Ian, did not have his passcode, and had in fact broken into his house.

Run, said my inner Murgatroyd.

I hung up the phone and dashed back to the kitchen, clambered out the window, and ran to the garden door which had, thank god!, a latch that could be opened from the inside.

Back on the street, I started walking to the tube, listening for the sirens and the thudding of feet chasing me down. I had visions of a savant CSI—or were they called SOCOs here?—lifting my prints from the door handle in record time and summoning a squad of heavies to head me off at the station before I had even made it to the bottom of the road. Instead, my phone rang. I began making mental lists of excuses I could give to whatever law-enforcement operative was going to be on the other end. 'Hello,' I said.

'You can't see me. But I'm here,' said a voice I had not heard for thirty-seven years. The Crooked Man! I dropped my phone onto the hard pavement. However, since I prudently invest in high-quality protective cases, it did not smash. I knelt down and scrambled it back to my ear. 'I saw what you did, criminal,' said the Crooked Man. I still could not speak. 'Do you know what we do to criminals? Shall I tell you?' And he proceeded to do so until I regained control of myself and hung up.

My heart didn't stop pounding a hundred beats a minute till I was back at my flat, and not for a long while after that.

I tried to douse my fear with gin but instead, like a jarred frog in a nineteenth-century museum, the alcohol kept it intact. What had I done? Fannied about like an idiot, and now Ian was missing, looking like he had tried to make an urgent getaway, there was blood in his house, and I had unleashed a supernatural terror who knew what I had done!

Was I responsible for Ian's death? What was the difference between me and a murderer?

13

At the Neele, Ian's absence had already started to scab over, the way traumatic events do. Just to mix my metaphors, we had mentally taped it off, like a crime scene. Things had only gone wrong inside the tape. Everything outside was the normal world, and that was where we were staying.

Someone—maybe it was Felicity, the administrator—did call the police and report Ian missing, and an officer came to the Neele to interview us. But everyone kind of blocked that out after it happened.

There was a general sense that he would turn up any minute, and that, even if he didn't, we had a new groove going. Nancy was forging his signature as needed, and generally picking up his work. One day I even found her sitting at his desk. Nobody wanted to pry. Conveniently forgetting my own rôle in all this, as one does, I began to get angry. If anything was going to get done, it was, as the phrase goes, *on me*.

Well, eff them all, I thought. I would go and see Oliver Manders at Arise, who had, Bunner said, lied about his friendship with Ian. If he knew anything about Ian's disappearance, perhaps I could get him to let slip some information by mistake.

I phoned Oliver's office, got past his assistant, and found him in an effusive mood. I told him I wanted to talk about curating my presence on the Arise website. He was delighted to meet me—as he would be, I suspected, for anyone who wanted to talk about *curating* things that were not museums.

I did love spouting media nonsense to people who took that sort of thing seriously. And I was after all a profitable author for them these days. He suggested 10.30 on the roof garden of their Shoreditch offices. Of course they had offices with a roof garden in Shoreditch.

I told Felicity I had a meeting and headed out. It was only a stroll across Finsbury Square and down the gullies of Wilson and Worship. These streets never quite felt safe for pedestrians, what with the nasty vans and viciously fast delivery bikes, but today there was something else. Something dangerous, travelling at my own speed, but never visible. Something following me?

I thought quickly about my line of attack. I had to be a little more incisive than I had been at the party. *How about Ian disappearing, eh?* Too easy to shut down. All he had to say was, *I didn't know that* and that was the end of the conversation. *I heard you were talking to Ian about my documentary a couple of months back.* That was more promising. Then if he said he hadn't, I could bring up Bunner straight away—*Well, but my friend Bunner said she heard you*—and if he said he had, well, I'd caught him in a lie—*Oh, but I thought you hadn't ever had a conversation with Ian until a couple of days ago.* That would be something. I wasn't sure where I would go from there, but with a good beginning, I could wing it.

The lobby of the Arise building might have been the showroom of an expensive home décor shop—except with less furniture on display and discreet metal detectors in the doorway. There was a raw concrete ceiling with recessed industrial lighting, and the walls were bare brick, except for one, which was covered in reclaimed Mediterranean tile; somewhere in Santorini, a restaurant was missing its floor. The reception desk was a huge sheet of butcher block on top of a pedestal faced with glazed bricks in gin-palace green. It was all virtuosically eclectic in a *comme-il-faut* Conran Shop sort of way.

I asked at the gin-palace desk; the lady made a telephone call, then directed me to a lift that would take me up to the roof garden.

I was walking across the vestibule. Then I froze. In one corner stood a figure, half-concealed in shadow. He wore a black hat and a long black coat. The sleeve of the coat stretched portentously in my direction, as if the figure were pointing the way to my doom, like the Ghost of Christmas Yet To Come. But no hand protruded from the sleeve. I stared in horror. I could not see his eyes, but it seemed to me that the Crooked Man met my gaze.

Then, all of a sudden, the spell was broken. The man pulled his arm out of the coat, which he had been in the process of taking off, along with the hat. Suddenly he was striding towards me with a jaunty wave. Like all famous people, he was smaller in person, but I recognized him instantly. He was wearing an orange T-shirt, and spotless jeans that probably cost a month's worth of my salary. His blond hair was buzzed. Given the size of his head, his body looked as if it wanted to be considerably huskier than it was, but he had pummelled all his body fat away with some kind of regime.

'Sir Ed—Sir Edward,' I stammered. I was in the process of chalking the whole hat-and-coat illusion up to my paranoid mind, but a part of my brain kept working on an inconvenient thought.

'Edmund,' he said. 'People get that wrong all the time.' He smiled and stuck out his hand for me to shake. 'Ed Ratchett.

A pleasure! And I think you're Agatha Dorn, aren't you? The woman of the moment!'

Sir Ed Ratchett would have been a national treasure, except he was a little too obviously avaricious in his pursuit of money.

'I like your lobby,' I said.

'Do you?' he said. 'I find it all a bit Conran Shop. We'll do better with the new place. Although that's on hold, isn't it?'

'I'm sorry to have been a thorn in your flesh,' I said with a smile.

'Oh no, not at all. And we're making lots of lovely money from your book, so that's some compensation. To what do we owe the pleasure, in any case?'

'Oh, I'm looking at trying to curate my presence on the Arise website a little more intentionally,' I said, smirking inwardly.

'I do think that's such a stupid phrase, *curate*—when you're not talking about a museum—nonsense, really, don't you think?'

'Yes, I suppose so,' I muttered, hoist with my own petard.

'Well, I shan't keep you!' said Sir Ed, waving me towards the now-open door of the glass lift. I went in.

'You know it's a funny phrase, *thorn in my flesh*,' he said. I waited for the doors to close. 'It's from Second Corinthians. Paul says that God has given him a thorn in his flesh in order to make his strength more perfect in the end. I wonder if that applies here?' As the doors slid shut, he said, 'Well, happy "curating!"' with audible quotation marks.

The idea that my mind had been attempting to form during my conversation with Sir Ed finally congealed. *He did the thing with the hat and coat deliberately*, I thought. *He knew I was afraid of the Crooked Man. He knew.* Then I followed that thought with another one: *How on earth would Sir Ed Ratchett know something like that?*

The glass lift travelled up the exterior wall of a huge central atrium, the centrepiece of which was a giant sculpture of a balloon-animal snake made of blue steel. By the time I got near the top, the people milling around the snake looked like dots.

The roof garden was overstuffed concrete raised beds with little walkways running between them. I had expected it to be filled with the expensively dressed-down clever boys and girls who were Arise's stock-in-trade. The presence of a repurposed ice-cream van displaying some kind of hipster frankenpastry suggested that it usually was; but now the roof was empty, except for Oliver, who was standing at the edge of the building. He was looking out towards Spitalfields, and the Christ Church spire that seemed always to define the landscape, despite the much taller buildings all around.

'Hello, Oliver!' I said. 'Do you know how they got the ice-cream van up here?'

'Agatha!' he said, turning round. 'I expect they drove it up the stairs.' He grinned, but there was something unconvincing about it. For one thing, he seemed to be looking past me. I turned round instinctively, and there was another man coming towards us—small, with a Top Man polo shirt and the grey, filmy skin of the perpetually hungover. He didn't look like the usual Arise sort at all. He looked like one of those boxers of the skinny variety.

'I've asked my colleague Tony from Product Management to join us,' said Oliver. This would not have been my first guess, if you asked me who the third man on the roof was—but then I supposed my privilege was showing. Oliver's expression didn't match his words, though. He looked distinctly unhappy about Tony's presence.

'So what can I do for you, Agatha?' said Oliver. 'Sir Ed's a big enough man that we can work with the editor of *The Dog's Ball*, even if it has cost us our campus! Besides'—He gestured around him—'our existing digs are really not too bad.'

There was something uncanny about the whole scene. Why was the roof terrace empty? My mind went completely blank. I couldn't think of anything to say. 'How about Ian disappearing, eh?' I said. Agh! Gah!

'Well, Ollie, looks like you owe me ten pounds,' said Product-Management Tony with what I found to be an unpleasant intonation.

'Ha ha,' said Oliver.

'Why do you think he owes me ten pounds, Agatha?' said Tony.

I paused. 'I don't know,' I said.

'See,' said Tony, 'Ollie said to me that you wanted to talk to him about something to do with the way your book—which as I understand it is not actually your book, as it happens, but a book by someone called Gladden Green—but passing over that—the way your book is presented on our website. Didn't you, Ollie?' Tony from Product Management was, I noticed, standing a little closer to me than I would have preferred.

'Ha ha ha,' said Oliver.

'But I bet him ten pounds that what you were actually going to want to talk about was your boss Ian Harcourt-Reilly. And look at that. It looks as if I was right, doesn't it?'

'I was just making small talk, really,' I said.

'Were you, though?' Tony said. He had been steadily advancing on me, so that my back was now almost up against the railing, here on the empty roof. I was suddenly quite aware of the wind on my skin. 'Well, that's fine. Why don't we finish up with the small talk and get to the business at hand: the website.'

I would have said that was fine with me, except that, in all the excitement, I had neglected even to look at the listing for *The Dog's Ball* on the Arise site. I found myself in the strange position of wishing that Tony from Product Management—and I was beginning to trust my initial instinct that this was not his actual position with the company—would continue to menace me so that I would not have to make up obvious lies to tell to Oliver. For a moment, my wish was granted.

Tony continued, 'From what Ollie tells me, he doesn't even know your boss, isn't that right?'

'I actually go by Oliver,' sputtered Oliver, with a dying fall.

'I'll try to remember that, Ollie,' said Tony. He made a sudden hissing sound, through his teeth. Oliver flinched, as if he had produced a knife. 'But you were saying?' Tony went on.

'What's that now?' said Oliver—'Oh, *right*. That's right. I don't know Ian at all.'

'That's right,' said Tony. 'So let's let that be the final word on *that* subject, shall we? Now, about that website?'

'Oh,' I said, flustered. 'I can hardly remember what I wanted to talk about now. Why don't we just forget it?'

Tony paused for a long moment, looking directly at me.

For an instant it seemed as if Tony was going to hoist me over the edge of the building. Instead, he said, 'No, that's quite all right, Agatha. Why don't I go and get us a little snack, and when I come back you'll have remembered all about it and you can tell Ollie and me.' Tony walked in a leisurely fashion to the pastry van.

Oliver got a panicked look in his eyes and put his finger up to his lips. He pulled a scrap of a receipt and a biro out of his pocket, scrawled on the paper, and handed it to me. Written on it was a name: *art-brute*.

Counting the *Raven* forgery on Ian's desk, this was the second time that individual had come up in the last few days. But what did Oliver mean? Was he telling me that 'Tony' was the prankster who had embarrassed the Neele three years ago? I pointed at Tony and mouthed, 'Him?' It didn't seem very likely, frankly. Oliver's eyes got big, and he gave me a grimace that communicated precisely nothing.

Now Tony was coming back our way, carrying a pair of cronuts or kouignoù-amann or some other nonsense that would have been grossly overpriced had he paid for them. He handed the oversized syrup-glazed things to me and Oliver.

'Now, Agatha, tell Ollie all about it.'

My mind was empty. Something about my book on the website. 'It's the thumbnail,' I said.

'Is it?' said Oliver.

'The thumbnail,' said Tony. 'What about it? Have a bite of your snack.' We did. 'And?' said Tony.

'It's too small,' I said, blowing crumbs of puff pastry out of my mouth.

'Thumbnail too small,' said Oliver, as if he were making notes, which he was not. 'OK. I think we can sort that out for you. Bigger thumbnail. Not a problem. That everything, Agatha?' He said my name, but he was looking at Tony.

'Yes, that's everything,' said Tony, after a pause. 'Now f— off with you, Dorn,' he said with a grin. I effed off just as fast as I could.

Except: one more thing of note happened on my way out of the building. As the glass lift made its journey back to the ground floor, I spotted Sir Ed Ratchett again. He was hugging someone as if they were a long-lost friend. Here's the thing, though: I couldn't be sure, because the lift was moving too fast, but it weirdly looked as if the person Sir Ed was hugging was Murgatroyd's girlfriend Dimitra.

14

Let's say Oliver had indeed been trying to tell me that Tony was art-brute. That was assuming for a moment that it was plausible for the goon type I had just met to be a notorious art-world prankster. Why? It would make a certain sense of the fact that Ian had apparently been perusing the fake *Raven* chapbook. But so what?

I tried telephoning Oliver to confirm straight away, but he was no longer taking my calls. But why not? Was he suggesting that *Tony* had forged the *Dog's Ball* manuscript? If so, how could anyone but I (and, presumably, Tony) have known that it *was* a forgery? How would *Oliver* have known anything about that?

What do I do now? I asked the Murgatroyd in my head.

Do what I would have done, Ag, she said. *Keep investigating. Find out who Tony is.*

I chalked the possible Dimitra sighting up to my adrenaline-hampered brain; the more crucial task was to try to discover Tony-from-Product-Management's identity. Back at the Neele, from the safety of my desk, I attempted to discover it.

I started with art-brute. I knew something about his somewhat legendary history as a prankster from the Poe business, and what the Internet threw up was mostly a rehash of that: calling the police on some poor innocent was a well-known troll prank, but in one case, he had gone one better and induced hundreds of tourists to cause the police to be called on them: in 1999, he had stolen the self-guided tour cassettes from the

National Gallery and replaced them with ones that instructed visitors to remove paintings from the walls in order to 'get a closer look', setting off every alarm in the place.

A couple of years after that, he had installed a whole menagerie of fake animals in displays at the Natural History Museum: jackalopes, mermaids, Bigfoot. Lots of them were masturbating or engaged in otherwise unsavoury practices. There were so many that it took a month for them all to be located and removed.

Rumour had it he had been nastier still. In online discussion boards, the name of art-brute was frequently tied to an incident in which a group of actors pretended to be terrorists and ambushed a charity event. The actors had blindfolded Ant and Dec, poked them with bayonets, and forced them to plead for their lives, streaming the whole thing online. He had never taken credit for that one, for obvious reasons.

In short, he was a clever boy with a sick sense of humour and a lot of time on his hands. People on the Internet adored him.

Searching for his identity proved much less fruitful. He had annoyed enough people over the years that serious attempts had been made to hold him to account. But he had covered his tracks extremely well. Internet theories claimed: he was a well-known rapper with a secret identity; he was a shop assistant in Yorkshire; he worked in private security—interesting!—and that was how he got access to all the premises after hours; *she* was an old lady who volunteered as a museum docent and hired an actor to play herself as a man in online videos; he was the Lizard People, the Illuminati. The usual.

I moved on to Tony. Arise appeared to have no corporate directory. It was possible to google around and find the names of the big cheeses—the C-suite people and the VPs—but nothing much else. And then, individual employees had LinkedIn accounts, or they didn't. Tony didn't—but that didn't mean anything, necessarily.

My next thought was that I might be able to locate an image of him online somewhere. Oliver had introduced Tony as a colleague he had asked to the meeting, but Tony had seemed rather to enjoy making it clear that he and Oliver didn't know one another, and that in fact Oliver was rather afraid of him. Nevertheless, I had to start somewhere. I image-searched Oliver Manders. It turned out he had been snapped by the *Tatler* at our launch as well. Then, I found his smug mug on a LinkedIn page: 'Senior Corporate Counsel at Arise'. A headshot from a site called *law.net*. A faraway image of Oliver standing at a podium from some kind of internal newsletter. That was, for all meaningful purposes, about it. My eyes were starting to get dry.

On a whim, I searched images of Sir Ed Ratchett instead. This time, there were thousands. Sir Ed posing with a scarf for a *fortune.com* profile. Sir Ed gesticulating at a panel discussion. Sir Ed gesticulating at a TED Talk. Sir Ed gesticulating at a conference. Sir Ed in an armchair being interviewed, with a giant picture of himself projected behind him. Sir Ed standing in front of his Learjet. Sir Ed next to Bill Gates. As I continued to scroll, the pictures took on more of a tabloid flavour. Sir Ed exiting a Tesla outside a restaurant. Sir Ed in a dinner jacket at some kind of function. Sir Ed with his ex-wife, the actress Veronica Cray, trying to put his hand in front of a paparazzo's lens. Sir Ed—but wait!—in the paparazzi shot—Sir Ed was surrounded by a security team—as, I suppose, he was in the others too, but in this unauthorized shot, they were visible. And there, in the corner of the picture, wearing one of those shiny suits that somehow manages to project the same energy as an English Defence League T-shirt, was Tony. Product Management, my foot! Tony was one of Ed Ratchett's bouncers!

Now wait. Neither now nor, if I was honest, before, had Tony looked like the type who would get a kick out of elaborately humiliating museums. But could he be? One of the rumours *was* that he worked in security. I wasn't sure I could see it.

From the picture, I cropped only the part that contained his face, and used that as the basis of a new search.

And there, a few images in, he was. Client Services Executive at an outfit called the International Protection Agency, which a moment's further research confirmed that Ed Ratchett retained for his personal security. 'Tony's' real name was Rick Fawn. He looked distinctly less hungover in his headshot, but there remained something unsavoury about him that no amount of grooming could conceal.

I googled the name, too. Of course there were any number of Richard Fawns online, but one result looked interesting. 'Court martial results from the military court centres'. The little preview blurb highlighted 'Richard Fawn 3 PARA', but when I clicked on it, all I got was a screen asking for a password I didn't have. Still, that was interesting. It was at least plausible that Fawn had got into private security after being kicked out of the military. That seemed like a likely career route into private security, I had to say. I filed the information away in the back of my brain.

Arguably more relevant than any of this, though, was the fact that Ed Ratchett had dispatched one of his personal bruisers to scare me off asking questions about Ian's relationship with his company. Here, I really *was* getting somewhere—this more-or-less *proved* it.

What now, Murg?

Didn't you make a list of things to investigate?

Frankly, I was rather rattled by my encounter with Tony. Perhaps there was another avenue I could pursue, rather than doing more apparently dangerous digging around Arise. The night of the *Dog's Ball* launch, I had started making a list of curiosities that bore investigating. I pulled it out of my desk drawer and took a look. Most of it was about why Murgatroyd had been poking about *The Dog's Ball*. This, of course, had to be set in the context that I was now convinced Murgatroyd had been killed. I had noted Ian's alleged prior relationship with Oliver. Thinking back to that night, I realized now that I ought to add something about Dimitra Leonard, too. *Murgatroyd used to say, always, she'd make sure I was comfortable*, Dimitra had yelled at me. Something like that. She told me Murg had told her she was going to give *her* everything. That was rather different from her claim to Ian that Murg was trying to destroy her beloved Gee-Haw. I added some notes to that effect.

What could that possibly have to do with *The Dog's Ball* though? Was Murgatroyd trying to raise money for Gee-Haw by selling stolen pages from the manuscript? Was Ian somehow involved in this scheme?

I couldn't make sense of it—but I did realize that amongst all this speculation was a lead I could follow—lord, was I a person who thought she was following *leads* now?—nevertheless, though, a lead I could follow without probable danger to life and limb. As Murgatroyd's executor, I had had some dealings with Mr Ronald Wells of Hammond & Wells, solicitors of

Palmers Green. It occurred to me that he might well know what Murgatroyd had done, or been threatening to do, or whatever it was, in Re: Gee-Haw.

I didn't quite know how to plan my attack in Palmers Green. It occurred to me that my brother Heri was someone who probably dealt with solicitors a fair bit, so I telephoned him and asked if there was some provision in the law that would force Mr Wells to tell me what he knew.

'Lord, Agatha,' he said, when I got through to him. 'I should just ask him. He might tell you to go to hell or, as you are Murgatroyd's executor and she's no longer here to object, he might just tell you what her plans were. There's no need for you to be an idiot about it.'

'It's always such a pleasure talking to you, Heri,' I said. But it did seem as if this whole thing might be a simpler matter than I had feared.

Hammond & Wells was one of those solicitors' offices that looks more like a shopfront than an office. It was half of a semi-detached Edwardian house on Green Lanes, the other part of which housed an insurance business. Next door was a forecourt full of clapped-out-looking used cars, with a large sign promising 'EZ Kredit'.

I knew what to expect, having been there before, but it was still a curious set-up. Once inside the building, the Edwardian frontage gave way to a reception area with two white leather chairs for waiting in, an ice-blue carpet, and a frosted-glass reception desk. Unfortunately, the design genius who had modernized the entryway had waved aside the minor difficulty that the whole hallway was only three feet wide. Consequently, by the time one had allowed for the leather chairs, there was only about a twelve-inch corridor along which one had to mince in order to access any of the actual offices. There was a middle-aged lady with a perm, wearing a green cardigan, behind the desk, looking as if she were dressed for a different office from this one. Making use of the appalling American usage of the word, she told me that Mr Wells would see me 'momentarily'. I thought about asking what would happen if it turned out that I wished to see Mr Wells for more than a moment, but I did not want to confuse her.

In any case, Mr Wells did indeed emerge after a short wait. He picked his way along the tiny corridor, shook my hand, and led me back to his office, where the building's stylistic whiplash continued. Either the project of modernizing the building had run out of money after they had done the reception, or Mr Wells had put his foot down when it came to his own room. For, as I recalled from my previous visits, Mr Wells's domain remained decorated in the style of the era when the building had been constructed, all tufted leather armchairs and shelves full of legal tomes. His desk, by contrast with that of the receptionist, had a top of green tooled leather and one of those stiletto-like letter openers on a stand that would have proven to have been the murder weapon, had Murgatroyd only been stabbed. Above the desk hung a photograph of a lot of young people in dinner jackets and the legend: 'Shrewsbury College, Oxford, May Ball Survivors, 1998'.

'What can I do for you, Miss, ah—' he said.

'Dorn,' I reminded him.

'Miss Dorn, that's right!' he said happily. 'What can I do for you? You're handling the estate of Miss —'

'Murgatroyd. Amy Murgatroyd.' No wonder Hammond & Wells was stuck in a tiny office next to a used-car dealership. They needed to get better at pretending to remember who their clients were.

'Ah, Murgatroyd, yes. That's right. There's, ah, a property over the way you'll be wanting to arrange to sell,' he said. 'There are a number of, ah, claims on the estate, if I recall.' *Now* he remembered. Maybe he had been getting phone calls from the manufacturers of penis-shaped pasta whom Dimitra had stiffed and referred to him. That would be enough to jog anyone's memory.

'Yes, in due course,' I said. 'I've been quite busy. I had a book come out, you know?'

'OK, well...' he said, disappointingly unimpressed.

'Anyway, what I wanted to ask you was—in my capacity as executor'—reminding him of my credibility—'did Ms Murgatroyd say anything to you about winding up the business she owned in Camden Market? It's called Gee-Haw. I believe they have accrued some fairly significant debts. This would have been some months ago.'

Given Mr Wells's apparent inability to remember who Murgatroyd was, I was not optimistic. And indeed, he sat for a long moment, seeming to rack his brains.

But then, lo and behold, it all seemed to come flooding back to him. 'You know, Ms Dorn, you're absolutely right, she did. I suppose you're wanting to dispose of things according to her wishes, are you?' I said that that was why I was asking the question. 'Yes, she did come to see me, asking questions about liquidating the business. I got the impression that, because the business was in trouble, it would be best for all concerned if she could wind it up with a minimum of fuss. I gave her some details about how to enter into a process of voluntary liquidation. But I didn't hear from her again after that—until the news of her death.'

I said that Murgatroyd had known she was dying and must have wanted to get things neatly squared away before that happened. What I did not say was that Murg had not—rightly, as it turned out—trusted me to be a good steward of her affairs. Perhaps she had been worried that Dimitra would have managed to prevail on me somehow to try to keep the thing going—and that Dimitra would have ended up losing the shirt off her back—or that I would somehow have gotten dragged into a great financial mess that could not be so easily solved. This was all terribly interesting, though. It meant that it had been in Dimitra's interest to stop Murgatroyd from dissolving Gee-Haw. And it confirmed that Dimitra had lied to me about Murg's intentions for the business.

'Now, Ms Dorn,' said Mr Wells, 'what I probably ought to do is to give you the information on liquidating the business that I had been intending to give her…' I thought about telling him not to bother, that Murgatroyd's estate remained fairly low on my list of priorities—but he had only been so forthcoming because he believed I was trying to set Murg's affairs in order, rather than trying to solve her supposed murder. In any case, he had bustled out of the room before I could say anything.

Wells seemed to be gone for an unusually long time. I kept myself busy trying to spot him in the Oxford photograph behind his desk, like a real-life 'Where's Wally?' puzzle. I was well aware that I had my own tree-trunk-sized chip on my shoulder about never having completed university, but there was something embarrassing about people who displayed photographs like this. Especially given the rest of Wells's faux-donnish office. A sentimental attachment to getting drunk, reading some books, wearing a stripy scarf, having some childish affair or other, and then constructing a whole identity around it for the rest of one's life! Honestly!

Before my bitterness could get up too much of a head of steam, I finally found him, with a good deal more hair, holding on to the post of a tent for support. I grinned slightly to myself, then stopped short. Wait a minute! Surely not!

'Here you are!' said Wells, coming back into the room with a sheaf of photocopied sheets. 'This will give you the information you need to get started, and of course I'm always here to assist you, though you may find you need to engage the services of a specialist insolvency practitioner.'

He went on with something or other about arrangements with creditors and telling banks and loans that might get called in. I smiled and nodded the best I could, taking none of it in. Instead, my eyes remained fixed on the picture behind his head. For, standing a little way away from the undergraduate Ronald Wells, there they were—much younger, but indubitably themselves—Oliver Manders and Ian Harcourt-Reilly, caught by the photographer mid-guffaw, like the great friends they surely were!

Look at that! said my internal Murgatroyd. *You've found something else out.*

15

Part of the problem was, the more I found out, the more con-
fusing it all got. Another part of the problem was, I was still
spending a good deal of time doing *Dog's Ball*-related activities.
Not only did these eat into the time I had for the avenging of
Murgatroyd, but I found them quite enjoyable. The day after
my visit to Hammond & Wells, for instance, I was booked
at a conference at Lowlands University, somewhere outside
Coventry, to talk once again about my great discovery.

I used the time on the train to chat with Murg about what
I knew.

What do you think, Murg? I asked her.

There was Dimitra. Murgatroyd had presumably wanted
to use her last weeks or months of passable health to put
Gee-Haw out of its misery in a mercy killing. To spare the
incompetent Dimitra from financial woes after Murg was dead.
It had to be something like that. I couldn't imagine Murg's
being guilty of having acted maliciously. But Dimitra wouldn't
have liked that. Not at all. Would she have disliked it enough
to kill Murgatroyd before she had a chance to liquidate the
business? It seemed absurdly melodramatic. But then, someone had faked Murgatroyd's suicide, so there was a certain
amount of melodrama inherent in the whole business. And
there was some sort of connection between Dimitra and Arise.
Even if I hadn't really seen her at the Arise offices, she had
mentioned them when Ian had tracked her down. They had

a guilty conscience, she said. They ought to pay her rent for her, wasn't that it?

You know I can't tell you what happened, Ag, she said. *It doesn't work like that. I'm just a mental construct you've come up with. But keep going.*

Speaking of Arise: Sir Ed Ratchett had had his security goon warn me off asking too many questions about Ian's connection with Oliver—a connection that I now knew dated back twenty years or so, all the way to Oxford. Why would he care about that? And the Crooked Man! My childhood terror had phoned me out of nowhere, also trying to spook me about looking for Ian? Why?

Go on.

Oliver had mentioned art-brute, the prankster who had humiliated the Neele years before. Murgatroyd, Ian, Oliver, art-brute—were they in on some scheme together to duplicate the manuscript of *The Dog's Ball*? And why? To sell it for money? Money to save Gee-Haw? Was one of them art-brute themselves? And so—what?—they had fallen out? Ian had killed Murgatroyd? Someone had killed Ian? But in any case, Murgatroyd hadn't been keen on *The Dog's Ball*—she hadn't wanted Clara to have anything to do with it. She had scolded me for getting so big-headed about it. And, again, what about Arise? Why would they care about any of it?

I can't make sense of it, Murg, I said.

You will, she said.

The whole thing felt a bit like the occasional Christmases when I would try to solve a Rubik's Cube. If I managed to collect a few squares of the correct colour on one side, suddenly the far side of the thing was in disarray. It was as if there was an angle on the thing that my brain didn't want me to consider.

Instead, I decided to put it out of my mind. It was a sunny day, and the train was making its way through the Chilterns, whose picturesque hills looked like an advert for the British countryside. *Should I move here?* I thought. Even the ham sandwich I bought on the train was strangely delicious.

And although the bucolic air was dispelled as we rolled into the outskirts of Coventry, my good mood persisted. I was Agatha Dorn, literary personage.

I had to take a taxi to the Lowlands Conference Facility, which was in the middle of nowhere. I imagined sending the receipt I would get to the conference organizers for reimbursement and felt, as I always did in such circumstances, quite decadent.

The conference centre was a very strange place indeed. It was as if a group of media consultants had been given a pile of money and a Travelodge. There were endless corridors with 1990s fixtures, punctuated by those tight-fitting fire doors that thunk and flub when you open them; there was AstroTurf on the walls. The only food available for miles around was from the conference-centre's cafeteria. It came in cardboard packaging with cutesy messages written on it: 'Go on, recycle me! You know you want to!' That kind of thing. They were supposed to distract from the awfulness of the food.

I made my way to the room where my panel was to convene. I was met at the door by the woman who had invited me, a graduate student named Sally Finch. 'Agatha Dorn?' she said. She was meek and diffident and extremely happy I had come. I was a good get for her.

'Yes,' I said brusquely, letting the silence that followed get awkward just because I could.

She gave the impression that she wanted to gush over the success of *The Dog's Ball* but was worried that gushing was not something academics did. 'Did you get here all right?' she asked. Well, evidently I had. She led me into the room, where the chairs were arranged across an op-art carpet that threatened to bring on one of my headaches; a wall made of blackboard behind the table proclaimed the bizarre legend: 'BREAKFAST LUNCH BRAINSTORM'. I dry-swallowed a couple of prophylactic Nurofen. 'I think we'll have a good turnout. *Edmund Swettenham* is here,' added Sally Finch in a hushed tone. Swettenham was Green's authorized biographer. I made a non-committal noise but was secretly gratified to see him in the last row. It seemed like a sign from Fraser Green that I was among the chosen.

Sally was moderating and introduced the panellists. My introduction, I noted with pleasure, was the most fulsome. The first speaker was a faculty member from Lowlands who was, he had told me, Sally's adviser. He argued that *The Dog's Ball* constituted a clear marker in Green's stylistic evolution from *Murder in the First Person* to *The Kingpin*. I grunted. *The Kingpin* was a barely warmed-over stew of old short stories Green had cobbled together in the aftermath of the Harrogate scandal. The second panellist was a male postgrad who argued in his opening paragraph that Green's fiction would have been more radical had she been able to imagine more rhizomatic structures of connectivity, after which I stopped listening.

But then, does anyone really listen at these things? Conferences are just events that organizations put on in order to demonstrate that they continue to exist, and sometimes to provide an excuse for people in the creative industries to go on holiday. Although it wasn't much like a holiday. As far as I could tell, the only things for miles around were some unattractive university buildings and an immense car park.

My paper, which was just a version of my usual spiel about finding the manuscript, seemed to go down very well. I got a hearty round of applause from the thirty-or-so people in the room, and most of the Qs in the Q&A were directed my way.

When I did the talks at bookshops, the questions were all the same: 'What was it like to discover the lost manuscript?' 'How did you feel when you realized what it was?' The questions at academic talks masqueraded as more intelligent. 'Could you say something about the social construction of the idea of the *lost work*—especially when it's handwritten—as a kind of sacred object?' 'I'd love to hear you dilate on the manuscript as it relates to something like Walter Benjamin's concept of the aura.' Neither the people in the bookshops nor the academics were saying what they really meant, and they were all asking the same thing: *Did it feel—for a moment—as if you mattered? What is that like? Did it feel like magic?* And I always wanted to say, *It did! Yes, it did!*

I was feeling great when, after the paper, Edmund Swettenham came up to talk to me. Swettenham had a haircut that made me think of the First World War, somehow, with severe sides and a scrappy top. He was wearing a navy-blue cable-knit jumper over a crumpled grey Oxford shirt. He radiated the same air of election as Nancy. He began to ask me about the provenance of the *Dog's Ball* manuscript. But after a while, it became clear that he wasn't just asking me about it—he was pressing me on it: How had I come to get hold of the manuscript in the first place? How well did I know the Cadigans? Had I gone back and checked that there *was* an Alexander Cust working at the

Pale Horse in 1926? I asked him why he seemed so sceptical: did he—I trembled to ask—have doubts about the book's authenticity?

'I mean, there are a few things that strike me as funny about it, that's all,' he said. 'I don't mean to be rude, but it's all a bit too pat for me. For one thing, she's supposed to have written a forty-thousand-word novella in eleven days, while in deep distress at the break-up of her marriage? That's four thousand words a day. It's not impossible but, well, it's quite a lot of words. Have you ever tried to write four thousand words a day, consistently? And have them come out as well as they did? It doesn't read like a first draft.'

'Sometimes stress brings out the best in us, I suppose,' I said.

'And then, Archie Green'—Gladden's first husband—'was always so adamant that she really *had* had a breakdown. He vacillated on the memory-loss stuff, which I don't think anyone ever really believed, but he was absolutely convinced that she had had some kind of major mental catastrophe—as were the doctors who examined her afterwards. I'm just not fully convinced she would have been capable of producing this perfectly formed text.'

'I mean, surely the Greens orchestrated all that, didn't they?'

'Maybe. That's never been my impression. And there's one more thing. On the first page, Captain Brown is driving a Lagonda, right?'

'Yes,' I said.

'Well, that's even stranger. Because Green never has Captain Brown driving a Lagonda—she never specified what kind of car he drives at all. They invented the Lagonda thing for the TV series.'

I felt as if I had been punched in the stomach. This was the kind of thing I ought to have spotted immediately. I couldn't believe I had overlooked it—if it were true. 'That's incredible!' I said. 'It must be a coincidence! What a crazy one, though!'

'Well, I hope so,' said Edmund Swettenham. There was a glint in his eye for which I did not care at all.

In an instant, all my good feelings swirled down the drain. Because that was it: the possibility that I had not been letting myself consider. What if *The Dog's Ball*—source of all my late good fortune, anchor of my poor fragile ego—what if it had been a fake all along?

That night, in the uncomfortable conference-centre bed, I thought about what I ought to do next. You'll remember that I took some liberties with the truth with Fraser Green when I was describing the steps I had taken to authenticate the manuscript. There were actually some things I could do fairly easily if I wanted to set my mind at rest. Or confirm my worst fears. That was the rub.

It seemed that the most useful thing I could do was to face my fears.

The next afternoon, I took Murgatroyd's manuscript page with me to work, headed to Special Collections, and had Bunner fetch *The Dog's Ball* box for me. Once I was alone, I reached into my pocket and pulled out my keys, which had a pocket-sized UV penlight attached to them. Never leave home without one!

Beginning in the 1950s or thereabouts, most paper was manufactured using what are called optical brighteners, chemicals that make the paper look extra-white. One thing about optical brighteners is that they glow under ultraviolet light. If you shine an ultraviolet light on a piece of paper and it glows, that means it has optical brighteners in it, which means that it was most likely produced in the 1950s or later, and in any case definitely not before 1936, when brighteners were used for the first time.

So, you can guess what's coming. I shone my UV light on several pages of *The Dog's Ball*, including Murgatroyd's scrap of a page, which were supposed to have been written in 1926. They glowed.

On some level, I had wondered if they would, ever since I found the page at Murgatroyd's house. She had been investigating the manuscript. Why? Because it was a fake. I had only failed to consider it before because I had refused to entertain the possibility.

The world seemed to spin around me. Oh, the Crooked Man, the Crooked Man had won! I sat with my head in my hands, wanting to throw up. How had I got myself into a position where so much depended on the success of *The Dog's Ball*? The life for which I had longed through all the years of being passed over and put down and ignored—it would all be gone. No more Mabel Palmer, whose services were being paid for from the *Dog's Ball* royalties. I'd be back in Palmers Green wiping dribble off my senile mother's chin till she died. This was not to mention the small matter of the survival of the Neele itself. Arise would be back with their compulsory purchase scheme at the first hint of a scandal.

All I wanted to do was go home and empty the gin bottle. But I had to think. Bunner would surely be back in a moment—was there anything else I could do that could help matters?

I pulled out Gladden Green's letter from the box—the one I had found before the manuscript, the one where she donated the novella to Cust—and shone my light on that. No glow. That meant—well, nothing definitive, but it meant that the letter *could* still be real. That was something.

Murgatroyd had been an archivist too; she knew about optical brighteners and all that. The lava lamp and the fragment at Murgatroyd's house suggested she had probably known about the fake too. And if she had been going to tell, well, was that a reason to murder a terminally ill person right before they died? It seemed plausible. In fact, the only marvel was that I hadn't done it myself.

Did you know, Murg? That it was a fake? And you didn't tell me?

I had my reasons, Ag—you need to believe me.

I had to come clean. There was no option. If all that was at stake was my reputation, that was one thing. But someone being killed? There was no way I could keep quiet.

But then, from a utilitarian point of view, I thought, *what course of action would bring about the greatest good? Who would be hurt if I spoke up? Clara. Mabel Palmer. Everyone at the Neele. All the readers who would no longer get to enjoy a lost masterpiece. And who would be helped? A tax-dodging mega-corporation. Wasn't the ethical thing to do to keep stumm, if you really thought about it properly?*

No, I had choices. I could in fact deny the Crooked Man his victory. Couldn't I?

But my train of thought was interrupted by a ping from my phone, followed by a series of other pings in quick succession. I was being tagged repeatedly on the Twitter account I had established as a publicity avenue for *The Dog's Ball.* Everyone famous had one. The first one was a link from *The Times Literary Supplement*: 'The Dog's Ball: Lost Green or Clever Fraud?'

My stomach dropped. *Oh, S—. S— S— S—.* I clicked the link. It was Edmund Swettenham, the biographer who had buttonholed me at the conference, asking if the novella was a fake. He started with the stuff about the recycled names, about which I too had worried a little at first. He must have had this all ready to go well before he said anything to me! The irredeemable piece of s—!

He repeated what he had said to me before about Gladden Green's mental health, and the unlikelihood of her being able to compose a forty-thousand-word narrative in eleven days. He wrote about the Lagonda, adding damningly that the car in the book seemed, from various passages of description, to be the two-litre Tourer featured in the TV show. This model, he went on, was not sold until 1931, five years after the supposed composition of the text.

My phone rang, with an unknown number. I ignored it.

There was nothing direct from the Cadigans. Bless their hearts, they must have refused to speak to him. He had been to Harrogate, though, and had not only failed to find evidence of an Alexander Cust working at the Pale Horse but had also failed to find evidence of his having existed at all. This seemed to me tendentious, since I had a large box of such evidence sitting at the Neele, but he, of course, would have discounted that right off the bat.

None of this was really conclusive. But, like a good showman, he had saved the best for last. He, unlike me, had had the paper and ink of the manuscript properly analysed — how had he got hold of it? He revealed that both the paper *and* the ink were consistent with a date much more recent than 1926. That was a nice way of putting it. Apparently the manuscript had been written with a number of Paper Mate gel pens. The final paragraph was cold. 'Knowing all this, it appears that the only question remaining is whether Agatha Dorn and the Neele Archive have been ruthless perpetrators of or bungling accessories to a spectacular fraud? Dorn's lack of attention to proper procedures of authentication might suggest either answer. But this will be a matter for the post-mortem.'

My phone rang again. Nora. Decline.

My email inbox was beginning to fill up with messages from addresses I did not recognize. I clicked on one. 'My daughter's name is Agatha,' it began, 'but I now wish that it was not, so that she would not have to share a name with a fraudster such as your bad self.' Things seemed to be escalating quickly. There was a text from Fraser Green: 'call me as soon as possible'. I did not. The phone rang again. It was my producer at the BBC. Again, ignored. Like a fool, I returned to Twitter. always thought @agatha_Dorn came off as a con artist—guess i was right #dogsballfake. This was from someone who, by his own admission downthread, had met me for five seconds at a book signing. But, you know, he felt like he could just tell. To get down the thread, I had to get through clearly a publicity whore—called it on day 1 and dont know about con artist but i know shes an ugly f—ing dyk3 lol. Those will get deleted because of bad language, so the joke's on them, I thought. It was cold comfort.

I had to get out. If I could get away, I could think and figure out what to do. Perhaps all was not lost. I stood up.

The door to the stacks burst open. It was Nancy. 'Agatha,' she said, her face furious, 'what the f— is this?'

Oh, Murg, I thought, *What have I done?*

PART THREE

16

There were ten minutes left. We had had customers all evening, and my feet were killing me. It wasn't as if there was a surprise new Harry Potter or something. It was just a freak rush.

So it was only Mark and I on late closing, and Mark was no help, as usual. His favourite activity was to hide in the stockroom and complain about what a dump the bookshop was and how quickly he was going to escape. He was right about the dump part. He had tried recruiting me as a fellow bitcher and moaner a couple of times, but I had refused to play. Now he left me alone. I despise self-pity. Could he not just take occasional nips of gin in the back, like I did?

Because Mark was hiding, a steady stream of vaguely annoyed customers was drifting to my till in the back of the shop. I belonged to the popular-science section, which smelled of the bins from the salsa bar next door. I got to clock out in seven minutes.

I hated having to bring back into circulation these phrases from retail jobs I'd had when I was sixteen. Late closing. Stockroom. Clock out. I hated being given late shifts with less than a day's notice—and saying, 'Oh yes, that's fine', because Broadstreet's could replace me in a snap.

But then, it was fine. I didn't have anywhere else to go these days. Sampson the Gelding, the Gatehouse speakeasy, had stopped letting me in. I could go to the pub. But, oh, wait, I no longer had any money, and no one with whom to go, either.

Or I could go 'home', to Murgatroyd's house where I was essentially squatting. The creditors would have to evict me. I had told the clearance company not to come. I wanted the piles of Murgatroyd's hoarded trash around me like a blanket, or a shield, against the Crooked Man, fragments shored against my ruin.

When I first got fired from the Neele, I tried to find a house share, but it had been a blasted nightmare. It was all these giant houses of children just out of university, and every time I turned up for an interview, their faces would fall, because who wanted a middle-aged housemate? Not only would I nag them about the washing-up, &c., but I would be the spectre at the feast: a permanent reminder that London might not be the backdrop to the heart-warming movies of their own lives; they too might be living in a ghastly falling-down shared house twenty years from now.

One of the girls in one house had had an especially pretty button nose. Behind her, in the living room, a boy was playing a shooting game on a console (*Reload!*). I had imagined taking a switchblade out of my pocket, putting it into the pretty girl's nostril, and slicing. Instead, I said that I understood that no one wanted an old lady for a housemate, but I promised to keep myself to myself and always pay on time. I said it as if it were a joke, but it was not a joke. They said they would let me know.

I might as well be at the shop as anywhere.

A woman with an I'd-like-to-speak-to-the-manager haircut was heading my way with a copy of—wouldn't you know it?—*Effervescent Arsenic*.

'I wanted a Père Flambeau, but this is all that was on the shelf!' I resisted the urge to tell her that, interestingly,

Effervescent Arsenic, which featured the unpopular Colonel Cuff as detective, had originally been adapted from a Flambeau short story, entitled 'The Cruel Orchid'.

'Do you not have any more?' she asked.

Of course we did. She must have looked in the wrong place. 'Did you try the next shelf down?' I asked.

'Yes, I looked on the shelf, thank you,' she snapped. I had impugned her ability to perform simple tasks. 'I meant in the back.'

Instead of leaping to my feet, I made a non-committal gesture. The woman continued. 'I wanted to read the "new" one, but it turned out to be a fake, didn't it? I suppose this will have to do. It's one of the ones with a suicide that's not a suicide, isn't it? I've read it before, but...' She raised her palms in surrender, as if I were personally forcing her to buy this book she did not want.

I told her it was 8.99, and she pulled out a £20 note, at which my heart sank further. At late closing, we had to make do with whatever was in the till. Only managers had access to the float. It was never a problem, because who paid for anything with cash any more? Not being trusted to make £11 worth of change was just one of the innumerable petty humiliations up with which I had to put. I opened the drawer, where there were, as I had known, just a few small coins. 'I've no change, I'm afraid,' I said. 'Do you have another means of payment?'

'No I don't,' she said indignantly. 'Can't you go and get change from another till or something?'

I told her that I was not allowed to.

'What you mean,' she said, 'is that it's five minutes till closing time and you can't be bothered. I'll just have to leave it.

I'll be going to Waterstones from now on. And I'll be posting about this poor service on Twitter. What do you think about that?' She flounced away. I barely noticed, though. What she had said about suicide had stuck in my craw.

I was going to write that, in the days after the *TLS* published the *Dog's Ball* article, things went from bad to worse, but 'worse' doesn't really cover it. They went from worse to worst? Here is a list of the important things that happened—I shan't dwell on them, if you don't mind: websites and newspapers said unpleasant things about the book, the Neele, and me in particular. *The Lost Green* got cancelled. The producer had the nerve to ask me for a comment for the BBC News website at the same time. I hung up on him. The Neele fired me. Why not, eh? In Ian's continuing absence, the Chair of the Board of Trustees did the honours, which was good of them. I shouldn't have liked to have been fired by Nancy. Less than a day after that, Arise let us know—let *them* know—that they would be renewing their attempts compulsorily to purchase the archive. No one said goodbye to me. Not Bunner. Not Nancy.

Upon confirming the details of Swettenham's article, Fraser Green decided to have *The Dog's Ball* pulped. Aeolian invoked a morality clause in my contract: apparently I had brought 'widespread public condemnation' upon their organization. I couldn't really argue. I was instructed to return all my royalty money, which I no longer had. I was the subject of what they call a 'pile-on' on the Internet. The number of people who decided that the whole thing was my fault reached a tipping point. I shan't reproduce any more of the messages I got, but you can imagine.

I upped my consumption of gins-and-water. Actually, that's a lie. The water part remained about the same as always. I began having to manage blackouts. That was just fine by me. As far as I was concerned, the less of my day I had to experience, the better.

At a certain point I deleted my social media accounts, changed my email, and bought what I believe is called a burner phone. I was fed up with being contactable. I got the terrible job at Broadstreet's bookshop on Charing Cross Road, and the days—months, now—slid by.

Worst of all, I was forced to sell my precious flat to a property developer. It was only on the market for a day. Residences in the Gatehouse are highly desirable, did I tell you? It was the only way I could raise the money to repay Aeolian and continue to fund Clara's care. Heri made no objection. I moved my somewhat meagre possessions to Murgatroyd's house. And so, one terrible morning, I bid farewell to my beloved vertical sink and headed to Palmers Green.

I gave up on poking about and drank until I believed the seal on the gas canister had not snapped between my fingers, the window of Ian's house had never been smashed, and Tony had indeed been a charming gentleman from Product Management. I googled: 'gin hallucinations', 'booze delusions', 'am I schizophrenic?' It turns out there are online quizzes for that. I took one. 'Moderate Schizophrenia!' the computer said when I had finished, with an asterisk. Under the asterisk it said, 'Since this online quiz cannot diagnose any disorder, it does not tell you whether you have schizophrenia or not.'

One of my headaches was on the table basically every day. I took to wearing a medical patch over the trigger eye to keep them at bay. I noticed Mark, that absurd hipster, looking at me with curiosity and approval. I wasn't talking to him, though. It occurred to me that Mark's eyes were a much steelier blue than I had ever before noticed. There was no way I was telling him anything.

What's going to happen to me? I asked Murg.

I can't tell you that, she said unhelpfully.

It is 1992, and I am home from uni. I am looking into our nasty gilt-edged sitting-room mirror for some reason. Clara is behind me.

'The plastic surgeon really did a wonderful job,' I say. 'You can't see that there was ever anything there.'

'Pardon?' says my mother.

In 1983, I had become probably the only child in the world truly to fall victim to a Halloween treat-tamperer.

We were home after a brief evening of trick-or-treating—just to the end of the road and back. It was the early days of the phenomenon. Heri had worn a bedsheet with cut-out eyes. I was wearing a black baddie's mask. The costumes were pretty basic in those days.

With her puritan's heart, Clara had allowed us each to eat one sweet, then proposed to put the rest of our haul in the cupboard for a future date.

'Wait!' I said. 'Can we eat a healthy one?' I pulled the lone apple out of my plastic bag.

'I suppose,' said my mother.

I bit down and felt something impossibly thin and sharp slice into my top lip. Blood began to flow onto the apple and down onto the floor.

The confused investigation that ensued alongside attempts to find something to stanch the flow revealed a razor blade, slid invisibly into the apple, just the way the tabloids breathlessly warned they might be.

For once, my mother's intransigence proved useful. At North Mid Casualty, the doctor on call had proposed to put a couple of stitches in my lip and get back to dealing with the glut of injured drunkards the occasion had generated. However, unwilling to accept the idea that her daughter should look anything other than perfect, Clara held a one-woman sit-in in reception until they agreed to send a plastic surgeon who could sew stitches sufficiently tiny that no scar would appear. It was one of the few things she had done for me for which I was thankful. Still, I cut my apples into prudent pieces to this day.

In 1992, looking in the mirror, I remind her: 'The razor blade, remember? In the apple?' When she remains confused, I rehearse the familiar story, by now told so often as to have become a piece of family lore.

'What a lot of rot,' says Clara. 'Those stories are just urban legends. Really, I don't know why you're such an incorrigible liar, Agatha.'

I am never 100% certain that I am in my right mind.

Back at Murg's, after work, I tucked myself into my armchair with a bottle, a glass, and the television, and settled in for the evening.

Just then, I heard an unfamiliar chiming from the bedroom, the ring of a mobile phone that wasn't mine. With annoyance, I heaved myself out of the chair and went to investigate. Probably the darned thing would never stop if I didn't.

On the nightstand sat Murgatroyd's pink Nokia, plugged in as I had left it three months ago, jangling and buzzing. Honestly, I rarely came into the bedroom. I preferred to sleep in my chair. I picked up the phone, and said, 'Hello?' No one was there. Probably spam.

But there was suddenly a glimmer of something in my mind I hadn't felt for a while. The mystery. I suddenly remembered that Tom Cadigan had called Murgatroyd's phone on the night I discovered she had been killed. The police had thought I was cuckoo when I brought it up, and I had let it lie, because I had not wanted to poke into the provenance of *The Dog's Ball* as much as anything else. But now? Well, I couldn't really make things much worse for myself, could I? At the very least, a little light googling of Tom Cadigan seemed like a way I might pass some time.

Tom Cadigan had a surprisingly small Internet footprint for someone I had pegged as craving fame. Perhaps I had him pegged wrong. One expected to find a de luxe personal website, long on style and short on substance, or perhaps an obviously self-authored Wikipedia entry, but there was none of that. He did not have a bio page at his new employers, Monkshood, which was not itself surprising, but the *Bookseller* had picked up the press release announcing his hiring:

Monkshood is pleased to welcome Tom Cadigan to the position of Head Graphic Designer. Of the appointment, publisher Dennis Clement said, 'As a freelance designer and consultant, Tom has overseen the design of a number of exceptional projects for Monkshood over the last several years, including the best-selling *Complete Do-It-Yourself*

Manual, the award-winning Facsimile Documents series for Arise, and the fourteenth edition of the standard medical text *Dodd and Mead's Pharmacology.* We are thrilled to have him as the head of the Art Department.'

Arse arse arse. My mind shot back to the old days at the Neele:
'What do Arse want today, Agatha?'
'Don't be vulgar, Nancy. Their name is Arise.'
'Quite so.' (Ian now.) 'We wouldn't want to get in the habit of calling them Arse, would we? Imagine if every time people heard the name Arise, all they could think of was arse arse arse.' And he had *sauntered away, singing* arse-arse-arse-arse, *to the tune of the famous bit of Beethoven's Fifth.*

Arise's resources provided the leverage with which they persuaded the government to let them have the Neele. And Monkshood was the company producing those resources, in part through the work of Tom Cadigan. Gladden would have called these 'certain suggestive points'. My brain seemed to stretch after a long hibernation. *The humble grey matter,* I thought, in a French accent.

You're back in business, said Murg.

17

In the morning, the itch to investigate was still with me. I thought, *I could at least find out if the call really happened.* Perhaps the mobile company could tell me if Tom Cadigan had really rung me that night.

After a fifty-five-minute hold—during which time I made myself late for work—I got a person. The person—'Paul'—eventually understood that I wanted the company's own call logs, and not for my phone—well, yes, it was my phone—but it had belonged to someone dead and had been left to me in a will so in that sense it wasn't *mine* mine. What I had to do was produce a copy of Murgatroyd's will, and also of her death certificate, and send them in to the telecom company, before I could get what I wanted. Well, that was fine. I was an archivist. I knew how to hang on to pieces of paper. I got copies made at the newsagent down the road and popped them in the post on my way to get yelled at, at Broadstreet's, for being two hours late. Something told me it was worth it, though. To set my mind at ease.

'Paul' had told me he would ring back as soon as they had received and processed the documents, probably within a few days. And so, for the next several days, my mind kept drifting to my own burner phone, wondering if I would find a message, wondering if it would ring with news. When I had heard nothing for a week, I decided—perhaps irrationally, though perhaps not, honestly—that this meant I was never going to hear anything. Nothing whatever would come of my attempt to infiltrate Murgatroyd's phone records.

More fool me.

It was night. Well, the living-room clock said it was after midnight, so it was technically morning, I suppose. I was in my armchair in Palmers Green. Pitch black. My eyes popped open as if there had been a noise in the room, though I hadn't consciously heard it.

I couldn't move. My muscles would not do what I wanted them to do. I wondered for a moment if I was dreaming, but I knew I wasn't. I sometimes mistake dreams for reality, but I don't think I've ever mistaken reality for a dream. So then I thought, *Well, maybe it's sleep paralysis.* Which meant it was important to keep calm, I think I had read once in a magazine at the doctor's surgery. If you kept calm, it would pass.

Then I heard the rustle. Even while I was terrified, I mused, in a detached way, that I was feeling the way people are described as feeling in sensation novels: *A horrid dismay thrilled my blood*, and so forth. *Oh,* this *is what it means when they say that sort of thing*, I thought. Another reason why I was sure I was not dreaming was: in nightmares, when the bad thing happens, you scream with all your might but out no sound comes. I couldn't even get that far, though—I couldn't even get my mouth open.

Part of the darkness detached from itself. A black coat. Suddenly I knew. *It couldn't be.* I directed my gaze upwards—my eyes still worked, you see—and shining from the darkness was a pair of steely blue eyes. I looked lower. And there, emerging from the folds of the coat, was the horrible stump. He waggled it at me tauntingly. *The Crooked Man.* Effing hell.

Now the other hand, which had on it a black leather glove, was moving towards me, holding—was it?—the tissue box from my bedside table? The hand passed the box purposefully in front of my eyes, in a way that reminded me of magicians demonstrating that there was no false bottom. I remained unable to move, despite my best efforts.

The gloved hand put the box down on my lap. Then it put a finger on my upper lip, its thumb on my chin, and jogged my mouth open. It reached for a tissue and put it in my mouth. The tissue turned immediately to a disgusting, clammy pulp. It reached slowly for another tissue, taking its time. The detached part of my brain noticed that there was something familiar in the figure's movements. The Crooked Man put a second tissue in my mouth, and a third.

After ten tissues, my mouth was full to straining and as dry as paste. I was pretty sure this was the worst thing that had ever happened. Something in the figure's manner suggested to me he was enjoying himself. He stood for a long moment. Then he turned to go. Was that it, then?

But, at the door, he turned back and spoke, in a whisper, for the first time. 'Might I ask you *please* to leave alone the death of Amy Murgatroyd? If you would?' Again, there was something familiar. A trace of an accent? He left.

One consolation was that the clock was in my field of vision, so I was able to mark the passing of time. I used the time to spin out worst-case scenarios. Was this a creeping paralysis that would eventually shut down my eyes, my lungs, and then *boom*, I'd be dead? Or was it going to be a locked-in-syndrome type of thing, like that man who dictated the novel by blinking in Morse code? Or had he been paralysed because of something else? I couldn't remember. Or would it be that my body would slowly, agonizingly come back to life, one finger would twitch, then another. Would it all even come back? What if I could move everything except, you know, my toes? Do paralysed toes rot and drop off? Is that what leprosy is? Does leprosy even exist any more? How do paralysed people urinate? Would I even know if I had wet myself already? I imagined the neighbour finding me in here, dead, lying in my own faeces. They'd be sorry, then, I told myself with a vengeful glee.

Shh, said Murgatroyd. *Keep calm.*

What happened was that after two terrifying hours, I found myself suddenly able to move again. Just like that. One minute I was paralysed; the next, I wasn't. It was as if someone had paused me for a while, then pressed play.

I hadn't really anticipated this, and for a moment, I didn't know what to do. I thought I had better peel the tissues out of my mouth, which made my flesh crawl. Gluey bits stuck to my palette like papier mâché. I retched, bringing up some bile and giving myself heartburn in the process. And, oh: it turned out I had indeed weed myself. Christ's wounds! What do people do, when this sort of thing happens? If indeed this sort of thing is a thing that happens to other people? I swung myself out of the chair and walked to the door, staggering a little, but not overmuch, considering. True, I whacked my head on a cabinet on the way, which left a bit of a gash, but still. I was only a little bit dizzy. My neighbour, Mr Something-or-other, talked like he'd been in the army. Lawd, would I never learn the utility of basic neighbourliness! I would knock on his door and begin, I supposed, the process of 'raising the alarm'.

*

It turned out there were no footprints. No fingerprints. The neighbours had seen nothing. The police were intrigued enough to call their medical liaison from the toxicology department at Guy's, who muttered to himself about early experiments in anaesthesia, but ultimately said there was no drug that behaved in quite the way I had described. The questions that came my way from the police stopped being about what I had seen and heard and started being about whether I had a tendency to have vivid nightmares and such. I said, 'Oh, and I suppose I like to stuff my mouth full of tissues for recreational purposes?'

My interviewer bit back a smart response. I was really ticking her off. But she, like everybody, was deeply invested in the project of *sparing my feelings*. Oh, how my feelings got spared! The crazy b— sincerely believes she has been through something terrible, that's pretty clear. But she's had a whack on the head, did you see it? And isn't she a time-waster, been on the phone before saying her girlfriend had been murdered, her boss had been kidnapped, all turned out to be nonsense? And did you see the empty pints of gin in the bin? Everybody's job was to calm me down enough that they could give me the number of a helpline to call and get back to the office. A man with latex gloves swabbed the inside of my mouth and put the swab in a baggie, then took the tissues that had been in my mouth and sealed them in a different baggie. That seemed promisingly serious, but then he warned me that it wasn't like the TV, love, DNA samples took months to process in real life. By that time I'd probably have received a bland letter closing the investigation, and a whole drawerful of leaflets with useless numbers to call.

*

For a lot of people this would all have been profoundly traumatic. Years of therapy and so forth. But not I, it turned out. Once everyone had left, I didn't feel violated; I felt awakened. I had been right about Murgatroyd! What's that you say? I was still in shock? Manic? This was the mental equivalent of a sugar high? Pish posh, away with you! I felt better than I had in months! I had a little gin to celebrate. When criminals threaten people to warn them off, does it ever work? I was back in the game!

The abrasion above my right eye, which I had acquired attempting to get to my neighbour's house, had already gone a little strange. There was an oddly shaped lump the colour of ordinary flesh, which worried me, since from the weird shape and the amount it hurt, you would think it would be some ghastly hue. The injury was lurking, waiting to kick in. *Or*, I thought, *perhaps it never will. Perhaps God is keeping me healthy for my quest.*

I knew exactly what I had to do next: I had to go to Harrogate, home of the Pale Horse and of the Cadigans. Broadstreet's could get bent. I would take the train now, immediately. I checked the schedule. Well, tomorrow morning, then.

There was one easy way to find out if Tom Cadigan had known Murgatroyd: I could ask him in person! Then there was the fact that Murgatroyd had been to Harrogate—Bunner had said so. Perhaps someone would remember!

What were you hoping to find in Harrogate, Murgatroyd? Why did you go?

Because Gladden Green's letter to Cust is written on old paper— which means that perhaps she did write a real Dog's Ball just not the one you found.

So it was important to find out if the story of *The Dog's Ball* was plausible, even if my manuscript was a fake. Did the hotel resemble the description given there? I'd have to look for myself. Edmund Swettenham had failed to find evidence of the existence of Alexander Cust. No matter, I would find it myself! If I went to Harrogate, went to the hotel, and talked to the Cadigans, everything would start to fit together. I must be the last person the Cadigans wanted to see, though, surely? The ego-crazed moron who had exposed their family to public ridicule? So what! I would sit outside the door till they let me in. There was nowhere I would rather be.

18

The Cadigans lived on Hickory Street, a steep hill off a ring road that was never intended to be traversed on foot. I had made the long walk from the station down a vestigial pavement stained dark grey with exhaust fumes from the cars that passed unconscionably close. I went by the usual assortment of car-stereo retrofitters and off-brand fried-chicken joints, whose emissions played badly with my hangover. At one stage I had actually to climb over a metal central-reservation fence. It had sucked all the romance out of the journey, really. Wasn't Harrogate supposed to be posh? Still, I enjoyed the feeling of 'powering through'. Being on a mission was giving me a sense of myself again.

Hickory Street's Victorian terraces would have gentrified nicely, but that hadn't happened yet. The brick frontages were black with some northern blight. The road culminated in a nasty-looking pub and a grimy Spar shop. It looked like the kind of house the Cadigans, a primary-school teacher and a media freelancer, would be able to afford. There was a little front garden walled off with decorative breeze blocks, as if we were supposed to believe we were in Palm Springs or something—and a *SOLD* sign tied to the blocks. I'd move too, if I lived here and I'd just gotten a job with a multinational. Mind you, given my current residence at Murgatroyd the hoarder's murder house, I couldn't exactly talk.

Alexander Cust's granddaughter, Lily Cadigan, said she hadn't thought she'd be hearing from me again. I remembered her, though. Her face was as striking now as it had been at the *Dog's Ball* launch. The way she had opened the door only the minimum distance necessary to maintain the appearance of civility suggested she was far from pleased at my reappearance. I remembered her monotone replies in interviews about *The Dog's Ball*. She hadn't wanted the media attention in the first place, and now look what had happened!

When it became clear that I wasn't going to go away, Lily invited me in. 'I'm just finishing up with a student,' she said, 'but there's coffee in the pot in the kitchen if you don't mind helping yourself. You look terrible, by the way.' I reached into my bag and made the coffee 'Irish'. A child was saying English words slowly out loud in an accented voice from somewhere in the back. I took my mug and wandered into the sitting room.

There was a shameful sofa and a small television. Above the fireplace was a black-and-white Expressionist print of some peasants suffering nobly—I'd have guessed a reproduction of a Käthe Kollwitz—ludicrously too small for the space. The walls were covered in a discoloured flock paper. Someone had had a go at painting over it in blue but had given up partway through. There was a cheap pine bookcase full to bursting, supplementary piles of books running the length of the rest of the same wall, and all of it was covered with white cat hair. The affront to my aesthetic sensibility began to make me feel quite unwell, but I determined to stick it out.

One corner of the room was quite different, though. It was home, if I was not mistaken, to a Herman Miller swag-leg desk, which must have cost more than all the furniture in the rest of the room combined. It was immaculately free of cat hair and topped with a new-looking MacBook Pro in space-age aluminium.

At this point there was a bustling noise in the hall. The front door opened and closed, and Lily Cadigan appeared in the sitting room.

'Harrogate loves to pat itself on the back for agreeing to host a tiny number of the refugees this country takes in. But then we mainstream the kids in the state schools and expect them to pass Key Stage One reading when they barely speak a word of English. Ninety per cent of them are at least bilingual in some other languages, but that counts for nothing.'

I nodded earnestly, since she obviously pegged me for someone who cared about such things.

I remembered the effect Lily Cadigan had had on me last time we met, when she had strangely impressed me with her refusal to make small talk. She was quite different from what I had originally imagined. Those human-interest pieces they did on the family in the papers painted her as a pleasant nobody, the sort of person who could have been a contestant on a home-makeover programme. But the blandness she had projected in interviews had been contrived, I realized, to hide her hostility to the whole business. What did she care about one more throwaway beach read in this fallen world where children had no idea from where their next meal was coming, and on her very own street! She had the sharp bones of a saint in an icon and seemed to exude an empathic anger of a kind of which I was instinctively suspicious. Were there really selfless people in the world? I could never quite believe it.

Part of the strangeness, I realized, was that my image of Lily thus far had been to a large extent based on my idea of the sort of person who would have married Tom Cadigan, who gave off a strong whiff of narcissism. He would have wanted a pliant little wifey who took up none of the air in the room. But that did not turn out to be what he had got.

The expensive desk and computer were his. The sitting room was an argument between Lily, for whom taste was an inexcusable indulgence, and Tom, who didn't see why people shouldn't have nice things. Had Lily thought she had married a martyr like herself, only to find out her husband merely had a thing for radical chic?

Lily asked what she could do for me, and had I finished making her family into a national laughing-stock? I replied that she wasn't the one who had got death threats, though I regretted it as soon as I said it.

'No, I dare say,' she replied, 'but we've all ended up looking stupid, haven't we? I'd rather forget the whole thing, really, but here you are.'

Suddenly it did not seem the moment to tell her all about Murgatroyd's death and the gas canister and the Crooked Man. Instead, I told her I felt terrible about the whole thing, and that I thought if I could find out who had faked the manuscript, and why, I could make amends.

With uncharitable sarcasm, she replied that I was quite the altruist. 'But, honestly, why keep raking it up?'

The front door creaked again, and this time two small girls wearing gingham school dresses and navy-blue cardigans tumbled in, shoving at one another. 'Mummy, Alice says Powerwolf is stupid,' cried one.

'Alice, that's not nice,' said Lily.

'They *are* stupid,' said the one whom I supposed was Alice. Her sister punched her in the arm.

'Betty!' said Lily. Tom Cadigan followed in behind, carrying two small rucksacks.

'Daddy!' wailed Betty. 'She's being mean about my favourite band. She's not allowed to say my favourite things are stupid! My favourite band is Powerwolf and my favourite song is "We Drink Your Blood".'

At this point, I almost interjected. If one had the bad judgement to have children in the first place, surely one could keep them from listening to filth.

'Jesus Christ,' said Lily to her husband, 'it's bad enough you let them listen to heavy metal in the car, but now they have to fight about it too?' At least Lily agreed with me. I knew there was a reason I had liked her!

'I'm not interested in banning things,' said Tom, with a wry note in his voice that suggested he was rather enjoying himself. 'Alice, why don't you try explaining to Betty *why* you think Powerwolf are stupid?' The girls flew at one another again. Lily looked as if she was willing her eyes to fire laser beams at her husband. Tom shrugged. 'I think it's so important that they learn to articulate themselves. Hello, Agatha!' he went on breezily, not looking like someone to whom I had last spoken, apparently by mistake, on the phone of a dead woman.

'Why are you wearing an eyepatch?' said Alice, spontaneously losing interest in the pigtail attached to her sister on which she had been yanking a moment before. 'We're moving house!' Betty was sprawling on the floor, bewildered.

'Yes, I saw the *SOLD* sign,' I said.

'We're going to move right to the middle of London!' Alice went on. 'We're going to go to a new school, and Mummy's going to be a teacher at the same school we go to!'

'Is that so?' I said awkwardly. The moment to explain that my eye covering was a jury-rigged migraine-prevention device appeared to have passed. I wasn't good at small talk at the best of times, but children really have no idea how to hold a conversation.

'I've been doing a lot of work for Monkshood, the book packager,' said Tom. 'They've decided to bring me in-house.'

'It means we have to move to London,' interjected Lily.

'It means we *get* to move to London,' said Tom. 'We're going to have a flat in the Gatehouse, imagine that!' I winced, I hoped only internally, at the thought of his gaining possession of a vertical sink.

'They've got me teaching hedge-fund managers' kids at Sir Carmichael Clarke's Foundation Primary,' said Lily. She made it sound as if she had been given the job of sluicing the Portaloos at Glastonbury. 'Alice and Betty, hang your bags up. I want you to start homework in five minutes.' I was being given my marching orders. But Tom was having none of it.

'To what do we owe the pleasure?' he asked me. 'Can I get you a cup of tea?'

I made the most of the opening. 'I've just had a coffee. But I was hoping I could I ask a couple of questions about Alexander Cust and the manuscript,' I said.

'Of course, ask away,' said Tom.

I turned to Lily, though. 'What was your relationship like, with your grandfather?' I felt profoundly stupid now for already knowing the answer to this question. My mind must have been somewhere else at the time. 'Did you know him well?'

She exhaled through her nose as if to say *here we go again*, but quietly, so as not to seem openly rude. 'I didn't, no,' she said.

It seemed as if that was all she would say, but Tom prompted her—'Tell the story about the macaroni cheese!' She glared at him again. 'This is a great story!'

'Well,' she said. 'He was a weird man. He lived in this dark little bungalow when I was a kid. We hardly ever went there. He didn't like children much, I don't think. He had divorced my grandma by then. One time we went there, he made us dinner. Macaroni cheese from a tin. It smelled terrible. It was all gelatinous, like one of those deep-sea creatures that have never been touched by light. We were sitting there eating it in the dark almost—I was pushing it around my plate. And suddenly my dad shouted, "Ow!" It turned out there were little nuts and bolts in with the macaroni cheese. Dad broke his tooth. I don't know if my granddad had done it deliberately, or if he was just mad, you know?'

Was Lily a fellow victim of the Crooked Man? Things like that were just his style.

I thought we were finished, but Lily went on of her own accord, warming to her theme despite herself. 'When I was older, Dad told me Granddad was angry because his life hadn't turned out the way he'd planned. He was bitter and hard to get on with, and people didn't like him. He and Dad fell out. Granddad told him he'd wasted his chance, getting married, having kids. *After all I've sacrificed for you*, &c. Granddad fancied himself as a great writer—but you know that. He put himself through university to get out of doing odd jobs in hotels. But he ended up right back there, as a desk clerk, instead of a porter. Couldn't get anything else.'

'He ended up back at the Pale Horse?'

'Yes, I believe so. He was retired by the time I knew anything about it.'

That was interesting—it meant it was just possible there was someone still there who had known him.

'Your father gave you the box of papers just before he died, yes?'

'Yeah,' she said. She was clamming up again. We were back in *haven't-we-been-over-this?* territory. 'Like putting the papers into an archive was going to make up for their sh—y relationship.'

'Had you seen or heard of the Green manuscript, or the papers where your grandfather mentions it, ever before that?' I asked.

'No,' she said. 'Like the letter says, he was supposed to keep it a secret.'

'What about the manuscript itself? Did you see that in there when you went to fetch the papers? Or could someone have snuck them in there later?'

Lily thought for a long moment, but Tom jumped in. 'They were there,' he said. 'They were definitely there when we opened the trunk.' He sounded sure, I thought, but then, why shouldn't he? He was the one who had taken the interest in the papers. It stood to reason that he would have a better idea of what was there than she would. And this was promising, somehow.

'Oh, Tom,' I said, as if I had just thought of it. 'This is a bit weird—you didn't telephone a friend of mine recently by any chance? You don't happen to know her, do you? Something odd happened with her phone.'

'I don't believe so—I don't think I know any of your friends,' he chuckled.

Lily was staring again. I couldn't decide if she had just thought of something, or if it was just leftover anger from before. Either way, it was time to go.

Then, as I was walking back to the ring road, I thought that had been a strange conversation. He hadn't asked about whom I thought he was talking or when exactly the call was supposed to have taken place or with whose phone something odd had happened. He had just said he didn't know any of my friends. How in blue blazes did he have the first idea whom I knew and didn't know?

19

I had imagined that I could walk to the Pale Horse, but when I found it on Google Maps, it became clear that I would need to take a taxi. I knew the hotel was not exactly in the town, but it turned out that it was more truly in the middle of nowhere, a place with the unprepossessing name of Upper Nidderdale. (By the way, if you imagine that a Green expert ought to have known such a thing, you would be wrong: it is entirely possible to possess unrivalled expertise in an author's work while having limited knowledge of their life, which is generally of secondary concern.)

It was getting to be teatime, and the sky was gloweringly low. The temperature had dropped to that damp cold that gets in your bones and interferes with your brain. But the cab, when it arrived, was no consolation. It was an ancient Ford Sierra driven by a bullet-headed man who looked as if he might run guns in his spare time. The Sierra had leather seats, which immediately made me uncomfortable. People think that leather car seats are luxurious, but to my mind there is something vaguely redolent of sex work about them, perhaps because, unlike cloth car seats, they seem designed to be able to be wiped clean.

In any case, I began to fear that the car was unequal to the task of getting us to the Pale Horse. As we shifted into the Dales proper, the road became death-defyingly narrow. It would drop off on one side or the other into sheer banks, from which we were protected only by a wire rope strung between flimsy bollards. Everyone else out here was either a sheep or driving a tank-like Land Rover at sixty miles an hour in the opposite direction. I winced each time another vehicle squeaked past, but the gunrunner did not seem to find these to be especially close calls. The road would jerk suddenly up and down at angles that were, to my way of looking at things, manifestly unsafe, but the driver said nothing, even when our wheels span on a patch of ice and I was sure we were going to plunge to our deaths. The low sky, untempered by the reassuring civilization of the town, had become extraordinarily depressing. I was not sure we would ever reach shelter.

Eventually, however, the steepest and narrowest track yet ejected us into a wider gravel path that ran through a stone arch. Despite the twilight, I could see some curious stone figures sitting on its top. An inappropriately muscular cherub, a woman in a face mask, and a man smoking a long pipe and leering nastily. Beyond the gateway, a tractor with a snowplough sat to one side. Beyond that loomed the Pale Horse. The hotel was made of blackened granite. It was squat and castellated, with narrow windows and what a Gothic novel would have called massy walls, and looked more like a fort than anything else, though I happened to know that it had been built as a stately home in around 1600. I hoped the original owner had refused to pay the architect. Over the door was the sandstone relief of an emaciated horse, after which the property had been renamed when it became a hotel in the early 1900s. If I'd been in charge of PR, I would have picked a different name and chiselled that creepy carving off the front while I was at it. I thought of Gladden fleeing up here in 1926, like something out of Wuthering Flipping Heights. She certainly had a sense of melodrama.

I paid the cabbie, who vanished instantly, leaving me to brave the terrifying entryway alone. I walked up, and cracked open the door—

—and found myself in the lobby of a bland, mid-range chain-style hotel doing a brisk trade. There was a worn maroon carpet with a crazy pattern traced out in goldenrod, dotted with large unoccupied armchairs. There was a set of plasma-screen TVs advertising the restaurant, the pool and gym, and so on, and a check-in desk with a faux-marble top. We might have been in Stevenage town centre, instead of in the middle of Britain's most godforsaken moorland. People in formal dress were milling about all over. Was it a wedding? There was something a bit odd about it, though I couldn't put my finger on what.

I got in line at the check-in desk, still reeling slightly from the journey. Suddenly, I realized I was standing behind three Père Flambeaus. Clerical collar, dapper little moustaches, the whole shebang. One of them was six-foot-four, but other than that, the resemblance was excellent.

'*Pardonnez-moi, monsieur,*' the first Flambeau said to the receptionist. 'You have perhaps the booking for a Père Flambeau?'

'Do you have the credit card you made the booking under?' replied the receptionist, who was wearing a name badge that read 'Goforth'. He gave the impression that he had said this many times today already. 'I have fifty-three bookings under the name Flambeau.' I wondered if I had fallen asleep at some point without realizing, and was about to awake, mortified, on the Cadigans' sofa.

But that's when it clicked. The clothes I was seeing all around me: they weren't just formal, they were *old-fashioned*.

Greenites.

Greenites are the cosplay arm of Gladden Green fandom. They are not for a moment to be confused with the scholars among whose ranks I count myself. You'd be amazed how many of this lot have never cracked the spine of a Green novel. Although they have all seen the TV versions. Today, though, I was grateful for the shallowness of their knowledge: few of them would be likely to know who I was.

'Is it a Gladden Green conference or something?' I asked when my time came.

'It is, madam,' said the unctuous Mr Goforth, pronouncing it *madarm*. 'You were perhaps under the impression it was a pirate-themed event?'

The blooming eyepatch again. I thought about trying to explain but gave him a little pursed-lipped smile intended to convey amusement and annoyance in equal measure. Goforth gestured at a flat-screen TV above his head, hanging incongruously next to a set of antlers on a plywood shield. On the screen was a list of the day's events:

11 a.m.–5 p.m.: The Shoppes at Steeple Aston: The Greene

Steeple Aston was the Cotswold village out of which Père Flambeau was constantly being called from retirement to solve just one more murder.

2 p.m.: Tisane Mixing Basics: Ballroom 1
7 p.m.: Murder Mystery Dinner: Olde Ballroom

These people were evidently under the impression that super-fluous 'e's conveyed old-world charm.

'Does madarm have a pre-booking with the hotel? Only I lament to tell you we have no availability on account of the conference.'

I was momentarily stymied. This would never have happened to Flambeau—the real Père Flambeau, I mean. Not that there is a *real*—well, you get the idea. Although it struck me at this moment that this *does* in fact happen to Flambeau, at the beginning of *Stamboul Train*. All the compartments on the train are full—but then Flambeau realizes that one of the bookings has been made in the name of a fictional character, who will thus surely not arrive.

'Do you have any no-shows?' I asked, feeling pleased with my ingenuity.

'It is, I fear, a smidgen too early to tell,' replied the receptionist. 'Unfortunately it is only 6 o'clock. We release unsold rooms at 11 p.m., although I shall gladly add madarm's name to the list. Madarm will be a trifling sixth in line.' Sixth? My smugness slipped away.

'How often do six people not turn up?' I asked.

'Oh, I would think there's a favourable chance,' he said, as if it was nothing, although if 11 came and there was no room, I'd be back in a taxi on the icy road, and this time in the pitch dark.

'But what if there is no room later?' I asked.

'Ma*darm*?' He looked offended, though it had seemed to me a reasonable question.

'It's fine,' I said. 'Put me on the list.'

'Very good, madarm.' He went to beckon forward the under-sized Captain Brown who was next in line, but I hadn't finished.

'Does the hotel keep old employee records?' I asked. Goforth looked desperately at the queue forming behind me.

'Such things are regrettably quite confidential, madarm,' he said.

'I mean, records from the 1920s. I'm told you had an employee who was supposedly given a novel by Gladden Green.'

'Ah,' he replied, taking on a weary expression. 'I am familiar with the story, but I am sorry to say that my father purchased the hotel only a few years ago, so we do not have any records from that time.' I thought of Edmund Swettenham's smug claim that the hotel had no records of Alexander Cust. He might, I thought, have mentioned that the hotel didn't have any records *at all*, since that put rather a different complexion on the matter.

'You sound as if I'm not the first to ask,' I said.

'Well,' he said, and shrugged apologetically. 'There have been a few. Journalists and such. A Mr Swettenham,' he said proudly. 'Gladden Green's authorized biographer.'

I glared. 'What about an Amy Murgatroyd?' I asked. 'Was there someone called Amy Murgatroyd asking questions about the novel, some months before it was published?'

'I'm afraid I couldn't possibly remember,' he said.

'You could if she stayed here,' I said. 'Her name would be in the computer.'

Goforth looked with a vague air of panic at the growing queue behind me. I gave him my most obstinate stare, hoping that he would decide that humouring me was the best way to get rid of me.

It worked. He tapped some buttons on his keyboard.

'Yes,' he said. 'We did have a Murgatroyd a few months back. One night. Single queen room.'

'But you don't remember what she wanted to know?'

'Well, I expect she wanted to know what they all do. *Was there a Cust here in the 1920s? Was he here when Green was here? Did he leave a sworn affidavit written on the wallpaper that he had come into possession of a lost masterpiece?*'

'And you didn't know?' I said.

'No,' he said exasperatedly.

I suddenly had one last idea. 'Is there anyone still working at the hotel who was here in the 1970s?' I asked, picking the latest possible date at which I thought Cust could conceivably still have worked on the desk.

'Well—' He glanced nervously at the queue again. He looked as if he didn't want to tell me the answer to my question, but his panic at the line of customers seemed to be clouding his brain and preventing him from coming up with a lie. 'I believe my father might have been here in those days,' he said hurriedly. 'He was employed at the property for many years before he purchased it.'

'Does he still work here?'

Goforth looked as if I had asked the one thing I shouldn't have. 'Mmmmh,' he said. I looked at him expectantly. 'I believe you'll find him on the Greene,' he said, as if I had outsmarted him. I made to move away. He called after me: 'Only—'

'Yes?' I said.

'You may not find him to be quite so—congenial—as myself, madarm.'

'Thank you,' I said. 'It's Agatha, by the way.'

'Madarm?'

'Agatha Dorn. My name. For the standby list.'

'Very good,' he said, not writing anything down.

I made my way out onto the 'Greene', where 'The Shoppes at Steeple Aston' were in full swing.

So you did come here Murg, I thought.

Yes, she said. *I was nothing if not thorough.*

They were not so much shops as tents, in two sad rows, with a channel down the middle. There was a stand selling sacrilegiously hollowed-out Green hardbacks, converted into little handbags. As an aside, I believe there is a special place in hell for people who carve up books to make knick-knacks. There was a moustache stand, where you could buy false Flambeau-style moustaches and, for extra money, have your photograph taken whilst wearing them. There was a stall devoted entirely to fascinators. I have never been a fan of any kind of dressing up. The illusion is never sufficiently convincing, and there is something hideous about the constant failure of the pretence. The Greenites were paying for Green-themed tat all around me, and their credit cards running anachronously through those little readers plugged into mobile phones were like nails on a blackboard. Everyone was trying their best to conjure up an air of jolly good-fellowship, but it wouldn't take, what with the cold, the looming dark, and the vaguely apocalyptic setting. Our moorings felt flimsy.

An ancient lumpy man with shoulders too big for his body and a neck like a turtle's was sitting at a table in a tent called Gladden's Tea Shoppe. Gladden's Tea Shoppe at the Shoppes. Gladden never used the awful word *shoppe* except satirically, and then to the best of my knowledge only once, in an unsung late novel entitled *The Flatmates*. And did these people not care that Green wrote a whole novel—*A Season At Brown's*, which, incidentally, directly preceded *The Flatmates*—skewering the kind of gum-ghastly period fakery on which gatherings like this were founded? I told you Greenites were morons.

The lumpy man's hair grew only in patches and looked like it would give you an infection if you touched it. His dirty shirt had one of those American mechanics' patches over the right breast pocket. It read 'Goforth'. This was the man who owned the Pale Horse. He was the only person in the whole grim landscape who looked as if he belonged there: his skin was as grey as the sky. The idea of his having that coxcomb on the desk for a son was hilarious.

I thought I would take the direct approach. I walked up to the table and sat down. 'Mr Goforth?' I said. He inclined his head slightly, in a gesture I took to be a nod. 'My name is Agatha Dorn. Your son said I could find you here.' Having established my credibility, I could move on. 'I'm wondering if I could ask you a question. Did you know a man named Alexander Cust who worked here many years ago? Possibly on the front desk, possibly during the 1970s?'

Goforth *père* looked me in the eye, and opened his mouth as if to speak, then he winked significantly and belched, all without breaking eye contact.

A waitress rushed over. She was holding a laminated menu, from which dangled a miniature magnifying glass on a piece of rustic twine. 'Can I help you, sir?' she asked, in a tone that implied she was on the point of calling the police. She must have been a temp, employed just for the Greenites' benefit. To be fair, it did look as if a feral transient had strayed into the conference in order to soil himself all over the rug. He turned his gimlet eye in her direction, and I saw an opportunity to ingratiate myself.

'This is Mr Goforth,' I said. 'He owns the hotel.' Goforth grinned at the waitress as if I were having a hilarious joke at her expense. She glared at me, thought for a moment, and stalked away. 'So, do you happen to remember Mr Cust?' I said to my new partner in crime. He gave me another eloquent look, this one telling me I had misjudged the situation entirely.

'Do I remember someone from the 1970s?' he said.

'Yes,' I replied.

'Nay,' he said. Then he got up, revealing a pair of obscene trousers, and stalked away.

20

After this failure, I had just one more card to play: Gladden's room. If I could establish that the room in which Green had stayed matched the description given in Cust's notes, that would not exactly *prove* anything but it would at least make it more plausible that the novella had *some* connection with reality. Was it the large, airy room Cust described so evocatively? What that would show, I didn't really know. Perhaps I just wanted to know exactly how completely I had been conned.

Alas, though, it looked as if here, too, I would be out for a duck. As I made my way back inside the hotel, I saw a small wooden sign pointing the way to 'Gladden's Retreat'. I headed what turned out to be quite a long way down one of the ground-floor corridors, which became quite cramped and dark. There I found a guest room with a plywood plaque outside, the twin of the one with the antlers above the check-in desk. This one read: 'GLADDEN'S RETREAT: In 1926, Gladden Green hid away in Room 105 in the Pale Horse Hotel. Her 10 day disappearance created one of the largest man-hunts in history.' (You have no idea, incidentally, how much it pains me not to hyphenate '10-day' in the above—but, in the name of historical accuracy, I preserve the hotel's illiterate verbiage.) Lest there be any doubt, the number 105 was right there on the door. Here, on the ground floor. Green herself had written in her note of her disappointment not to have been on the ground floor. And Cust wrote in detail of himself dragging Gladden's trunk up the stairs to a Room 105 on the *first* floor. So even his notes were a fraud?

As I was torturing myself with the knowledge of how easily I could have checked this before pushing publication of *The Dog's Ball*, a steely blue flash appeared in the corner of my eye. I started with horror. The Crooked Man had followed me here!

I heard footsteps coming closer. I wanted to spin around and confront the phantom, but I was rooted to the spot—this time by fear alone. I felt breath on my ear—he was right behind me! I willed myself to move.

'Arrr, Jim Lad! You know that plaque is wrong, right?' said a voice that I knew issued from a mouth full of bright little teeth.

'Nancy?' I gasped, spinning round. There she was, as large as life, wearing a blue flapper's gown with a sequinned headband, whence had issued the terrifying glint.

'Agatha!' she said. 'It's so *wonderful* to see you! Have you come as some kind of *zombie pirate*? What on earth are you doing here? I've been trying to call you for *ever*!'

'I got a new phone,' I said. Propriety, as well as ordinary curiosity, dictated that I respond in kind, but instead I said, 'What do you mean, the plaque is wrong?'

'Well, in the eighties, the Pale Horse got taken over by an American company who renumbered all the rooms. In American hotels, the ground floor is the first floor—plus, the first number of each room corresponds with the floor it's on—so one-oh-five ended up down here. When Mr Goforth bought the place, he forgot, or didn't care, and had the plaque put up outside the renumbered room. But in the twenties, one oh five was actually on the first floor, looking out over the green.'

I had lots of questions, but I settled on: 'What are *you* doing here?'

'I asked first, remember,' said Nancy. 'But come on—let's have dinner. You can tell me all about it.'

She marched me back down the corridor towards the Olde Ballroom, where the Greenites were filing through the double doors in their monocles (plastic) and wigs (murder-victim blonde). They looked like they were going to a fancy-dress party at the next-door neighbour's, especially by contrast with Nancy, who looked as if she had just stepped off the dance floor at the Cotton Club.

At the door, a teenager in a Pullman porter's uniform hailed each diner with an unenthusiastic invitation to step aboard the Stamboul Train and handed out a meal ticket.

'I don't think I'm on the list,' I said.

'Balls!' said Nancy. 'You think anyone's counting?' I thought they probably were, but I also had infinite faith in her ability to waft away any difficulties that came our way with a bat of her lashes. I let her hustle me past the fake porter.

'How's disgrace?' she asked breezily.

'Ignominious,' I said. I was furious with her for dropping me like a hot brick when the s— had hit the fan, but it was easier to go along with her pretence that we were still long-lost pals. Besides, I wanted to know what was going on.

We reached a table and sat down. The places had been preset with glasses of nasty house white. Nancy got to work on hers. 'These people are really something, eh?' she said. 'Still, since my life mostly consists of packing boxes these days, I'll take what I can get.'

'Packing boxes?' I asked. 'Are you moving?'

'You didn't know? Oh, come on, Agatha, how can you not have known! They're kicking the Neele out of the Gatehouse, right? We're boxing our whole lives up.'

'Right,' I said. I supposed that I did know they'd been given notice to get out. It was just that I had unplugged from everything. There was a pregnant pause. 'So—why *are* you here?' I asked. I had been hoping the answer would have arisen naturally, so I wouldn't seem rude, but when the conversation dried up, it was literally the only thing of which I could think.

'Well now, this is awkward,' said Nancy, 'because do I assume that you really don't know, and tell you, or do I assume that you *do* know, and have been avoiding all my messages because you're so furious about the whole thing? And on the assumption that you're going to be angry with me, it's important that I hit *just* the right note with what I say to you next.'

'I haven't had any messages,' I said. 'I bought a new phone and got rid of all my accounts. I have literally no idea about anything.' I remembered why I used to hate her. On the other hand, I *was* flattered at the idea that she had been trying to contact me.

'Oh, well. I'm doing a *podcast*. On—' She screwed up her eyes in mock shame—'literary mysteries.' I expect I made a face. 'Oh god, Agatha, I'm so sorry I took your idea. But there it was, the big romantic unsolved mystery of *The Dog's Ball*—what was the story with this fake manuscript?—and there I was, you know, close to the action. And no one could get hold of you.' She paused. 'It's doing quite well. Apparently I'm what they call a *microcelebrity*. There was an article on the *Guardian* website.'

Of course there fudging was, I thought. In my head though, I didn't mince the oath.

'I've been trying to reach you for months and months!' She went on, 'But nobody knew where you were! You just disappeared!'

'Wouldn't you have?' I asked.

She said that she supposed she would, but I didn't believe it. She'd have found a way to come out of the whole thing freshly scrubbed and smelling of cold cream.

Nancy. She always got you in the end. I wanted to pour my horrid glass of wine over her head and eff off back to London, but that would have been an unconscionable waste; and besides, I couldn't resist. 'What have you found out?' I said.

'Well, to be perfectly frank, until today, not a lot that isn't already in the public record. That's really why I came here—to see what I could find out about Alexander Cust—whether he worked here. Whether he even really existed.' Unlike me, I noted bitterly, she had not failed to discover the existence of the Greenite conference.

'He existed,' I said. 'Swettenham conveniently failed to mention that the Pale Horse doesn't have records of *anyone* who worked here, not just Cust.'

'Well now,' said Nancy coquettishly. 'It just so happens that they *do*. The current owner, Mr Goforth, was here at the same time as Alexander Cust. Isn't that incredible?'

I clenched my lips. Wasn't that just like her, to throw it in my face? If it had been I, I would have kept stumm about it just to spite me.

'He's just come in—don't look! He's kind of a funny chap. He doesn't like anyone to acknowledge him at all. You'd think he cleaned the toilets or something by the look of him. But I suppose I managed to make a connection with him, somehow.'

Aaaaaaaaaaaaaargh! I looked, of course. Has anyone ever told you not to look and then you did anything other than immediately look? If so, you're a better person than I. And there he was at the back of the ballroom. Horrid-trousered old Mr Goforth, who had just made a fool of me. He raised a glass satirically in my direction.

'Look, he gave me this,' said Nancy, producing a leaf from an ancient hotel memo pad. 'It's a duty rota from 1969 with them both on it—Goforth here, and Cust over here!'

A pair of guests were eyeing us warily. I assumed that I had taken one of their seats, and I was about to be asked to leave. They moved towards us, and I felt my buttocks tense. But, instead of asking for their seat back, the woman began asking me in a loud and affected voice whether I didn't find it outrageous that the Stamboul Train was entirely booked up this evening, and had I been able to secure a berth for myself? 'It's completely unheard-of for the entire train to be reserved!' said the man in an equally ridiculous tone. I froze in sudden panic.

'It's a bit...' hissed Nancy into my ear. 'Audience participation!' When I still didn't respond, she turned to the man. 'Yes, we secured a berth, thank you very much,' she said. 'Look, here's our ticket.' She waved the chit the 'porter' had given us on our way in.

'Outrageous!' cried the woman. 'I, Countess von Kramm, unable to secure passage on the Stamboul Train, and this riff-raff accommodated without a murmur.' There was general giggling. I wanted to point out that the Countess von Kramm wasn't even in *Stamboul Train*, and that if she had turned up, Flambeau would certainly have had something to say about it, but that was Greenites for you. No attention to detail whatsoever.

Perhaps thankfully, at that moment a spotlight appeared at the main door, and in came Flambeau and the director of the railway, ready to finagle Flambeau onto the train and set the plot in motion.

'What I haven't been able to do,' said Nancy, ignoring the actors, 'is track down the Cadigans. They seem to have gone quiet since it all kicked off. I'd love to find out what they think about it all, but they're not returning my calls.' She smirked. 'Maybe they threw away their phones, too?'

I glowed inwardly. I knew something Nancy didn't know. I needed to play it cool. I didn't need to impress Nancy, for goodness' sake! I shouldn't tell her till I knew what the information could get me...

'I saw them this morning!' I blurted. 'They remember the manuscript's being there when they first opened the box!'

Blast it!

'Agatha, you're brilliant!' she said. 'Of course you saw them! This all adds up to a fairly serious probability that there was indeed an Alexander Cust, and that he did write about being given a manuscript by Gladden Green!' Nancy paused. 'You know what we should do? We should record something about this while we're here!'

'Who's this *we*?' I asked.

'You and I,' said Nancy. 'You should be a guest on the podcast!'

'Excuse me, monsieur,' boomed an actor with an unconvincing American accent on the far side of the ballroom, '*Je crois que vous avez un erreur!* I think you have made a mistake!'

'God almighty,' said Nancy. 'Shall we order room service instead?'

*

196

I was not excited about being a guest on the podcast. In the first place, I had not yet decided if I had forgiven Nancy for ditching me after *The Dog's Ball* went pear-shaped, let alone stealing my podcast idea. Second, I had misgivings about appearing in any kind of public medium again, after last time.

In the third place, my lack of self-confidence tends to read as diffidence—something that is responsible, as several people have told me over the years, for my lifelong failure to live up to my potential. This means I am not at all charismatic, which is a problem, for radio.

And in the fourth (and final) place: I don't know if you know this, but if you are recording for radio in a hotel room, you have to create a little structure out of blankets and pillows to record inside, so as not to get reverberations. This is true. You can google it. Thus, I had to be interviewed in essentially a small child's den not more than five feet across and three feet high. It was very hot, and I had to sit uncomfortably close to Nancy. For some reason I could not fathom, this disturbed me beyond for what I could account by my hatred of human flesh generally, with its fluids and smells. Even behind the patch, my eye began to throb with the pre-migraine sensation. That caused me in turn to self-medicate from the minibar. There was no gin, so I went with whisky.

But that began to make everything feel better.

As the booze got going, the whole enterprise began to gleam at me like the sequins of Nancy's headband. It began to wink at the tiny, infinitely seductive possibility of rehabilitation—more than that—recognition!—at having the world look back at me once again in the way at which I longed to be looked.

We turned on the recorder and Nancy began to ask me

things. Between the panic and the gin, it all went by in a flash, and at a certain point, Nancy announced that we had finished recording, which meant I must have said things to some degree of satisfactoriness.

It was not really that late yet, though—and so we ended up raiding the minibar once more. And besides, she said, I really ought to stay on her sofa, since I didn't have a room, which was reasonable now that we were, one supposed, once again best buddies. There's something wonderfully conspiratorial about drinking miniatures, I think.

So we sat in the blanket den, drinking spirits and chatting like we used to, until at a certain point Nancy said it was time for bed. I hauled myself up. Nancy sat on the floor grinning and holding her arms up towards me, asking me help her up—so I did that—and we found ourselves standing quite close to one another, face to face.

It suddenly felt utterly imperative that I did in fact find a room of my own. With no ceremony, I fled the room and stumbled back downstairs in search of Goforth (Junior, the oleaginous one), who was as luck would have it still on the desk and who had, praise be, an empty berth available. I secured the room with what I thought was a decent impersonation of sobriety.

The next morning, I got up early, made my way back to Harrogate by way of a taxi more salubrious than the one that had carried me hither, and boarded the train to London. I spent the journey first googling Nancy's podcast—it was called *The Body in the Library*, which was a better name than any up with which I had come for my book—and then musing gently about features on the *Guardian* website. It wasn't till we pulled into King's Cross that I realized I never had seen Gladden's room.

21

It was the next day. I pressed a Freezy-Soothe cooling gel sheet over the gimp eye and held it in place with my patch. Then I popped a couple of Nurofen Max Meltlets. It was true, the bump on my head did not seem to be getting better. It was looking distinctly lesion-like, with the yellow beginnings of crustiness. But that was small potatoes. I was ready to detect!

There were four or five messages from Andy, my manager at Broadstreet's, waiting on the burner phone. Well, he could eff off, thank you very much. After everything I had learned in Yorkshire, I had some more investigating to do. The only problem was, I had no idea what to do next. At a certain point, though, I remembered a book I had bought during the course of my diploma, momentarily interested in the accuracy of Gladden Green's depiction of the police. And, come to think of it, I hadn't seen it in years. A rummage of middling length later, I had in my hand *The Crime Writer's Guide to Police Procedure*, open at the chapter entitled 'The Investigation Begins'. '"Trace, Interview, and Eliminate (T.I.E.) enquiries are the cornerstone of murder investigations",' I read. I had vaguely remembered something about this. The first thing was to track down, or *trace*, anyone who could plausibly have done the murder.

That's good, Agatha, said internal Murgatroyd.

I'm not entirely useless, I replied.

I never said you were, said Murg.

But here I ran into my first problem. Because actually, what did I know now that I didn't know before? I knew Cust was real. He might have met Gladden Green in 1926. She might have given him something she had written. Tom Cadigan knew who Murgatroyd was and possessed her telephone number. But I didn't know anyone new whom I could ask about anything. As far as Traces went for Murgatroyd—I hardly had any idea who her friends were. Clara was mad. Dimitra had told me everything she was willing to, and I didn't think another run at Tom Cadigan would achieve anything at the moment. As for Ian, I knew nothing about him except what I had learned through work. No one at the Neele knew anything—we'd established that when he first went missing. I suppose I had a sense that Ian had high-up connections in government. But I couldn't very well ask the Prime Minister if he knew where Ian was. What was there for me even to do?

Then it occurred to me that there was one person to whom I hadn't spoken about Murgatroyd: Mr Whatchamacallit, the military-sounding neighbour who had found her, to whose door she had affixed her note. Which, now that I thought about it, she would not have done, not if she had in fact been murdered. It was possible—likely even—that Mr Armed Forces Man had seen something without realizing, and perhaps I could find it out.

There being no time like the present, I went to knock on his door. Then I thought, after the business with Not-Mrs-Hernandez, I really ought to see if I could find out his name first, in order to make an appropriate impression. I looked about for an idea. There was a big grey polyethylene rubbish bin next to a gleaming white garage door. The door had no handle. *Motorized. Fancy*, I thought. It seemed plausible that my man might have thrown away unwanted post in a bag that had made its way to the big bin, and that such post would likely feature his name.

Checking to make sure he was not in sight, I went over to the bin and took off the lid. Immediately I realized that I might have bitten off more than I could chew. In the bin, a mess of white kitchen bin bags bulged with goo and rottenness. There were no pieces of paper or envelopes in sight. I supposed I could try searching through just *one*. I tore open the top bag and began rootling. And, it turned out, I was in luck. Underneath a waxed box coated with some kind of hideous orange slime that smelled as if it had once been dairy-based, I found exactly what I was looking for: a pile of junk mail. I pulled it out and squinted at the top envelope. *Easterbrook*, it said. He was Mr Easterbrook! Perfect!

'Are you going through my bins?' said a gruff voice. 'Get out of it! B—y vagrants!'

'Mr Easterbrook!' I said turning round, one hand dripping with noisome orange gunk. There he was, wearing beige slacks, a maroon tank top over a tattersall check twill shirt, and a forest-green woollen tie. As you do, when you've retired. I couldn't endorse his fashion sense, but I admired the commitment to propriety.

'Colonel Easterbrook,' he said imperiously. 'And how do you know my name?'

'I'm your neighbour,' I said, 'Agatha Dorn.' I put out my sludgy hand, then thought better of it.

Colonel, though! That gave me an idea.

'What?' He looked closer, and decided it was me. He had, you may recall, last interacted with me a few days before, in the middle of the night, when I knocked on his door to report having been terrorized by the Crooked Man. 'Oh,' he said. 'Well. So it is.' He had adopted the tone I was coming to recognize as the I'm-talking-to-a-madwoman voice. 'Are you all right, dear?'

I said that yes I was, and thank you. Then I asked if, his being a military man and all, he could find out why someone might have got kicked out of the army. That was my idea, you see—I wondered if he could find out any more about Rick Fawn for me, as well as answering questions about Murgatroyd. He hummed and herr-ed and said he didn't really think, hmm—but that wasn't quite a *no*, I thought.

Then I asked him if he knew that the woman who had lived next door to him before me, the woman who died, had been my friend. He said that he didn't, and how interesting. I was not certain he believed me, though.

'This is going to sound strange,' I said, 'but am I right in thinking she pinned a note to your door the night she died?'

'You don't want to go worrying about all that, my dear,' said Colonel Easterbrook. 'Horrid business. If I were you, I would rest up after the nasty shock you had the other night. You look like you could do with a rest.'

'Oh, I will, thank you,' I said. 'But supposing I did want to worry about all that? Would you tell me about it?' He looked as if he was trying to figure out what would be the fastest way of getting rid of me.

'Well,' he said, 'I suppose so. It was early evening. I was watching the television, I think, after dinner—I'm retired, you see—and I thought I heard someone messing around with the front door.' I could picture the living room now. Spotless wing-back chairs with antimacassars.

'Did you go and look?' I said. 'I suppose you can't have opened the door, or you'd have discovered the note before she had had time to kill herself.'

'Well, I looked through the window first.' I looked behind him at a round window next to the front door, with a small lace curtain. I bet he loved to peer through that thing. 'I assumed it was kids playing a joke. But then I saw someone on the pavement, walking back towards Miss Murgatroyd's house, which must've been her, although at first the coat made it hard to tell. Makes sense, really. Children nowadays are off shanking old ladies and what-have-you, not playing Knock Down Ginger.

'But then I did open the door,' he continued. 'To see if any damage had been done.' He was warming to his theme now, I was glad to note. 'When I read through the letter, I assumed it was a joke. Well, Miss Murgatroyd had always been a perfectly good neighbour, and it didn't seem in character. But then you never could quite trust her. She was a lesbian, you know. Burned incense. I went back inside. But after a time I thought perhaps I ought to go over there and see if anything was going on, and that's when I found her on the bed with that hood on her head. Selfish, if you ask me. The coward's way out. And a lot of stress and bother for people who have nothing to do with it. Mind you,' he went on, 'better than those idiots who jump in front of trains. I was stuck for two hours on the Piccadilly Line once because some moron had gone under the wheels.'

I wondered how long he would go on if I didn't stop him. I thought, *You selfish warthog. If you'd have gone over right away, you might have saved her!* But only if she really had committed suicide. If the murderer had had any sense at all, he would have made sure she was thoroughly dead before putting up the note. 'Forgive me, Colonel Easterbrook,' I said. 'Could I get something clear? You said a moment ago that you saw someone walking who must have been Murgatroyd. Were you not sure?'

'Well, I don't see who else it could have been.'

'But if you had to swear to it?'

There was a pause. I said, 'You said she was wearing her coat?'

'Yes,' he said. 'B—y great heavy thing.'

'If I was going to kill myself, and just popped next door to deliver a suicide note, I don't suppose I'd bother putting on my coat, do you? Even in winter? I'd just go in whatever I was wearing. And I wouldn't bother with the pavement, I don't think. I'd just go over the lawn.' I gestured at the unobstructed green swath that led to my house. The grass became disgracefully ragged at the point where the Colonel's property gave way to mine.

His manner had changed subtly. His former desire to shake me off as fast as possible seemed to be morphing into curiosity. 'You know there was something. It may have been nothing—just the light playing tricks. But since you ask, I *did* think there was something strange.'

'Go on,' I said.

'Well—it's ridiculous, really—she was swinging her arms as she walked and, as she went under the street lamp, she looked for a second as if she only had one hand.'

What a triumph! This was the best detective work I had done yet. I had Traced Colonel Easterbrook, Interviewed him, and come away with a revelation. I mean, I hadn't excluded him from my enquiries as such, but come on! Murgatroyd had been murdered by the Crooked Man! In retrospect, I thought, nothing could have been more obvious. He had stalked me all my life, and now he had murdered my friend.

'Do you really think there might be funny business involved,' said Colonel Easterbrook, looking quite excited by the possibility.

'I think it's possible,' I said.

'My goodness,' he said. 'And—' He seemed to have made a hundred-and-eighty-degree turn on the whole thing. All of a sudden he was thrilled by the idea of being part of an investigation of some kind—'you were asking me before about a chap who was kicked out of the army? Does that have something to do with this, too?'

'It may do,' I said conspiratorially. 'Chap named Rick Fawn,' I continued, doing my best to mirror his bluff manner back to him. 'Been working in private security for the last few years, but he was with—' All I had was the abbreviation I had found online, with no real idea what it meant—'Three Para. Is that right? Three Para?'

'That's the Third Battalion of the Parachute Regiment, my dear. And I may be able to find out something. I'll let you know if I do. Let me have your number.' He put out his hand, as if I was going to give him a business card, or something.

My hand was still covered in gunk from the Colonel's bin, but I thought I had a pen in my coat pocket. I pulled it out with my other hand, grabbed his hand, and wrote my mobile number on his palm. He got a little bit of the she's-a-crazy-lady look back in his eyes again. 'Sorry,' I said. 'You might have to wash your hands. Write the number down first though.' Colonel Easterbrook nodded and retreated.

Although it was still early, I felt that a drink was in order. And the Blue Boar opened at eleven. By the time I had walked there, it would almost be opening time!

22

You would think that I had enough problems—between the drinking problem, the problem of Murgatroyd's death, and the problem of the *Dog's Ball* fiasco. I realized, however, that I was developing an ever larger money problem as well. The last of Andy's messages told me I had been fired from Broadstreet's, and it wasn't as if I had any savings on which to stay afloat. If I was going to carry on investigating, I needed cash. As I racked my brains, I could think of only one way to get some, but it was not going to be pleasant.

I pulled out the burner phone and dialled my brother's number.

Heri met me at his consulting rooms on Harley Street. I had been there only once before. But then, I had never been to Heri's house, so his meeting me here felt positively intimate.

Heri's office was like a museum. His panelled walls were painted duck-egg blue. There was an eighteenth-century landscape in an ornate gold frame above the white-painted fireplace. His desk was made of varnished wood, bow-fronted, with a pattern inlaid in carved veneer. We could have been sitting in the same room two hundred years ago, except for the sleek computer sitting on the desk's glass top.

'You made it sound urgent,' Heri said.

'How are the children?' I said. I thought I'd ease my way in using small talk, although it is not really one of my skills.

'Oh, fine. Madeleine was caught shoplifting from Selfridges and I had to try to extricate her from that—or rather, my expensive solicitor did. And Aubrey is in danger of being expelled from Harrow because of his appalling behaviour, so I am supposed to donate a lot of money to prevent that from happening. Heribert Dorn, everybody's milch cow. I exist primarily to ooze cash for people from my great udders. What do you want, Agatha?'

'I need to borrow money,' I said quietly. Dear, oh dear.

'Of course you do,' he said. 'I assume your archive decided to fire you after you dragged their name through the mud.'

'I did have another job,' I went on, 'but…' I hesitated. It was true, we were not close. But Heri was my brother, and I was suddenly overcome with a familial feeling. It seemed to me that if anyone would understand what I was doing, he would.

'Well,' I said, 'here's the thing…' And I told him all about it. The seal on the helium tank. Tony from Product Management. The Crooked Man's terrorizing me. The trip to Harrogate and the Pale Horse.

When I had finished, there was a pause. Then Heri started to laugh.

'My god, Agatha,' he said, 'you've really graduated from pretending to crank call yourself, haven't you?' This was a reference to my childhood terror of the Crooked Man's telephone calls. I noted that Heri had evidently taken my mother's side on that issue and decided that I had been faking the whole thing all those years ago. He continued, 'That's the stupidest thing I've ever heard!'

'I could have lied,' I said, hurt. 'I could have just told you I hadn't found another job yet and needed some cash to tide me over. But I thought, *No, let's trust Heri. He's my brother. He'll understand.*'

'That's not the silliest decision you appear to have made lately,' he said.

'Well, thank you. Thank you very much.' I had nothing in the way of a clever comeback.

'Oh, don't get your knickers in a twist,' Heri said. 'I'll give you some money if you like. At least you have an entertaining story, unlike my horrid children. You're in luck. I just had a rather rum patient pay me for his operation in cash.' Heri went over to the picture over his fireplace and pulled on one side, revealing a safe behind. Just like that.

'You have a safe behind your picture?' I said, incredulous. 'Is this an exclusive medical practice or a casino?'

'For goodness' sake don't bite the hand that is about to feed you,' said Heri. 'I run an extremely reputable operation.' He pressed some buttons and opened the safe. Inside were several bundles of notes wrapped up with elastic bands. Heri took two and threw them to me. I have never been remotely gifted at anything athletic. I caught one, miraculously, but as the other came at me, I flailed at it, dropped the first, and both bundles of £20 notes ended up on the floor, forcing me to scrabble around for them. Heri snorted, enjoying himself.

'That should be two grand, Sis,' he said. 'Will that do you for a while?'

I said that it would.

'Let's not forget that you owe me, then,' he said. 'And for God's sake spend it on staying alive until you can get another job and not on this ridiculous "murder" investigation.'

'Thank you, Heri,' I said. I thought that he might make a crack about how we only saw each other if I needed something, but he held off. After all, it was as much his fault as mine that we were hardly in touch.

All the way home I felt as if the money in my satchel must be somehow visible to everyone else on the train, and they were merely waiting for an opportunity to jump me for it. At the first opportunity, I went into the bank and self-consciously deposited it. I was sure the cashier thought I was a crook. There were few reputable ways to obtain £2,000 in cash. Or, rather, just under £2,000. I kept hold of a little bit for a trip to the pub on the way home. After all, I had to celebrate—thanks to Heri, I could carry on the investigation!

The burner buzzed with a text. I fumbled around and found it.

'I would ask if you've seen Twitter, but you're a hermit these days, so there's no point.' It was Nancy. I groaned inwardly. Had I somehow succeeded in being cancelled for a second time? 'People are being really nice about your bit on the podcast! You should check it out!'

It was later the same day. Judging by the gloaming out the window, it was evening. I had apparently made it home from the pub. I was pretty sure I wasn't sober though.

Eventually I made it to Twitter and searched for my name. I had deleted my account, but they still let one look. 'Really nice' might have been an exaggeration, but it was certainly different from the vitriol I had had a few months earlier. For example: 'DORN REBORN!' 'Used to think Agatha Dorn was just a grifter but it turns out she's way weirder……in an amazing way!' '@bodyinthelibrary, did you just reverse-milkshake-duck Agatha Dorn??' I had to look that one up.

'What on earth did I say?' I wrote.

'Oh, come on,' she replied.

I called up the episode and listened. It turns out I hit the perfect sweet spot between poignant and hilarious when I drink whisky. I should have tried it sooner. I had mused at length on the connection between my deep-seated feelings of parental disapprobation and my desire to publish *The Dog's Ball*. I had unaffectedly expressed my remorse at allowing my greed to overwhelm my judgement. But also I had said 'Paper Mate gel pen' several times in an amusing tone. I had described in detail the disgusting pressed duck at Fraser Green's ghastly flat. I had discoursed on the beauty of the vertical sinks in the Gatehouse. I had not been who anybody, including myself, had thought I would be, and this had proven, it seemed, to be a novelty.

'So nice, right?' buzzed Nancy.

When Nancy opened the door in Manor House, she did a double-take.

'I'm hilarious when I drink whisky,' I said.

It was a little later the same evening.

'Agatha,' she said awkwardly. 'It's great to see you.' There was an awkward pause.

'I've been investigating,' I said. 'I want to record some more pods.'

'OK.' She paused, unsure what to do. 'Why don't you come in,' she said. 'Here, have a sit-down. I'm going to get you a cup of tea.'

I sat down on the blue sofa. But I must have nodded off, because the next thing I know, I was waking up in the child's bed in Nancy's guest room.

It was Saturday morning. I took an inventory of the state of myself. Eye and head both got a solid D+. The belly was bad, too. But I had slept. And I hadn't fully got going with the booze after I got to Nancy's, so that made a difference. I felt like caca, but something was different. It was like the pain had been hiding, not daring to come all the way on lest I hit it with more punishment. But now, for some reason, it was sticking its little head out and nosing about.

In my semi-conscious state I allowed myself to spin out a daydream in which I rose, showered, and found Nancy preparing breakfast for us both. When would I remember never to be optimistic! This was basic Crooked Man defence stuff. *One oh one*, as I expect Nancy said when she was at Yale.

For, in fact, as I staggered out in the clothes in which I had gone to sleep last night, and indeed for the last several nights, I found my hostess wired into at her laptop.

'Hi, Nancy?' I said.

'Oh, right, Agatha—you're here,' she said. The *You're My Favourite Person* show was on hiatus. The beams of her sun were shining on other pastures; none was to spare.

'Yes—thanks for letting me stay,' I said. She said nothing. 'Do you have any food?' I said.

'What?' she said. 'There might be some coffee in the kitchen. Or you can make yourself one if you wash out a mug.' When I didn't move, she went on, 'Sorry. I have some work stuff. I'll be with you in a bit.' I looked at her screen. She was carrying on a correspondence with a ready-to-prepare food-box manufacturer who wanted to give her a not insignificant amount of money to advertise on *The Body in the Library*. 'I just have to deal with this, and a couple of other media things.'

Never did I *deal with media things*, in the zone like this, first thing on a weekend morning, not even at the height of *The Dog's Ball*. This was another difference between the likes of Nancy and the likes of me.

I wandered into the kitchen, which was not the pastoral haven of my imaginings. Digging in the lukewarm water in the sink, I pulled out a mug and washed off the dregs and the soap scum. The coffee maker was empty, but I balanced the old grounds on the heaving bin and started another pot. I'm writing about the coffee as if that was the first thing I did in the kitchen, but actually the first thing I did was notice the selection of spirits on top of the fridge. As I drank my coffee, they pulled at me, like the hook at the neck of a bombing vaudevillian. I resisted, though. I was going to be good. I was going to be like Nancy.

'Agatha, you're a saint,' said Nancy, seeing the coffee as she made her eventual way in. 'Listen, you seemed in a bit of a state last night. Do you have anywhere you have to be?'

'No,' I said truthfully. For indeed one of my recent messages from Broadstreet's Andy had been to tell me that if I did not come in for my next shift, I need not bother coming back. That had been a couple of days ago, and I was pretty sure they had not been weekend days.

'Do you—' She seemed hesitant, but she went on—'do you want to hang out here today? I have to go to work, and then I have a meeting in town, but you're welcome to—' She searched for a phrase less indelicate than *sober up* and ended up with the scarcely better 'dry out'.

It struck me that there was nothing I would rather do. What a thrill it is to spend a day in someone's house, and them not there, don't you think? Assuming they haven't just committed suicide and left you the terrifyingly overleveraged house in question. I wanted to play it debonair, so we chatted over the toast made out of some heels of bread I found until Nancy left.

Now what was I going to do with myself? Naturally I made for the bookcases. What did *wunderkinder* read, I wondered? You could trace out the elements of Nancy's life on the shelves. *The Oxford Anthology of Sixteenth-Century Verse* and *Paradise Lost*, complete with undergraduate annotations ('Ship is a metaphor for the journey through life!'; 'Passive voice. *Interesting!*', double-underlined). Fredson Bowers. S. R. Ranganathan: postgrad texts for aspiring archivists. The Dickinson scholars, the competing editions—Johnson, Franklin, Higginson and Todd. The complete works of her toxic adviser, Anne Beddingfield, books whose titles dared you to read them with a straight face: *The Metastatic Glyph* and *Em-Dash En Abyme*—that sort of thing. And then, a series of titles related to the new venture, which had about them a charming naïveté: *Podcasting for Dummies* and *So You Want To Start Your Own Podcast!* Swettenham's biography of Gladden (Grr). *The Dog's Ball* (groan). In fact, a complete set of Gladdeniana, one that, I noted enviously, rivalled my own. I took her copy of *The Dog's Ball* and put it in my pocket. My contribution to erasing any evidence that the dratted thing had ever existed.

Somehow, though, among all this, Nancy herself was nowhere to be found. No covert passion for thrillers was in evidence unless you counted the Greens. I couldn't tell you what she liked to read; only what she needed to have read. Was that her secret? Was there literally no inside, nothing to her at all but grit and grind and eyes on the prize?

I had a hankering for a gin but somehow, today, I was sure I ought to abstain.

Cleaning up would be a good start. I took a shower and performed sundry secondary ablutions. I located a bottle of that yellow Dettol and splashed it around on my head lesion. I hadn't cleaned my clothes in so long they were beginning to get something of a rough-sleeper quality to them. You know when you live in the city and you blow your nose, it comes out grey? My entire wardrobe was getting a bit like that. I decided to borrow a few things of Nancy's instead. Nothing distinctive. I didn't want her to come home and think I was Single White Female-ing her. Everything Nancy owned seemed expensive, but I found some non-threateningly own-brand-looking tracksuit bottoms and an oversized navy sweatshirt that read 'KALE'. This get-up—what do they call it?—loungewear? *athleisure*? Ugh, worse!—it was about as far from my standard brindled look as I could imagine. And yet. There was something comforting about it, like wearing a big blanket. In America, I understand one can buy wearable blankets. This feels like an almost over-apt metaphor for America generally, especially if the wearable blankets were to turn out to be mass-produced in, you know, Vietnamese sweatshops, which I was ninety-nine per cent sure they would. I wondered if Nancy had such a garment. That might be something I would like, too. I was in a big blanket kind of mood.

As penance for the borrowing, I thought I would tackle Nancy's flat. In *Cymbeline*, when innocent Innogen turns up at the cave of the incognito princes, they tell her, 'You must be our Huswife.' Rancid Agatha no longer, I would be Innogen-Huswife, awaiting my nacreous Nancy.

On the hot-wash setting, and with a double helping of Ariel, I laundered my garments. I took on the noisome kitchen. Doing dishes by hand, on one's own, can be really quite meditative. Those yogis who used to charge celebrities thousands of pounds to learn transcendental meditation in the sixties—were such people still around?—they could get, you know, Beyoncé, to promote manual washing-up as a cure for depression, and regain their millions. Were automatic dishwashers to blame for our rolling mental-illness pandemics? It was worth considering.

In any case, by the time the flat was sparkling, and I sat down to relax with Thomas Johnson's *Complete Poems of Emily Dickinson*, I was in a better mood than I had been in forever. I was hardly even thinking about the fortificatory swig I could, if I wanted, take from the bottle of vanilla extract in the cupboard to the left of the sink.

This was the point at which Nancy arrived home. She was carrying a Chinese meal for two in waxed-cardboard pails—hipster facsimiles of those New York square *frusta* that must have cost three times as much as your ordinary corner takeaway. Was she back to trying to be nice to me?

'Oh, Agatha,' she said, looking at the flat. 'You really *are* a saint! And now we don't have to eat out of the boxes! Did you—did you *clean my flat* while I was at work?'

I said that I supposed that I had.

'Whatever for?'

'I felt bad about being an uninvited drunk. And about borrowing your clothes.'

'You're barely recognizable!' She laughed.

*

Over a dinner in which she tactfully uncorked a bottle of artisanal sparkling juice instead of our usual booze, Nancy presented a surprising proposition. 'So listen,' she said, 'I've been putting together a deal with BBC Sounds to commission a second series of *The Body in the Library*. We're a good way along with it. They're going to pay me to license it—a lot of money. Eighty grand. That's not, you know, to buy Learjets—a chunk of it will need to cover the cost of making the show—but there'll be a fair bit over.'

'Congratulations,' I said, unsure whether or not I was sincere.

'But,' she said, 'I need a partner. The show's not quite right the way it is. I need someone else. Agatha, I want you to come in with me on this. Split the money, everything. After all, I *did* steal your idea.'

I paused.

Careful, Agatha, said Murgatroyd's voice in my head.

I know, I said, peeved that internal Murg didn't trust me to be sufficiently wary.

'Are you sure?' I said. She was doing this out of guilt and pity. 'This seems kind of impulsive. And kind of stupid, honestly. I'm just a tipsy lady with whom you used to work.'

'No. You have a skill set I don't have. You got the Cadigans to talk. You found *The Dog's Ball*. And besides, people loved you on the show, remember?'

'I feel as if you're overstating this,' I said. 'People didn't like me that much. I was a novelty act. Would you have even thought of this if I hadn't willy-nilly appeared on your doorstep last night?'

'Look,' she said, 'that doesn't honestly matter. I know it sounds crazy, but I don't really know how to explain it. I just have a really strong feeling about this. There's nobody else I can make it work with. It has to be you.'

It is difficult to maintain a rational perspective on things when someone is telling you what you desperately want to be true, but I had a go. 'There are lots of other people around,' I said. 'I don't understand, why me?'

Now it was her turn to pause. After a moment, she looked as if she had come to a decision. 'You're the only one. There's nobody else,' said Nancy.

23

The next morning (when Nancy and I really did eat together a charming breakfast of *pains-au-chocolat*) I finally felt sufficiently at ease to share my Murgatroyd-was-murdered theory. In my head, the BBC money was a perfect opportunity to kill two birds with one stone: we could solve the *Dog's Ball* mystery together, redeeming my spoiled reputation, and at the same time I could devote myself properly to discovering who killed my friend.

But as usual, I should have thought it through. When I had finished, Nancy's face was sympathetic. Not to my theory, but to my sickness. 'Oh, Agatha,' she said. 'I never knew it had got so bad.' She put her arms around me; I gritted my teeth and let it happen. I did not yet know her well enough to let on how I despised hugs.

Too late, I realized how insane it had all sounded: I turned on a helium tank when I was concussed and thought I broke a tiny plastic seal; a mysterious call came, but there was no record of it; I was attacked in a scenario out of a nightmare, except that there was no evidence it ever happened. And I thought a monster out of a Green book had killed my friend. By the time I was done, even I was half-convinced the whole thing was a delusion.

'I need to do this,' I said to Nancy. 'I need to be sure what happened to Murgatroyd. And Ian is still missing, right?' Nancy shrugged in agreement. 'I need to run it to ground.'

There was a long pause. 'Agatha,' said Nancy, 'I don't think you do. Your ex killed herself, and you were so busy being, you know, fired, and caught up in a national scandal, and, oh, vilified in the national media, that you haven't processed it. I knew I was right to ask you to do the podcast with me—I told you!—I didn't know why I was right, but I knew I was, and here's why: the season the BBC wants to buy—it's not going to be on *The Dog's Ball* at all. We're going to wrap that up. And then we're going to move on to other mysteries. What killed Edgar Allan Poe? Is there really a lost Shakespeare play out there somewhere? I didn't tell you yet, because I wasn't sure how you'd react, but this is *perfect*! You can stop thinking about Gladden Green entirely! It'll be like a *rest cure*—well, not a rest cure—a *work cure*! And we can get you a therapist, and keep you away from the booze, and...' She was off, spinning a fantasia, leaving me behind.

'Listen,' she said eventually. 'I have to go to work.' Why did it not surprise me that Nancy worked on Sundays? 'But I have a mission for you. To dot the I's and cross the T's on *The Dog's Ball*. Lily Cadigan's mother has turned up—Cust's daughter-in-law. Remember? She was nowhere to be found when everything was going on. I had been leaving messages, and she finally called me back! She had taken herself off on some kind of *grief holiday* after her husband died, and she just came back. She says she knows things. She's kind of a weird one. That's why I need you to talk to her.'

'Because *I'm* kind of a weird one?' I said.

'I'm not the one who said it!' smiled Nancy. And off she went—to the Neele, one supposed, though who knew, really?— leaving me with a number, an address, and her usual confidence that everything would turn out just the way she planned it. The address for a Biddy Cust was on Hanway Place, in the middle of the West End, which was intriguing for an elderly lady who had seemingly previously lived in a 1960s ex-council house in Harrogate.

Unlike Nancy, apparently, I needed a minute. I was back in my own clothes, which were feeling and smelling much better. The Dettol had stained the cut on my head yellow, but I thought it was losing a bit of its former impetigo look, which was good. My hunting hat and my tweed jacket should most likely not have gone in the tumble dryer. Both had gone small and stiff, and the jacket had congealed into feltiness. I decided to believe that they would ease themselves back to normal with a bit of wearing. My trousers had also come out at something less than their original size. I no longer felt like a homeless person, but I did feel a bit like a refugee. My eye was in decent condition. I felt shipshape enough to forgo the pirate patch. I needed an effing drink, but I was still full of resolve to be a Good Girl.

Staying at Nancy's, as I appeared to be doing, was giving rise to existential questions. Was I a crazy woman, haphazardly but unmistakably drifting down and out, sick, unemployed, drunk, obsessed with solving a murder that had never occurred? Or was I a maverick, pursuing truth and justice when no one believed in me, even at the cost of my own well-being? I should have bought myself a cat way back, when Nancy got the curator's job at the Neele, and saved myself all this anguish. But then I would have had (ugh!) hairs and poo and cat puke all over my flat at the Gatehouse—I understand there are things called *hairballs* that cats produce. I didn't even want to think about those. No, a cat was not a price I would have been willing to pay, even in retrospect.

The flat on Hanway Place was sandwiched between an empty shop with one of those vacant-property metal grilles instead of a door and an extremely expensive Chinese restaurant, outside which celebrities were sometimes photographed. Mrs Cust, over the phone, had agreed to have me visit immediately and ask questions. Something felt odd. I couldn't put my finger on what. As per usual. Maybe it was—would *you* invite me round, just like that? I know *I* wouldn't. Or perhaps it was simply that feeling I seemed to get more and more when I was out and about these days, that someone was watching or listening. Anyway. Mrs Cust's buzzer was the bottom one of a series; the others were blank. An industrial-grade camera loomed above the heavyweight door; when she opened it, there was a laminated poster behind her whose headline read: 'We Have Rules To Make You Safe'. She saw me staring, and said, 'Oh, don't worry about that. The upstairs is some kind of facility. I have the downstairs. You must be Agatha. I'm Biddy, by the way.' She turned jauntily, and led me through an excruciatingly kick-in-able laminate door, down a flight of stairs carpeted in a material that was now of an indeterminate dun; perhaps it had once been some other colour?

She was an unlikely customer for the setting. She was wearing a chain necklace of large gold links, and a silk blouse whose pattern had more chains on it, with some anchors thrown in for good measure. She looked as if she had bought the outfit from the gift shop on a cruise ship. She looked thrilled to bits to be living in one of the worst flats I had ever seen, and that was saying something.

It was carpeted throughout in the same awful stuff as the stairs. The low ceiling was one under which I could only just stand—although I am tall, to be fair. It was dark, too, the sole natural light coming from a series of window wells glazed with those three-inch-thick armoured-glass bricks. After a few minutes I noticed, too, that the whole place shuddered every time a train left Tottenham Court Road tube station.

This time to look around was brought to me by the fact that she had, without asking, headed to the kitchenette to make me a mug of nasty builder's tea. The default expectation that one ought to be glad to have tea at any time grates on my nerves more than I can express.

After a bit, though, in she came, determined to tell me all about the marvellous time she was having. 'Can you believe it?' she said. 'You read in the papers that no one can afford to live in central London any more except Russian oligarchs, but here I am! I saw the advert on an Internet website and came down here right away and said I would take it, immediately. The rental agent said I was very lucky to get it.' She was absolutely right about that. The fact that such a flat had been available for a cost she, a mortal, could afford, was nothing short of a miracle.

I felt a pang of something—guilt? (but why?)—this guileless old lady who had been here about a week and a half was going to get home-invaded by a druggy from upstairs before the month was out.

'Mrs Cust,' I said, 'I was hoping to ask you about your father. About the book that Gladden Croon was supposed to have given him.'

223

'Oh yes,' she said. 'I was away for all of that. But wasn't it interesting? I read about it in the papers—a few days behind, of course. I have always liked detective stories immensely, although I tend to watch them on television, rather than reading the books. It's a much easier way to get the same story, I think.' I clenched my teeth in an attempt to maintain a polite visage. 'But I've seen all the Gladden Green adaptations. They're so clever, aren't they? I never guess whodunit!

'But anyway, I went on a long holiday, you see, after Albert died. It's a horrible thing to say about one's husband, isn't it, but when he died I felt finally free.' She didn't sound as if she thought it was a horrible thing to say at all. 'He never let me do much of anything when he was alive. We'd go to Torbay for a week every summer and that was about it as far as quote-unquote fun went.

'And so when he died, there was a little bit of money, and I thought, for the first time in my life, I'm going to get away. I'm going to go somewhere really exotic and stay there for as long as I want. Only it turns out there aren't many places you can go to where you don't have to come back. So I went to the island of Jersey. You'll think I'm silly, but I thought Jersey seemed very glamorous, you see, because of *Bergerac*!'

Shamefully, I had had the same thought, about the same nineteen-eighties detective serial, at the mention of Jersey. I wasn't giving Mrs Cust the satisfaction of telling her that, after her nonsense about preferring TV programmes to books. But maybe Nancy had been right. Maybe this old lady and I were weird in the same way.

'It turns out,' she went on, 'that Jersey is not terribly glamorous after all. It's mostly potatoes and tax exiles, and none of the tax exiles wanted to get to know *me*. I didn't want to go back to Harrogate, though—so I thought, I'll put the house on the market, and I won't go back until it's sold, and I have the money, and I can move somewhere else entirely and never go back there again. And that's what I did. And so here I am.'

She did not seem to notice that I hadn't asked to hear any of this.

'I'm quite different now from how I used to be,' she continued. 'I stay up late. All night sometimes, watching television, or reading. I swear, now. I was in the supermarket—they have these little ones here, called Express and such—and the girl asked me how many apples I had in the bag. *I haven't got a f—g clue, love*, I said. We laughed. You haven't touched your tea.'

'Oh, I'm just waiting for it to cool,' I said.

'Did I underdo the milk?' she said. 'Oh s—.'

'Please, it's quite all right,' I said.

'Your friend—'

'—Nancy—' I said.

'—Nancy. She said in her message she wanted to know about the fake novel. She wondered if I knew anything about it.'

'That's right,' I said. 'We're making a radio programme.' It seemed to me that, despite her second youth, Mrs Cust might well be unfamiliar with the concept of *podcasts*.

'And—I'm terribly sorry, remind me of your name again?'

'Agatha,' I said.

'Agatha, that's right—what is it you wanted to know? I'm afraid I wasn't terribly close to Albert's father. No one was, really. He was such a strange, bitter man.' This was a story I had heard before. 'And what an embarrassment for my family, the whole thing. It rubbed my daughter Lily up the wrong way from the start. I've never felt any sort of attachment to the idea of a family reputation, luckily. But it was a bit of a shambles, wasn't it? And there was that poor woman who thought she had discovered the whole thing, and then got crucified, I read about her in the paper, what was her name?'

'Agatha,' I said.

'What a coincidence!' she said. 'She was Agatha and you're Agatha!'

'Yes, unfortunately,' I said.

'Fancy that!' she said. 'I bet you're glad you're not her!'

'I am she,' I said.

'Oh!' she said. There was a pause. 'Oh!' she said again. I wondered if she was going to show off her swearing skills again, but finally she merely said: 'Well!'

'Nancy and I are trying to find out how the manuscript I thought was by Gladden Green came to be written.' There was an awkward silence. 'It's for the BBC,' I added, in an attempt to regain some credibility. 'Did he ever say anything about it to you, while he was alive?'

'Oh no,' she said. 'I had never heard of anything like it until I saw the papers in Jersey. I knew nothing about it whatsoever. You probably know an awful lot more about it than I do.'

So that was that, I thought. I came all the way out here to listen to a doolally old lady's voyage of self-discovery, and I was going to leave with nothing to show for it. I thought I would look up the name of someone who could install a security door for her and be on my way.

'I'll tell you one thing, though,' she said. 'Penny to a pound he wrote it himself.'

'What?' I said. 'Who?'

'My father-in-law. That was him all over. A terrible liar about things like that. As long as I knew him he had an autograph framed, up in the cloakroom, that was supposed to be Harry Houdini's. "To Mr Alexander Cust, unrivalled porter and fellow artiste", it said. Albert's mum said he had it on the toilet wall ever since he met her—in 1913. And he would tell the story of how he had met Houdini at the hotel in 1911, and won his confidence by making a wonderful impression, because of his charm and professionalism, and had shown him a poem he had written, which Houdini had apparently admired terribly, and Houdini had written him this note. Every time he'd had a sherry or two, that story would come out.

'When he died, I wanted to sell it. Albert didn't want to do it. He never wanted to do anything. But I had a friend who ran an antiques shop, who said you could get a thousand pounds or more for an autograph of Houdini, that they were very collectible. So I took it off the wall and took it on my own down to the shop—and he had to show it to another colleague who could authenticate things like that, but, long story short, it wasn't Houdini's autograph at all. It was nothing like it.'

'Do you still have it?' I asked.

'I do. Why do you ask?'

'I'd just like to check something, if it's OK with you. I shan't damage it.'

'I suppose so. I'll get it for you. After all, it's not like it's worth anything to anyone, is it? Albert's dad made the whole thing up. Albert never let me forget that. But it sounds just like the story of this Gladden Green book, from what I understand.'

And she was right, of course. It did.

24

I realized that I had been hoping, by some miracle, the manuscript would after all turn out to have been written by Gladden Green. Perhaps Cust had transcribed a lost original for safekeeping? Perhaps there had been some mistake in the ink analysis? The revelation that Alexander Cust was a liar and a forger did not render these already-unlikely scenarios *less* likely, as such. It wasn't *proof* of anything. But, simply, it made sense. Just as he had with 'Houdini's' note, Cust had written *The Dog's Ball* himself. That would be the big reveal for the podcast—I knew it would be enough for Nancy. And then, that would be that. *It wouldn't have to be, Agatha,* you may be thinking—*You could carry on the hunt on your own!* But when I said it would be enough for Nancy, I was projecting. What I meant was, it was enough for me. After my visit to Mrs Cust, a forlorn hope was extinguished somewhere in my brain.

Nancy, as predicted, was thrilled. 'Oh, wonderful!' she said. 'This is perfect. You and I have a meeting at the BBC tomorrow. I think this will clinch it for us.' I must have been doing a sad face, because she said, 'Agatha, aren't you ever happy?'

I bit back the clever-clogs comment an old version of me would have made. 'I really don't know that I should work on this with you,' I said. 'I've been a bad-luck charm my whole life.'

I didn't want to give up searching for the person who killed Murgatroyd. But was there really a choice? On the one hand, I could follow my conspiracy theories all the way to the psych ward. On the other, I could be part of something successful; I could do well—I could be *recognized*—for once in my life.

'You have a unique mind,' said Nancy, as if that decided it. Then she patted my hair. 'Good girl,' she said again. Then, 'Well, I must be turning in.'

I did too, but slept restlessly, for some reason. Nancy's patting of my head kept replaying itself in my consciousness. I was on the island of Jersey and Nancy was a wealthy tax exile in need of a housekeeper to clean the worst flat in the world. Unfortunately, all she had with which to pay me was an autograph by Houdini that I could sell for a thousand pounds. My unique mind fussed in the dark and would not shut down.

The first thing that happened in the morning was that my burner buzzed, and Lily Cadigan's name appeared. Two days ago, even yesterday, I'd have leaped to the phone, with its faint but irresistible possibilities of revelations about *The Dog's Ball*, about Murgatroyd and Tom Cadigan. And, if I'm honest, the idea of interacting again with Lily's angular face. But this morning, I wasn't so sure. Now there was Nancy, whatever that meant. Oh god, I had to stop thinking that way. *Keep your guard up, Agatha!* But Nancy was right. I had to let it go. It was done. I couldn't let it drag me under any more. There were new opportunities, if I would just turn away. But I answered. It would have been rude not to do so.

'Is that Agatha Dorn?' said Lily's voice.

'It is,' I said.

'This is Lily Cadigan.' I knew it was. I might have said so in the first place. But do you ever do that thing where you act as if someone's name didn't come up on your phone because they might think it was weird that you had put them in your contacts? Anyway. 'Do you have a minute?' she went on.

I said that I wasn't sure I did. I had a really important meeting for which I was in the middle of getting ready. 'Sorry,' I said. It came out sounding more insincere than I had intended.

'Oh,' she said. 'Well, I had just remembered something a bit strange. About the manuscript. I wanted to talk to you about it. But I can call again. It's nothing, really, and if you're in a hurry...'

Remembering the outspoken woman I had met in Harrogate, I had put my guard up straight away. But this Lily sounded almost like a different person. I was sorry I had been so brusque. 'That's OK,' I said. 'I'm sorry I'm in such a rush. But, listen, I should tell you that I've decided it's probably better if I give up on trying to figure out any more about what happened with *The Dog's Ball*. It was beginning to drive me crazy a little bit. You said it yourself, when I came to Harrogate: better to forget the whole thing.'

'Yes, I did say that, didn't I?' She suddenly sounded a bit more like her previous self. 'You did have an air of mania about you. But you know, you're right. I've just been brooding on something stupid. But you're right. Forget it! You know, I'm glad I called you. You've ended up cheering me up.'

'Well, OK,' I said, bemused. 'Happy to help!' And she hung up. Look at that. I'd ceased investigating for all of eight hours, and already I was brightening people's days!

I was roiling inside on the tube to Oxford Circus but maintained a poker face. I had had three cups of coffee, on account of not having slept. I was wired and jittery, and the brief optimism that followed my call with Lily Cadigan had worn off, replaced by a nagging feeling. Nancy was a bag of nerves, and unmistakably in business mode. All morning she had been schooling me on the ins and outs of the planned series. *What a roster of episodes would look like. The sound-design concept. Why we needed them to bring the production in-house rather than just licensing it.* Having a passing acquaintance with media nonsense, I did my best to look like I was absorbing it. I realized I had never before seen the work she put into being on all the time, the jangledness and the planning. More than the filthy lair of a kitchen, more than when I had looked at her bookshelves, I thought, now I was seeing her truly.

I had been to Broadcasting House before, back in the days of favour, but the new, down-at-heel me felt even more out of place amidst its oversized DUPLO-block style than I had the first time. Then, the mismatch between me and this hive of striving modernity had felt like a lark; now, I just felt like an interloper.

Nancy asked for Hattie Reedburn, her commissioning editor at BBC Sounds, who appeared after a shortish wait. A practised observer, I noticed that Nancy momentarily looked crestfallen when she saw Hattie, and for a moment I wondered why, but then I saw it. Hattie was wearing her coat. That meant we were meeting in a café, instead of in her office; it meant no deal would be done today.

Chit-chat in which I took no part happened on the way to the café. Hattie Reedburn looked closer to my age than Nancy's, but she and Nancy looked more alike than Hattie and I. Hattie wore thick-framed glasses with a rubbery navy patina, and her hairstyle involved a severe fringe. She looked, though, as if she were trying to disguise the fundamental farmer's-wifeliness of her physiognomy, with its yeoman's cheeks that would have rosacea on them before the decade was out, and the thick, wheaty hair that topped it.

The coffee place was designed to look like the kind of café that might have lived on the main street of whatever village from which the teenage Hattie had escaped, only to return for alternate Christmases, but done askew, so one would know that the establishment was exhibiting its skill at pastiche rather than its lack of taste. The coffee was vastly better than it would have been at the village café: the pastiche did not extend into the kitchen, thank god.

I got wheeled out right off the bat—Hattie was just thrilled to meet me at last, Nancy had talked so often about me. She wrote her mobile number on the back of her card and handed it to me. Now I was among the chosen. When she spoke, her voice and manner matched the haircut and glasses; the farmer's-wife overtones disappeared entirely. Nancy led with the revelation of Biddy Cust—my great discovery that was going to wrap the whole thing up. Hattie thought that was terrific. And had Hattie heard the episode where I was a guest? (She had.) Wasn't I hilarious? (I was.) Wasn't I *just* the person to balance out the show?—On that point, Reedburn seemed to reserve judgement. But that was the gist: I was to be the comic to Nancy's straight (wo)man, the pundit to her commentator. The Morecambe to her Wise. It was not a rôle that came naturally to me, I have to say. I smiled and nodded and played nice, though.

The conversation segued into considerations of jingles and audio beds, and I began to zone out a little. My body was a mess generally, what with the four cups of coffee and the no booze. It was bad form, but I realized I had to excuse myself to go to the loo.

As I approached the table some moments later, something in the conversation made me stop. Instead, I lurked behind a rubber plant.

'I'm not sure,' Hattie Reedburn was saying. 'She doesn't seem so funny in person.'

'Well, OK,' said Nancy, 'but in the end, funny isn't the point, is it? I know you wouldn't put it this way, but at our last meeting, I essentially heard you tell me I needed a gimmick. Well, here's the gimmick.'

'I think what I actually said is that podcasts are stories, and stories need a *so what?* and a character. And unfortunately for you, the character of upper-middle-class Oxbridge supergirl is a little bit played out.'

'But so, even if Agatha's not that funny, *she*'s my character—crazy, alcoholic old hag—that's a pretty great character, right?' Nancy replied. 'And then the *so what?* is, she redeems herself by helping me solve these mysteries. Who doesn't love a redemption story? And the Twitter feedback when she was on before was really very positive.'

'Yeah, OK, OK. I see it. I might see it,' said Hattie. 'And she is a good gimmick.' Nancy smirked. 'She really just turned up in the middle of a conference in the Yorkshire Dales?'

'Yes!' said Nancy. 'With a fricking eyepatch and a head wound!'

'Jesus,' said Hattie.

I emerged from behind my rubber plant. Hattie and Nancy plastered on identical *here-she-is!* smiles. My head felt light.

'I'm afraid the gimmick has to leave,' I heard my mouth saying as I shot out of the café.

I speed-walked all the way to Euston Road on autopilot before I registered my surroundings. Satisfied that Nancy would not have come this far after me—if she even thought I was worth bothering with—I swerved into an Irish pub as nasty as my mood. It looked like the kind of place there would be fights later, which was to say, perfect. A barman, who seemed not to have seen natural light in months, served me the first of what I intended to be a good number of gins-and-water. It was a good job it had been a morning meeting. The day was still young!

My phone buzzed with a number I did not recognize. Reedburn, no doubt. Well, blast them. Both of them. I would be damned if I would pick up. A couple of swigs later, it had stopped. I had been Crooked Man-ed good and proper this time. Gatling Crooked Man-ed. Effing eff. My unique mind! Ha! The only one! God's wounds!

I felt in my pocket. The keys to Murgatroyd's were still there, thank god. The very thought of going back to Nancy's!

I would never get it, would I? It would never click. Good things simply did not happen to the likes of me. Ugh, I could scorch my brain black and plough it with salt, and yet the next day, up would peep the foolish shoot of hope. Agh!

Speaking of which: I would go back to Murgatroyd's and get rid of all her junk. I'd live at the house till I could sort out the sale, then I'd get rid of it and pay the debts, give anything left over to Dimitra, let her waste it again. Find some horrible children to be my housemates, find a new job at a bookshop, or a dirt farm, or an ash heap. Hadn't I read that in South America, shanty towns sprang up inside giant landfills, running on barter economies of found garbage? That sounded about my speed. I could just work there without complaining until I died.

Agatha, said Murgatroyd.

Shut up, Murg, I thought. *You don't get to say you told me so.*

I was just going to say I'm sorry, she said.

Then I tuned her out. I was going to get drunk.

25

It was a day for which the word 'bracing' was invented, a day whose weather made one proud to be English. It was cloudy but not miserable. The wind blew at just the right speed and temperature to conjure the fantasy of being the captain of one of the little boats, off to rescue our brave boys from the beach at Dunkirk. As the breeze changed direction, the smoke began to fill my nostrils, and now I was Baden-Powell boiling a campfire kettle for a troop of weary Scouts, who had reached the top of the mountain at last. (Quite where I was supposed to have got firewood on the top of a mountain, whether or not Baden-Powell ever really went up a mountain with boys, these were mere quibbles.)

The fact that the smoke had the acrid smell of plastic, from Murgatroyd's burning foam-rubber sofa cushions, did not bother me one bit. It was a new start, a new day.

Three hours earlier, I had awoken on Murgatroyd's bed, on top of the once-pink chenille bedspread. I was still in the too-tight clothes that had been through Nancy's tumble dryer. I felt like hell and damnation. Waking up hungover, one has to wait a minute to see how rotten it is going to get. I hoped against hope, but I could sense a bad one coming. Yet, I had apparently made it back to Palmers Green, so that was something. I rummaged in my pockets. They were fat with the flimsy curls of credit-card receipts, ledgers of yesterday's bad decisions.

So it had come to this. Of no fixed abode, I was in no one's employ, had no friends. I had made a fool of myself in a hundred different ways, in public and in private, in search of some hidden truth that was all in my mad head. I was drunk and broke. I hoped this was what they called rock bottom. I wasn't sure I could manage going much lower.

No: we were going to improve things. I remembered my plan of clearing out Murgatroyd's house. There was no time like the present. I went to sit up and didn't quite make it. Maybe there was no time like a few minutes from now. I had to catch my breath.

So Murgatroyd had discovered *The Dog's Ball* was a fake? So what? It didn't mean she didn't kill herself. So Arise was involved in some dodgy dealings of some sort? Wasn't everyone? And Ian had, who knows, disappeared to fulfil his lifelong dream of locating the source of the Nile. The rest of it? My moderate schizrenia, like the calls coming from inside the house and the razor blade in the apple. All in my head.

I managed to slink to the kitchen and eat a couple of slices of Value white bread. That was an improvement. There was a pain in my gut, but I would do, for now. I surveyed the room. The pile of 1980s bank statements from the cabinet on whose door I had gashed my head were still lying on the floor where they had fallen, next to what was now a dried pool of my blood. Good god! They had to go. Everything had to go!

I scooped up as many of the bank statements as I could carry and took them to the back garden. I happened to know there was a bottle of absinthe above the sink, and somewhere there was one of those long-nosed Bic lighters you use for starting barbecues. I located both, poured the booze on the papers, and set them on fire. Internal Murgatroyd wailed in distress, but I refused to listen. Paper doesn't burn for long, so I did the best impression of running I could manage with my throbbing head and my acid gut and returned with a pile of new documents just in time to keep the thing going. There was no difficulty about finding them. You just opened any drawer.

After a few rounds of this, I was puffed out from running, and knew I wouldn't be able to keep it up. To give myself more time, I needed something more substantial. Well, for a start, there were those hideous elongated 'African' statues Murgatroyd had got, no doubt, from Camden. If they had ever really seen Africa, which I doubted, it was as they were being churned out by the hundreds to flog to gullible tourists. But they were hardwood of some kind, which meant they'd smoulder forever.

With the statues ballasting my bonfire, I did a couple more rounds of papers. I burned the James Patterson from Murgatroyd's nightstand as well as several other substandard thrillers.

I burned Hattie Reedburn's card, and I burned Nancy's copy of *The Dog's Ball*, which had been still in my coat pocket.

Then I started in on her clothes, which I had always mostly hated. And while I was at it, I manhandled her wardrobe out the door and disassembled that too. It wasn't difficult. It was cardstock-thin particle board coated in white and pink vinyl from the IKEA in Wembley. I remember when we bought it. We rented a Mini to go out there and get furniture. When we were done, there was no room for me left in the car and I had to get the bus back. Onto the fire! This was the life. I felt my psyche getting cleaner and cleaner.

I burned things for at least three hours. I got as far as the sofa cushions. The sofa itself I was unable to move on my own but asking someone for help would have ruined the whole thing. And, in any case, whom would I ask? Maybe I could take it apart and bring it out in pieces? I wondered if Murgatroyd had an axe I could use. Now that would be fun.

It was at about this point that I realized I was going to have to prioritize. I was suddenly getting very tired. Murgatroyd had an awful lot of stuff. There was no way I would manage it all today. The crucial items to burn were the nonsensical 'clues' on which I had founded my 'investigation'. I burned the Chinese medicines. I burned the Catholic prayer card. Murgatroyd's pink mobile, phylactery of certain of my murder fantasies, crackled and turned black on top of the pyre.

There was one thing left that definitely had to go: the helium canister. I trotted to the bedroom and fetched it, treacherous broken seal still hanging slack from its neck, and heaved it onto the fire. The flames began to lick around it. I headed back to the kitchen for a cup of coffee, satisfied at last that my work was done for the day.

As I drank my coffee, a curious whining noise began to come from the garden. I started for the window, but—before I got there, thank god—it shattered with a boom. Gobs of molten plastic appeared on the far side of the kitchen as I found myself sprawled on the floor. When the shock subsided, I checked for pain around my body. Nothing beyond the usual. I began to laugh. Maybe it had not been such a good idea to put a canister of pressurized gas onto a bonfire, after all. But you had to see the funny side. Now everything connected with the so-called murder was blown to smithereens. Now, perhaps, I really could start over.

This was the moment at which my burner phone rang. I pulled it from my coffee-soaked pocket and pressed the button:

'Ah, Mrs Dorn?' Correcting him seemed like more trouble than it was worth. 'This is Paul at Linkscom.'

'Yes?'

'Regarding your, ah, enquiry, we have received your documentation regarding the call placed to your phone on the date and time in question.'

'I'm sorry, what?' I asked.

'Yes, you had contacted us about a call placed to your phone on the evening of the fifteenth of September? Number of a, ah, Mr Thomas Cadigan?'

Murgatroyd's phone. The call I must have imagined. I had had to send Murgatroyd's will. I had completely forgotten about it. 'Yes?' I said. My instinct was to run and get the phone. But, of course, this was the very phone I had just not only burned but also blown up. Uh-oh.

'Yes, it does not appear as if there was any call placed from that number on that evening. From Mr Cadigan's number.'

'He didn't call me?'

'That's correct, madam.' Oh, thank god. That would have been awkward. But as it was, the call provided final confirmation that I had been correct in my decision to give the whole thing up. That was good Crooked Man thinking. I was regaining my pessimistic edge.

But wait, as the infomercial says: there's more. As I cast around for somewhere not covered in coffee or toxic ash to put the phone, I spotted a voicemail icon on the screen, which I had not noticed before. I hadn't been paying much attention to my mobile over the last couple of days. I had had other things on my mind. I reasoned that I might as well listen. What was the worst that could happen?

Or so I thought. 'Agatha?' said the voice on the recording. 'Agatha, are you there? If you're there, I need you to pick up.' Inconceivably, the message was from—who else?—Tom Cadigan. He sounded panicked. 'Agatha? It's Tom. From Harrogate—well, London now. It's Lily—my wife Lily—she's—she's killed herself. I think she's killed herself. She's on the bed here right now, with a plastic hood over her head, hooked up to some sort of *gas canister*. She's not breathing. But she left a note. The note says, "If you want to know why, ask Agatha Dorn." Is this your idea of *revenge*? Christ, I know I screwed you, but *this*? I have to go. I can hear the ambulance.'

Oh fuck. Fuck, fuck, fuck.

PART FOUR

26

Tom Cadigan thought *I* had killed his wife? Nauseated, I thought of those angular cheekbones, to which I had taken a mini-shine, lying lifeless inside a plastic hood. Tom Cadigan thought I had *killed* his wife? I mean, even forgiving his not knowing that I had been a little struck by Lily, it didn't seem to him out of character for me? And I was supposed to have done it in revenge for the *Dog's Ball* disaster? Certainly, as you have seen, the whole business had brought my entire life crashing down around my ears. But even so, *murder* seemed a disproportionate response.

Somebody was doing murders, though. It never seemed quite real when I thought it. Somebody was doing *murders*. *Killing people!* Somebody, it suddenly seemed clear once again, had murdered Murgatroyd, and then murdered Lily Cadigan in precisely the same manner, apparently with the particular aim of involving *me*.

Not knowing what else to do, I set about cleaning things up. I took a fish slice and began to prise the exploded plastic blobs off the cupboards and the worktop. In a couple of places, the blobs were so securely fused that I could not remove them; in a couple of others, the blobs brought the formica away with them when I scraped them off, revealing the chipboard beneath. All in all I was not sure when I had finished that I had improved matters. There was less plastic attached to the cupboard, just as there is less evidence of a wound on one's arm if one picks the scab off. But, as also in the case of the scab, the effect was no less ghastly. It looked like the kitchen had a skin disease. I turned my attention to the window. I found a roll of gaffer tape and an ancient cardboard file box; I disassembled the box and tried to tape it over the broken place. The rest of the pane came away as I tried to secure the tape. This was not going well.

I was on my way to the sitting room to search for a bigger cardboard box when I realized what had been troubling me. What, specifically, about Tom Cadigan's call, I mean. Plenty of things trouble me, though I cannot always remember what they are; there's just a vague feeling of sadness that accompanies me at all times.

It was his certainty that I would be out for his blood. *Is this your idea of revenge?* he had said. Because *I screwed you.* But he hadn't. If anyone had screwed me, it was I. Or perhaps the minor mountebank Alexander Cust. Maybe it was a figure of speech—perhaps he thought I would naturally blame him for his having brought me *The Dog's Ball* in the first place, even though he had no idea that it was there?

Or had he screwed me? Did he think I had *discovered* something?

The doorbell rang. Grumpily, I went to get it. It was my old friend PC Dorothy of the Metropolitan Police. News of the circumstances surrounding Lily's death had evidently moved fast. I was glad they had sent Dorothy, though. She was a dunderhead, but she and I had seen Murgatroyd's cadaver together. Being in the presence of a corpse with someone forges an unbreakable bond. We were practically sisters.

'Excuse me, madam, might I speak with Ms Agatha Dorn?' she said.

'Dorothy, you know perfectly well that I am she.'

'Ah, excellent, madam. Can I come in?'

'I identified Amy Murgatroyd's body, remember?' She looked nonplussed. 'We spoke at length on the phone on multiple occasions? You refused to countenance the idea that Amy had been murdered?'

'May I come in, madam—Agatha?' she said.

I showed her through to the kitchen. 'Sorry it looks like a bomb site,' I said, trying to be funny. Not a chortle. 'I suppose people don't usually mean that literally, when they say it, ha ha,' I persevered fruitlessly. PC Dorothy eyed the wreckage suspiciously. 'I had an accident with a bonfire,' I went on. Somehow, this did not seem to help.

'Ms Dorn, are you acquainted with a woman by the name of Lily Cadigan?' she said. I said that I was. For a moment, I considered attempting to speed things up by laying out the history of the whole business, but I feared it would do no good. 'And might I ask the nature of your acquaintance?'

I began to go into it all, slowly, in bite-size pieces with which I thought Dorothy might be able to cope. She asked about my movements during the morning. I tried to explain about all the burning of things that I had been doing. At the end, she thanked me and said that she would need to schedule an appointment for me to sign a formal witness statement. Then she said that an investigating officer might have to interview me at the police station, and they would set up an appointment for that too. I didn't like the sound of that at all. A passage from *The Crime Writer's Guide to Police Procedure* floated to the front of my mind: 'The PACE codes of practice use the word *interview*, but a better word would be *interrogation*. The author should understand: criminals know that it is never advisable to participate in an *interview* without a solicitor present.' I told her I would await her call.

After she left, I fired up Google again. Things felt as if they were coming into some kind of focus. Tom Cadigan had worked, essentially, for Arise. Tom Cadigan got a big promotion—all the way from freelance piece-worker to Head Designer. On the basis of what, exactly? Designing a couple of textbooks? Then I remembered, bitterly, his telling me that the Cadigans had bought a flat in the Gatehouse. Which was now owned by Arise. Come to think of it, it seemed highly unlikely that even head graphic designers made the kind of money you'd need for a Gatehouse flat.

I wondered what it was possible to find out about the sales of people's flats. I had visions of having to engage a solicitor—who could then, I supposed, do double duty when I was arrested for the murder—oh, God's foot!—it wasn't funny! But in any case, it turns out to be worryingly simple to discover things about people's property online. The Phone Book website gave me the Cadigans' new address: Flat 103, Chesterton Tower, Gatehouse, London EC2Y 8JG.

My heart almost came out through my chest. It was my literal former address! The Cadigans must have bought it from the property developer! I remembered him telling me they were moving to the Gatehouse, but what were the odds? Sometimes the gods are needlessly cruel.

A little additional googling revealed that you can get a copy of someone's property title, with the sale history, purchase prices, everything, for the princely sum of £3. And up it comes, right on your computer! This seemed like it ought to be some kind of grey-market, dark-web shenanigan. But no, the information was right there, being provided to you by the British government itself! Someone ought to tell the government what the government was up to.

I don't know what I thought I would find. That Arise was the true owner of the flat? No, surely not: some bribe, that, to let someone live in a flat that you yourself owned. That they had sold it to him for under the market rate? But would they be so obvious? And what, exactly, was it for which they were supposed to be bribing him?

In any case, I paid my £3 and spun the (metaphorical) wheel. The conveyance history of the flat appeared on my screen. *1960… The Corporation of London… transfer of the property… 1982… Mr Somebody-or-Other*, and so on and so forth until—wait, what? 'Transfer of the property in this title dated 29 August, 2016 made between Phillipa Haymes and Agatha Dorn…The price stated to have been paid on 29 August, 2016, was £1,950,000.' My heart began to sink still further. This was not right. It hadn't been in 2016, but 1997, and not for anything remotely resembling that quantity of money. And I had never heard of a Phillipa Haymes. Something dubious was going on. And then, the next entry: 'Transfer of the property in this title dated 1 May, 2018 made between Agatha Dorn and Thomas Cadigan… The price stated to have been paid on 1 May, 2018, was £1.' That would be £1 (One). A whole £2 less than the cost of the land record itself.

My spirits hit the floor. I was far from clear about what was going on, but one thing seemed glaringly obvious: someone had made it seem as if I had acquired a de luxe property for a great deal of money and given it to Tom Cadigan. Why was

I supposed to have done such a thing? I wasn't yet sure, but it wasn't likely to have been for any ordinary, above-board reason, now was it?

I wondered what would happen next. Dorothy had not made it sound like a dawn raid was imminent, but then perhaps that was a ruse. Crooked Man thinking dictated that I should always anticipate the worst. No Bad Surprises. The possibility of having good surprises is always outweighed by the danger of having bad surprises. Therefore, better to have no surprises at all. If you miss out on good things that way, so be it. *Prepare for the worst but hope for the best*, they say, the idiots. If you're hoping for the best, you're not really preparing for the worst, are you? I say you should prepare for the worst and hope for the worst too. Then, when the worst happens, you won't have been humiliated by your optimism. So at least you'll have that going for you.

In my particular case, this suggested to me that I ought to leave Palmers Green immediately. If the worst that could happen was that the storm troopers or whoever were going to batter down my door at 5 a.m. the next morning, then I was not going to be here for it. I packed my duffel bag, something at which I was getting good, since I had essentially been living out of it for the last three weeks and headed for the door.

27

I had no idea where I was going. My initial, improvised idea was that I would head to a Premier Inn or some such and hole up there until I could figure out what was going on. As I headed down the garden path, however, a shadow seemed to move, and something light blue glinted from across the road. The Crooked Man!

As quickly as it had appeared, the glint disappeared. I suppose appearing and disappearing quickly is in the nature of glints. Had it not disappeared quickly, it would have been merely a light. In any case, I wondered if it had been the flasher of a police car in the next street reflecting off a nearby window or something. But that set me thinking. Were they watching me? Was PC Dorothy staking out the house? I mean, if she was, she surely wouldn't be out there with her blue lights on. But even if she and her brethren were not watching me, if the whole point was to hide, I couldn't very well just turn up at a hotel, pay with my credit card, and not expect immediately to be found.

I stopped and attempted to look as if I had left something inside. How would one shake off a pursuer, did I suppose? I had a little think. It seemed like the kind of situation in which Green's detective duo Bitsy and Bob might have found themselves, but I couldn't recall any tips among their exploits off the top of my head. In *The Hidden Foe*, I recalled, Bob tails his adversaries into 'the mean streets of Soho'. But, as I remembered, they do nothing to try to shake him off.

I found a winter hat and an old donkey jacket amongst what was left of Murgatroyd's possessions and shoved them in my bag. Then I set out again. There was a cashpoint at the Asda; I couldn't avoid leaving a record of withdrawing money, but I could at least do so near to the house and avoid placing myself in a new location. I drew out the most it would let me, a measly £300. With the cost of the hotel, that would only last me a couple of days. I wished I had kept more of Heri's money in cash instead of depositing it in the bank. I headed into Asda, had a quick browse, then made for the loos, where I traded my hunting hat and tweed for the donkey jacket and the bobble thing. I had to say, I was thinking very fast. I was quite impressed with myself. I knew, from my regular trips to the gin aisle, that this was one of those supermarkets with tills at the front *and* the back. My hope was that PC Dorothy did not know this. I grabbed a pint of Beefeater—solely to avoid attracting the attention of any security guards watching for people leaving without buying anything—moved through the queue, paying cash, and left the shop by the set of doors through which I had not come. Clever Agatha, eh? From there, it was a mere hop, skip, and a jump to the bus stop, where I took the first bus into town. As the bus pulled away, I thought I saw a strangely moving shadow not unlike the one I had spotted outside Murgatroyd's house. But then, I was all keyed up. I told myself there was nothing about which to worry.

Once I arrived in the centre of town, I had to grapple with the problem of where to stay.

I didn't fancy the mean streets of Soho overmuch, but it did occur to me that there were, unaccountably, a large number of bad hotels in Bloomsbury, where it might be possible to disappear, at least for a couple of days, while I tried to figure out what was going on. Walking to the British Museum and such, I had long wondered how one of the most expensive parts of town managed to sustain such a concentration of the kinds of crappy businesses big money had forced out of every other postcode. I hoped they hadn't all been turned into posh coffee shops since the last time I had been that way.

I was in luck. As I rounded the corner of Guilford Street, I spotted a grimy-looking terrace with a sign advertising the Hotel Mariposa. The poor building's Georgian sash windows had been ripped out and replaced with plastic double-glazing in the wrong size, and the intervening space had been filled in with breeze blocks. Adjacent bars of a hanging neon-butterfly sign flashed incongruously from side to side. Was one supposed to believe that it was fluttering? I didn't see how anyone could. A plastic sign screwed to the wall advertised 'Bed and Breakfast (with private facilities)', and a phone number wonkily assembled from adhesive numbers. I felt sorry for the violence the proprietors of the Mariposa had enacted upon the elegant eighteenth-century structure. It was as if someone had forced Beau Brummel into a 'Fat Willy's Surf Shack' T-shirt. Besides, why would you need to put your hotel phone number on the front of the hotel? Surely if you were in a position to read the number, you were also in a position to walk inside and simply ask for what you wanted? It was exactly for what I was looking.

In the narrow hallway, a receptionist who resembled a potato wearing a too-large building-society cashier's jacket affirmed that a room was available, that she would accept my hard cash to the tune of a mere £83, and that she required no confirmation that my name was the one I gave her, Una Nancy Owen. I was taking a chance with the alias—perhaps she had read *Catch a Tiger by the Toe*! But I wasn't worried: the receptionist didn't look as if she had ever read any kind of book. Better still, there was Internet access 'in the lounge'.

I headed to a staircase whose carpet seemed patterned after the haunted eponym of Charlotte Perkins Gilman's 'The Yellow Wallpaper'. I wondered on how many trapped spectral madwomen I trod on my way across its ghastly coils.

'If you want to know why, ask Agatha Dorn.' But I had no idea. It seemed horribly likely that she had been planning to tell me when she had telephoned the other day. I tried to tell myself that ruminating on *that* was an idle endeavour, but since when has telling oneself something ever achieved anything? I wanted to ask Tom what *he* thought it could have been about. That didn't seem like a good idea, though, on balance. In fact, I could not think of anyone whom I could ask who might not also have a crack at murdering me, too.

Although, actually, I thought—what about the girls? What about Alice and Betty Cadigan? Could their mother have confided in them, or might they have overheard—what? They struck me as just the kind of precocious little pitchers who might have ears of the requisite size.

But how to find them without, once again, tipping my hand to their father? That turned out not to be a hard problem to solve, either. Buttonhole them at school! They had told me in Harrogate that they were going to Carmichael Clarke's, next door to the Gatehouse. I could accost them during school hours somehow, ask them if they remembered, what they knew. I could present myself as a detective, working on the case of their mother's death. That sounded like the kind of thing children would like.

Now, however, things got more difficult. I knew Carmichael Clarke's fairly well from the outside—I used to walk past it every day on the way to work. Despite its polished-slate accent wall and asymmetrical arch over the entryway, it had, like all schools in the city, the appearance of some kind of upmarket secure facility—which I suppose it was, in truth. Like a really top-notch open prison for the very best class of white-collar criminals. Although it was lined with birch trees and the shrubbery of a pupils' garden, the school's fences were ten feet tall and made of a wire whose mesh was fine enough you could barely get a finger through. What was more, most of the fences didn't just go up, but had overhanging sections jutting out from the tops at right angles, to make it impossible to climb over even if you had, you know, a grappling hook. The absence of barbed wire was about the only concession the institution made to the notion that the academy was a place for the education of children.

It was imperative to keep out the paedos, I supposed. Even a ninja paedo would have had trouble getting into Carmichael Clarke's. I thought back to my own middle-of-the-road sub-urban primary school. Anyone could have walked in; indeed, the thought of the Crooked Man's accosting me at school had occupied a good portion of my daydreams. Were there just fewer nonces in my day? Or were we tougher, was this the coddled generation about which one was forever hearing? Neither, surely. Perhaps we have become rather less willing to be fatalistic than once upon a time—the idea of risk was increasingly intolerable. I wished it had been more intolerable to me when I had foisted *The Dog's Ball* on Fraser Green. Ah, well.

All of which was to say that I didn't fancy my chances of just sidling into the playground and taking the girls off round the back of the building for a quick word. No. I would need an 'in'. But what kinds of people could get themselves inside primary schools at a moment's notice?

28

The Mariposa's breakfast room had a tiled floor, a bad print of Tower Bridge taking up the entirety of one wall, and Union Flag bunting in the large window. A buffet table seemed to have been covered with a bedsheet rather than a tablecloth. On the table were the makings of what one might have imagined an English Breakfast to be if one's only experience of the thing was a second-hand account from a tourist whose language one did not speak. There was a plate with rolls of Value ham, a bowl filled with warmish hard-boiled eggs and another with chopped-up pieces of frankfurter. Since I had slept in, not needing to begin my mission until mid-morning, it was all beginning to congeal. Nevertheless, having only the £300 I had withdrawn from the ATM, minus the £83 I had paid for my night's stay, I did not feel it was prudent to forgo the breakfast. I therefore left for the City feeling quite queasy, which was the first bad sign.

I had imagined walking authoritatively into the office, but that plan foundered at the first hurdle: I couldn't even get onto the school grounds without shouting my business into an intercom at the locked gate. However, announcing that I was a counsellor had the desired effect, and the gate buzzed open.

Inside, things were immediately less prison-like. The parents who sent their children here may have been millionaires, but at the end of the day, a primary school is a primary school.

The receptionist who had let me in was wearing a headscarf and heavy mascara. Opposite her, a bronze plaque with a hieratic profile of Sir Carmichael Clarke glowered incongruously down on the primary colours in which the school had been painted. Surrounded by laminated posters demonstrating joined-up writing, he was a relic of a sterner time. Given that I understood him to have made his money running a rapacious government-condoned racket in Mandatory Palestine, I wondered how his ghost felt about his current office-mate. Filled with impotent rage, I hoped.

The atrium area into which I had been admitted seemed strangely free of children, though I did spot one toting a plastic-wrapped brick of milk cartons across the way, in the direction of a wall mounted with masks that pupils had made of their own faces. Cut-out paper letters above the display read: 'MARVELLOUS ME'. In fact, though, they were embarrassingly bad and not marvellous at all. If I ran a school, I shouldn't display terrible artwork all over the place, for fear that prospective parents would think I was running an institute for the mentally disabled.

In any case: I waved my piece of paper at the receptionist and said I was here to see Alice and Betty Cadigan. I had mocked up a letter indicating that I was a counsellor who was there to work with the Cadigan children after the traumatic death of their mother.

'Did you have an appointment?' the receptionist asked with a suspicious look. This was not in the plan. 'These kinds of things have to be set up with an appointment in advance.'

I said of course I did, didn't she see it written on the paper?

She said she meant had I set it up with them in advance with an email?

I said no, and was that a luxury they had in the private sector? Hoping to play on her liberal guilt.

That got me somewhere. She asked if she could see some identification, but the heat had gone out of her. I made a pantomime of patting down my pockets and said I must have left it in the car, but I was just here to offer the Cadigan girls some support after the terrible death of their mother, wasn't it a tragedy? The receptionist began to tear up and said that everyone had been devastated. I nodded in what I hoped was a supportive way.

'They're in 3-B,' she said. 'Across the hall, up the stairs, and on the right. But there's a room right off the office here you can use with them.'

'For what?' I asked.

She looked confused. 'To *talk to them*,' she said. Now the suspicious look had come back into her eye.

Right, I thought. Because of course I wouldn't just have a little chat with them in the corner of the classroom. They probably covered that on day one of the school-counsellor course.

As I tromped up the stairs to 3-B, I heard a musical voice leading the children in responsive phrases. '*Ni hao*,' said the voice. 'Nee how,' chanted the class. I knocked on the door.

'Come in!' said the teacher's voice. I opened the door on a small host of eight-year-olds in red sweatshirts, all looking up at me like dogs at the shelter. 'Let's say *ni hao* to our visitor, everyone.' The teacher, a large, jolly woman with a blonde bob, looked at me. 'What's your name?'

'Agatha,' I said.

'Let's say *Ni hao, Agatha*,' she said. They did.

It occurred to me that, as someone who was both wanted by the police and not in fact a school counsellor, I probably ought not to have showed my face to a whole class full of tiny witnesses. Also, I should probably not have announced my real name. But hindsight is twenty-twenty.

Taking the teacher conspiratorially into a corner, I explained what I was doing here and showed her my piece of paper. She made an exaggerated serious face, called the Cadigans up to the front, and told them to go with me to the office.

In the corridor, I asked the girls if they remembered me from my trip to Harrogate.

'Yes,' said one of them—I had no idea which was which—'You're Agatha Dorn, Mummy and Daddy's friend with the eyepatch.'

'Yes,' I said, 'I'm afraid I forgot to wear it today.'

'Did you come to make us feel better?' said the other girl—let's go with Betty—'Everybody is trying to make us feel better because Mummy killed herself.'

'You did very well, to remember my name,' I said to the one I had decided was Alice.

'Well,' she said, 'Mummy used to say it. She would have a glass of wine and she would wave it about and say, "F— Gladden Green!" and then we would all together say, "And f— Agatha Dorn!" and Mummy would laugh and drink her wine.'

Well! Lily Cadigan's cheekbones still lingered in my memory, but her foisting of this vulgarity upon her children took her down in my estimation straight away.

'Why did your mummy shout to, you know, Agatha?'

'She said f—,' said Betty.

'Mummy always said silly things,' said Alice.

That was as may be. But why had Lily Cadigan had it in for me?

We were almost back at the reception area now. The receptionist with the mascara saw us coming and came out of her little area with a key to open up the conference room.

'But then she changed it,' said Betty. 'After you came to visit us, we did "F— Art-Brute! And f— Daddy!" But only when Daddy was at work.'

'No, stupid,' said Alice to her sister. 'I invented that and you're an idiot!' Betty punched her sister in the arm, bringing back the memory of her doing it the last time I had seen her.

'You're stupid and Mummy invented it,' yelled the other.

'Girls!' said the receptionist, who had the door open by this time. 'Let's be kind while we're with the counsellor.'

'She's not a counsellor!' said Betty. 'She's Mummy's friend Agatha Dorn.'

'F— Agatha Dorn!' they chorused together.

'Don't be silly,' said the receptionist. 'And we use kind words at school.' But she said it half-heartedly.

I made to go into the conference room with the two girls, but Betty hadn't finished. 'Tell Miss Mansour about when you visited us when we lived in Yorkshire!'

The receptionist turned to me again. 'I'm sorry, did you say before that you had some identification with you?'

'In my car.' Drat and blast! Now they'd done it!

'Could I ask you to go and get it for me?'

'Of course,' I said, flustered. I started to wander towards the exit, but I was suddenly in a bit of a daze and was making myself more suspicious by the minute.

'Actually,' said Miss Mansour, apparently now not wishing to let me out of her sight, 'could I ask you to wait in here for a sec? Girls, you can go back to class.' Alice and Betty turned and headed back towards the stairs with the random and incurious acquiescence that descends upon children on occasion.

I saw the key still in Miss Mansour's hand and guessed at her plan: she was going to shut me in the empty office while she called the rozzers.

Quickly, I pulled myself together, shoved past her, and bolted for the door. I made it through and went on towards the street gate. The receptionist had not followed me outside. She must be back in her office calling the police—or worse, pressing some kind of lockdown button—but I saw with relief that the gate had a panic bar on it. *Thank god, lockdowns are about keeping people out, not keeping them in*, I thought as I planned to crash through it.

With horror, I saw that a police car was already parked by the gate. I must have been wrong. Miss Mansour must have called them as soon as I arrived. But she still let me see the children? No time to wonder about that. I turned around and spied a back gate, also with a panic bar. No one had yet exited the police car. Walking fast, I made it out of the school grounds, then began to run.

I hadn't run this fast in years and had got less than a street away when I began to pant and stagger. Also, I could hear sirens. Not that one can't generally hear sirens in this part of London, but these seemed very close.

I had come out of the school on the Aldersgate Street side, near the Museum of London—which is to say there was nothing around but the exterior walls of the Gatehouse and an underpass—no businesses into which to duck, for instance. Nothing for it but to keep going.

A police car roared past me beneath the underpass. Was it for me? It seemed a bit much—but then I was a person of interest in a murder—and presumably the safety of extremely rich people's children was now also felt to be at stake, so all bets were off. Luckily, the light was awful in the tunnel; I turned my face towards the wall, and the car didn't slow down.

But more sirens were coming my way. With unusual presence of mind, I pulled Murgatroyd's woolly hat out of the donkey-jacket pocket, put it on my head, and shoved the jacket itself the best I could into a bin next to a row of Boris Bikes. Then I staggered onwards.

On the far side of the underpass—at last—I found an upscale coffee bar and sought sanctuary.

I ordered a black coffee and attempted to regain my composure by taking a seat amidst a row of intimidating white bar stools, the only place to sit in the whole coffee shop. This proved quite difficult, since the stool seemed to have been designed with the sole aim of making it impossible to get comfortable, like the victim's chair in an interrogation room. My legs were too short to reach the little footrest, and the undersized seat was canted downward so that one constantly slid off. More police cars whizzed past, but none slowed down, and no one looked in my direction.

I had hoped this might be the subgenre of pretentious café that made use of a Chemex flask, but, alas, it was the kind that made their black coffee with an espresso machine. Thus my Americano, having been made primarily of steam, was excruciatingly hot when it arrived; I would have to wait forever for it to cool down. That was OK, though. I needed to wait out the police. And I needed time to think.

Now, you might imagine that my trip to Carmichael Clarke's was an unmitigated disaster, characterized by a series of schoolgirl errors on my part. However, that is only partly true. I realized that I had also learned some useful things. First, I had discovered that, after my visit to Harrogate, Lily Cadigan had transferred her rage about *The Dog's Ball* away from me and onto her husband and onto the forger art-brute. That was weird in itself. Because why would Lily have thought that an online prankster would have had anything to do with any of this? And hadn't I more-or-less established that *Alexander Cust* had written *The Dog's Ball*?

Second, Lily had telephoned me while I was at Nancy's, presumably to tell me what all this was about. So that bore out the idea that she had given up hating me. But what had changed? Let's say that Lily had, as I had, realized that Tom had inadvertently admitted to knowing Murgatroyd. But then what? Why did it matter?

By this stage, my coffee was cool enough to drink and the sirens seemed to have gone.

Once again, I was faced with a choice: a) throw myself on the mercy of PC Dorothy and assume that everything would come out in the wash? Or b) continue attempting to unmask the murderer myself?

In favour of option b) was that, besides the bad things that other people were trying to pin on me, I had now actively done bad things myself. I had impersonated a school counsellor (while announcing my name to a room full of small children) and run from the police. Turning myself in might work out very badly for me. Also, as a detective, I was mostly incompetent. In favour of option a) was the growing dangerousness of it all. As badly as things might end with the police, by continuing to go it alone I had every chance of ending murdered myself. It was a lose-lose, to be frank.

I didn't know how to decide. Then the phrase that had come to me so insistently as I was first searching Murgatroyd's house drifted back into my brain: *In for a penny, in for a pound; in for a penny, in for a pound.* My subconscious looked as if it had decided for me. Who was I to tell it *no*? I shrugged, got off the torturous stool, and began walking back to Bloomsbury and the Mariposa.

29

When I returned to the hotel, I went back to Google, and resumed my investigation into Tom Cadigan. For a while, things were fruitless. As I have noted before, there was remarkably little of him on the Internet. He was a graphic designer. He worked for Monkshood. He designed things for Arise. Apparently I had given him an expensive flat for one pound. Was there more out there about him and me? Had someone laid a whole trail of his and my corrupt dealings together? I tried '"Tom Cadigan" "Agatha Dorn"' and '"Thomas Cadigan" "Agatha Dorn"'. Nothing except the old stories about *The Dog's Ball*, thank god. I tried 'Lily Cadigan'. There was even less about her than of her husband. I wondered, momentarily, if some of the Mariposa's coffee might help, but decided against it. I wondered about giving up and taking a nap.

Come on, Ag, keep going, said the inner Murgatroyd. *You're about to get somewhere.*

I had a last-gasp idea. I returned to the *Dog's Ball* story in the *Mail* with the tiny picture of Tom Cadigan, the only one I had of him, and grabbed the image. For a man in his hour of triumph, he was grimacing rather. Then I located something that turned out, excruciatingly, to be called *FRIZZ: Facial-Recognition Image-Zearch Zervice* (just typing those madcap Zs caused my stomach to turn over). I ran it with the picture of Cadigan. The first page of results was all pictures of a minor television actor who resembled my gentleman. But, a little way in, there was a picture of what might have been Tom Cadigan himself.

The link was to a page in Reddit: 'r/autographs'. Clicking through brought up a bigger version of the picture. It really did appear to be Cadigan. 'DO NOT BUY AUTOGRAPHS FROM THIS MAN TOM CADOGAN OWNS PENNS IN YORK THEY ARE FAKE', shouted the caption. A blurb had been written by a Reddit user calling himself Mr RegularNoodles. It was dated 2013. The gist of it was in the headline, really: RegularNoodles had purchased a match-day programme autographed by Alan Ball (a famous footballer, apparently) from a memorabilia shop in York. Subsequent investigations revealed that the Portsmouth FC programme on which the signature had been inscribed dated from 2008, the year after Ball died.

Subsequent commenters had continued the theme: 'f— penns evrything they sell is fake', opined one Potatoez. Staxxxr and SOOpi concurred, with a similar degree of forthrightness.

As someone who had been the target of online scorn herself, I instinctively felt sorry for this Cadogan, who had been most likely simply trying to do a day's work for day's pay in the rugged autographed-entertainment-memorabilia business. But then I caught myself.

Was it that easy to disappear? Just change a *single letter* of your dratted name and move twenty miles down the road? It was ludicrous to think of it. And yet that seemed to be precisely what had happened. Why on earth choose such a flimsy alias?

I googled 'Cadigan'. The first listing was not a name at all, but a definition: 'Cadigan: a placeholder word such as *whatchamacallit, thingamajig, yada yada*'. Tom Thingamajig. He had changed his name as a prank, an *eff you* to anyone who might have come looking for him. And he had saddled his kids and his poor lamented wife with a stupid joke for a surname. There was a sick sense of humour at work here.

Returning to Google, I looked for 'Tom Cadogan forger', and the floodgates opened. Well, maybe *floodgates* is a bit strong, but there was certainly a lot more about 'Tom Cadogan' than there had been about Tom Cadigan. The rise and fall of Penn's in York had been dramatic enough to make the regional paper of record. Cadogan had inherited a well-established antique shop from his boss, Mr Penn, and transformed it into a thriving memorabilia outlet. But incidents like the one recounted by Mr RegularNoodles had happened once too often, and Cadogan had been forced to shut up shop. In fact, he had disappeared overnight, apparently without trace, leaving a troop of angry creditors and cheated patrons in his wake. There were more photographs, too, just in case there was the slightest remaining doubt that Cadigan and Cadogan were the same man.

No wonder Cadigan was grimacing in the photo from the *Mail*! I remembered the night of the *Dog's Ball* launch, when he kept disappearing whenever a camera was near. As much as he craved fame, he couldn't allow his picture to get around. It must have been pure torture for him!

I had another brainwave. Since the deflating meeting with Biddy Cust, I had forgotten all about the fake Houdini autograph. It hadn't seemed worth bothering with. But I still had it in my bag, and now a thought struck me. I fished it out, along with my trusty UV penlight. Lo and behold, the paper glowed!

It was late, but I thought it was probably safe to phone up Biddy Cust. If she didn't answer, she was probably out clubbing. But she did answer.

'Mrs Cust?' I said. 'It's Agatha Dorn.'

'Agatha!' she said. 'How wonderful! Did you make your radio programme?'

'Not yet,' I said. 'How have you been?' Here I found myself on the receiving end of a substantial monologue about the glories of late-night fried-chicken shops, which I will spare you. 'Listen,' I said, 'it's about that Houdini autograph.'

'Oh yes,' she said. 'Did you have it analysed? Is it a fake, after all?'

'It is,' I said. 'But I think it might once not have been.' Before she had chance to ask about what on earth I was going on, I jumped in with a follow-up. 'Mrs Cust,' I said, 'let me ask you a couple more quick questions. Are you sure that your father-in-law had the autograph on display in 1913?'

'Well, I wasn't there, dear, but that's what Albert and his mum would say. And the story got told a *lot*.'

'And when you tried to have the signature authenticated the first time, was that after Lily and Tom were married?'

'Oh yes, dear.'

'And did Tom Cadigan know that you had it?'

'Oh yes, he did—it was on the wall of the downstairs toilet, my dear, I think I told you.'

I hung up. If Biddy was right, the autograph in my possession could not have been the one that hung on her father-in-law's wall in 1913—the paper was too new. I looked at it again, trying to gauge how decent a forgery it was. The afternoon light shone through the lounge window and illuminated the paper. And that's when I saw it. The watermark was an image of Harry Houdini doing something disgusting with a grinning Trollface cartoon.

Only one explanation really made sense. Tom Cadigan was art-brute.

Probably should have realized that sooner.

Tom Cadigan—forger, con man, Internet troll; maker of an 'award-winning Facsimile Documents series' for Arise, who had benefited mightily from the exposure of *The Dog's Ball* as a fake.

Suddenly there was a new and extremely clear front-runner in the *Who-wrote-The-Dog's-Ball?* stakes.

My phone rang. An unknown number. Here was a quandary. If I answered it, it could be the police. And what would I say? *Oh yes, I'll gladly come in for an interview, as soon as I come out of hiding, and oh, by the way, yes, that was me impersonating a social worker in order to get access to two minors earlier today.* On the other hand, last time I had neglected to answer the phone, I had missed the news of Lily Cadigan's death. On balance, I thought I might answer.

'Miss Dorn?' said the soldierly voice on the other end.

'Colonel Easterbrook!' I was inexplicably overjoyed to hear from him. Perhaps I was encouraged by the memory of how he seemed to find Murgatroyd's murder to be part of a thrilling game rather than something that was liable to get me imprisoned.

'Have you solved our mystery yet?' he asked.

'I'm working on it,' I replied.

'Well, I have something that might help you. I asked a couple of chums, and I found out some details about your man Richard Fawn. Very nasty piece of work, this Fawn. Dismissed with disgrace about ten years ago. Shot an unarmed Afghani that the redcaps could prove wasn't Taliban. Some talk that he'd shot a few more that they couldn't quite get him on before that, too. You think he brought his murderous ways back home with him, eh?'

'I'm beginning to,' I said.

'Well,' he said. 'Could be. Could be. Hope I've been able to be of assistance. You let me know how it all turns out.'

I assured him that I would.

Suddenly, I felt as if almost all the pieces were in my possession. Murgatroyd investigating *The Dog's Ball*. Ian. Rick Fawn. Arise. Tom Cadigan. All the sides of the Rubik's Cube slotted into place for the first time! I had to be sure about Cadigan, though. I was in enough trouble that I couldn't go to the police without being sure. If he had written *The Dog's Ball*, there was bound to be evidence on that space-age laptop of his. Luckily, I happened to know where he lived.

I bounded down the stairs of the Mariposa—and almost lost my mind. At the reception desk, there, talking to the potato-shaped clerk, was PC Dorothy! How had they found me? Had someone spotted me on my way back from the school—or was it?—I looked down at the mobile phone, which was still in my hand. Had they *tracked* me using it?

Carefully, I left it on the stairs. Then I backed into the breakfast room, where I hoped the large bunting-filled window could be opened. Through the door, I saw Dorothy's feet heading up the stairs. To my room, I presumed.

It looked as if I might be in luck. The window did at least have a sash with a catch. Heading over to it, I tried to push it open. It had a layer of paint on it. It wiggled but did not budge. I tried again, working it back and forth. I had to say, this was not an auspicious beginning for someone about to try to break into her adversary's flat. Suddenly, the old paint gave, and the catch swung around. I heaved, and the window began to rise. Upstairs, I could hear feet heading back towards the stairwell. Dorothy had not found me in. I heaved again. The window did not want to rise high enough to accommodate me! Now the feet were on the stairs! I shoved one more time, with all my strength. The window creaked and opened all the way. I sort of rolled out and landed on the pavement on my feet. As I did so, I saw Dorothy pass by the breakfast-room door again, but, mercifully, she did not look in. I put on a burst of speed and made it (I hoped) around the corner before she came out of the hotel door.

30

My adventure at Ian's house notwithstanding, I was not the kind of person who would have the first idea about breaking into someone else's flat. Now, one might say that I was lucky, since my task for the day was to break into my own erstwhile abode.

On paper, this was what they call a *no-brainer*. If there was cast-iron evidence of Tom Cadigan's guilt in the matter of the forged *Dog's Ball* manuscript, the best place to look was definitely his computer.

However, the more I thought about it, the more impossible the task of getting at the MacBook seemed.

Because I used to live in the flat, I knew that the catch on the bathroom window, which faced the balcony, was broken, and I was willing to bet that Tom Cadigan had not got around to having it fixed. But was it any use having this information? How was I to get onto my former balcony? I tried to imagine myself dressed in black, *Mission: Impossible*-style, rappelling down a rope from the Chesterton Tower roof, or the balcony above. It seemed to me that I lacked the requisite degree of spryness. Plus, if I was going to come down from above, I had to get into the flat upstairs, which, again, how did one do such a thing?

Or could I perhaps get Tom Cadigan out of the flat *with* the laptop, arrange to meet him, and somehow steal it? It seemed unlikely that he would be keen to see me at all, let alone come with incriminating evidence in his possession. Could I get him to think he was meeting someone else? No, this way of thinking was a dead end.

Could I simply go in the front? Another thing I happened to know was that the flat, in my day, had had a puny Yale latch on the door, of the kind that one was given to believe could be pried open with a credit card. Cadigan was sure to have had new keys made, but would he have changed the lock itself? Maybe, maybe not. I filed this option away for further consideration.

The next problem was simply that people in the Gatehouse *knew me*. All right, I had kept myself to myself, but that didn't mean my face wasn't familiar; it didn't mean people weren't aware that I had moved out. Would they know I wasn't supposed to be there? That I didn't belong there? What if I saw Not-Mrs-Hernandez, or one of the others from Sampson the Gelding?

I had two choices. One, I could attempt to disguise myself. In Gladden's books, disguise is easy to pull off, and always a matter of less, rather than more: characters just have to wear clothes they don't usually wear or adopt mannerisms not their own. Ostentatious disguises are invariably red herrings. So, what? I could simply wear Nancy's sweatshirt, if I still had it, or take myself to Debenhams, buy some flowery dress or something I would never wear, then walk down the access deck like whatever was the opposite of an embittered old drunk, and Bob would be my uncle. Or two, I could go as myself and, if I met anyone I knew, tell them I was coming to see Tom, tell them, I don't know, a parcel had been delivered to my old address or something, and that I was coming round to get it.

What would Murgatroyd have done? I thought.

274

This last, I thought, was the path of least resistance. No disguise, no windows, no abseiling; just I and my credit card to jimmy open the lock.

And so, a medium-sized walk later found me heading back to Chesterton Tower. Several police officers were milling about near the entrance to the lifts. Was this just ordinary police milling, or were they looking for me specifically? One looked in my direction but without (I think) seeing me. I ducked back behind a concrete outcrop. How was I going to get up without their seeing me? I looked around for a solution. While there were police officers between me and the lifts, there was none, I noticed, between me and the door to the stairwell. Surely there had to be another solution than hacking up thirty-three flights of stairs! But a few more moments' consideration failed to turn up anything. And so it was with a heavy heart that I traipsed over to the stairwell and began the long climb up to my old floor.

By the time I emerged, I was puffing and plodding. So much for being inconspicuous! I had had to stop several times on the way up for a bit of a sit-down. I cursed myself for not having thought to bring a bottle of water, and also for not having kept up a sensible exercise routine for the last fifteen years. In the old days, anyone stupid enough to sit on the steps faced a game of Russian roulette as to whether or not they were going to find themselves in a patch of partially dried wee. The present occupants, thank the lord, seemed to hold themselves to a higher standard. That was one thing to say for gentrification.

As I made my way down the access deck, the feeling of being watched returned. Probably I was still nervous from seeing the police downstairs. And, I reasoned, it was the uncanny effect produced by returning to an address at which one no longer lives, in this case compounded by the new view from the deck. Although the Neele had not yet moved out, Arise had begun building in the parts of the complex they had already purchased. What had been a grass courtyard surrounded by low-rise apartment buildings now contained a series of giant glass spheres, reinforced with steel beams in hexagonal patterns, in which no doubt Arise employees could imagineer or synergize or whatever it was they did. I felt a little as if I were walking through a parallel universe.

I paused to look down at this weird moonscape.

A hand put itself on my shoulder and pulled me backwards into the stairwell, where no one would see what happened.

It was 1979, and I was seven years old. We had just got home from Fine Fare. I remember the strange lab-coat affairs the cashiers wore. Clara, who never tired of telling us how short we were of money since Dad died, could occasionally be prevailed upon to purchase a pudding of some kind. Only of the most basic sort, however. We could never stretch to Viennetta, or anything else on the silver salvers of the Bird's Eye Sweet Trolley advert that, to the young me, represented the height of sophistication. In the matter of choc ices, only the cheap kind with the thin 'chocolate-flavoured' coating were on the cards.

I must, however, have been given at my friend Julia's house a superior choc ice, with a thick coating of real chocolate that made a satisfying crack when one bit it. And so, on this occasion, I had thrown an explosive tantrum when Clara had reached for the usual box. I wanted the good kind. I lay on the floor and beat my fists and feet on the brown speckled tiles. (As an aside, I remember even at that age wondering why anyone would decorate a food shop with tiles the colour of dirt.)

These antics usually had no effect on Clara, who was made of steel. But she must have got especially little sleep the night before, or some other, more significant battle must have been going on in some other area, and she decided this was not the hill on which to die today. She picked up the superior choc ices, slammed the freezer door, and yanked me up by my collar. Heri, that sneak, looked mortified at my behaviour when Clara was looking, but grinned at me when she was not.

At home, I clamoured for an ice cream immediately. Again, ordinarily this would not have flown, but the main point, the buying of the pudding in the first place, having been conceded, what the heck?

Glorying in my triumph, I unwrapped my prize. (Heri had priggishly refrained, saving his treat for the appropriate after-dinner slot.) I bit down. The real chocolate made the wonderful crack it had at Julia's house. But then—something hard and disgustingly out of place. I spat it into my hand. It was a bone—a grey, spiky chicken bone. Nauseated, retching, and crying, I threw the ice cream and the bone on the floor.

Wicked Agatha! Selfish, ungrateful Agatha! What a waste! What a waste of money we didn't have! The bone could not be found, and Clara dismissed its existence out of hand. I got a smack on the back of my head, cleaned the floor, and was sent to my room. No puddings of any kind were purchased at our house for a long time after that.

Although I would not read about him until many years later, it was at around this time that the abstract concept of the entity

I would eventually know as the Crooked Man began to form in my mind. So it made sense that this was the memory that would flash before my eyes as the Crooked Man pulled me into the stairwell in Chesterton Tower, having finally got me at last.

'Jesus Christ, Agatha! Do you *want* the police to find you?' I was so surprised not to have been murdered that it took me a moment to figure out whose voice it was.

'Ian?' I said. I turned round. He was unshaven and wearing a long-sleeved T-shirt and cargo shorts, but not in bad shape. He looked like he was on his gap year.

'Come on,' he said, and began to jog down the steps. He was in considerably better condition than I was, and had to keep stopping while I caught my breath. 'You want to trigger another burglar alarm? I had a hard enough time keeping it quiet when you broke into *my* house.' I had to admit I hadn't thought of that.

After an age, we reached the bottom of the stairs—I don't think Ian knew there were police watching the lift—I think it just didn't occur to him to take it. We headed out towards Silk Street, and I had a horrible feeling I knew where we were going.

When we reached the door of Sampson the Gelding, Ian produced a key and let us in.

'You have a *key* to this place?' I said. 'God's blood!'

'I've been staying here,' he said. 'It's the most discreet place I could think of.'

'They have—rooms?' I said.

'It's a *club*,' said Ian, as if he didn't understand why I had asked, although it would not have occurred to me in a million years to place Sampson in the same category as those St James's establishments where certain kinds of rich people stay when they are *in town*.

Downstairs was empty. 'D'you want a drink?' Ian asked, heading behind the bar. Without waiting for my answer, he pulled out two glasses and filled them from an oversized bottle of red wine.

'You're not dead then,' I said.

I sat down at a table on one of the white plastic lawn chairs.

'No indeed,' said Ian. 'Here.' Ian joined me and handed me one of the glasses of wine. He took a large swig from the other. There was an awkward silence.

'I'm assuming you're going to tell me what you've been doing all this time,' I said.

'Yes, of course,' said Ian. 'Sorry. I was waiting for you to ask. It seemed rude to just launch into it.'

'Jesus,' I said.

'Right, well,' he began, 'I've been hiding.'

'So it would appear,' I said.

'From a lunatic who works for Sir Ed Ratchett,' he said.

'Would that be a man named Rick Fawn, by any chance?' I asked.

'Yes,' he said. 'You've encountered him, then?' I told him the whole story about Oliver and Tony from Product Management.

'Oh dear—poor Oliver,' he said. 'Still, better than being murdered, I suppose.'

I agreed. 'Shall I tell you what I think has been going on?' I said.

'Be my guest,' said Ian.

'I think that Fawn has been bumping off anyone who knew that the *Dog's Ball* manuscript was a fake. My friend Murgatroyd figured it out, and he killed her. And I think you knew, too.'

'You got me,' he said. 'I did know. But not till after it was too late to do anything about it! Oliver told me, on the night of the launch.'

'Your old college chum,' I said.

'Indeed. You *have* been doing some sleuthing,' he said.

'For a while, I thought you were Arise's man on the inside,' I said. 'Though if that were true, I wasn't sure why Fawn would have killed you. But then it occurred to me that, if there were a plot to take over the Neele by turning it into a national laughing-stock, and if that plot involved murdering people, there were unlikely to be many people who knew about it. Not Oliver, for instance. I couldn't believe he would have gone in for killing middle-aged lesbians. And so, not you, either.'

'Oliver and I had been working together to save the Neele from Arise!' said Ian. 'Oliver didn't really want the Neele to be relocated. His family had been major donors over the years. But, you know, sometimes you have to do things for work, and he got put in charge of trying to buy out the Neele so Arise could put their campus on the site. However, Oliver and I, on the quiet, were really just trying to run the clock out on the whole thing. We thought by the time he had finished giving presentations, we'd have either found a way round it or Sir Ed would have got bored and moved on to something else.

'What changed, though, was that this bruiser Fawn began hanging round the building the whole time—not just Sir Ed's office but lurking anywhere that had anything to do with the Neele takeover. Oliver starts discreetly asking questions, and discovers that someone has gone straight to Sir Ed with a plan to embarrass the Neele by planting a fake manuscript for us to discover and make fools of ourselves.'

Ian's phrasing reminded me of that awkward moment when Ian and Oliver had been whispering together about *The Dog's Ball*'s having 'gone to her head'. That's not what they had been saying, though. They had been saying that someone had 'gone to Sir Ed', with the fake manuscript.

'And who could it have been except this dubious character who had shown up?

'I confess I may have gone a little crazy. I started seeing this Fawn—I thought I was seeing him—hanging around the Neele. And then I got kind of obsessed with the idea that Fawn might have been responsible for all our misfortunes—that he could have been art-brute, who forged the Poe edition—I told Oliver about that.'

So that was why Oliver had decided that Fawn was the forger.

'The more I think about it though, the less sense it makes,' Ian continued. 'For one thing, it's rather hard to imagine that this ex-army hard man is also a forger and an Internet troll. And for another, Ed Ratchett was about to get his compulsory purchase. Why would his own bodyguard mess all that up?'

'Well,' I said. 'I think you may have the wrong end of the stick about some of this.' And I told him all about Tom Cadigan.

'*Cadigan* was—*is*—art-brute,' I concluded, 'freelancing at Arise, making historical facsimiles for the schools project. When he found out the company wanted to buy the Neele, he came up with this scheme to ruin our reputation that was very much in line with his own interests and sense of humour. He must have doubted that the company would give him the go-ahead to do such a thing, so he simply did it. Then he presented it to Sir Ed as a fait accompli and used the company's goodwill to buy himself a plum appointment at head office. Worked out very well for him so far.'

'That does make more sense,' agreed Ian.

'That's why I was trying to get to his flat!' I said. 'Except you stopped me!'

'Ah,' he said, 'I see. You really would have got arrested, though. The police have been keeping very thorough tabs on Cadigan's flat. I know because I was watching too—in case Fawn came back for a little more murdering.

'So what now, Flambeau?' said Ian. 'What's our next move?'

'*Our?*' I said. 'By my count, you knew *The Dog's Ball* was a fake and let me get hung out to dry anyway. You let me believe you were dead *and* that I was going crazy for believing I had burgled you. What makes you think there's an *our* here?'

I got up and began walking towards the stairs.

'Just wait a minute,' he said. 'You blackmailed Fraser Green into publishing the book and giving you royalties without checking its provenance properly. And you did indeed break into my house and destroyed my window in the process. And if I had told you where I was, I would probably be dead right now. So I don't really see that you have the moral high ground. Plus, the police are out there, and I don't believe that you have a plan for what to do next—I certainly don't—so don't you think two heads might be better than one?'

I paused. He made a good point. On the other hand, I was livid, so there was that. On balance, I decided he was right. I came back and sat down at the garden table again. 'Why was there blood in your house?' I asked.

'What?' he said.

'There was a trail of blood—on the stairs.'

'Was there?' he said. 'Oh, right. I got a nosebleed, what with the stress of having to flee for my life. I don't think I took the time to clean it up.'

'A nosebleed!' I said, remembering how I had pictured Ian grievously injured, being dragged over the stairs by a terrible assailant. 'Never mind. So what *is* next?' I said. 'I still think we need to figure out a way to get to Tom Cadigan.'

'That sounds right,' said Ian. 'I just don't see how.'

As it turned out, however, we didn't need to make a plan, because at that moment the street door clanged open and Tom Cadigan appeared at the top of the stairs, holding what appeared to be a bone-handled steak knife.

'Agatha Dorn!' he said.

31

'What did you do to my wife?' said Tom, advancing into the room.

'Well, this is handy,' I said. 'But how—? Didn't we lock—?'

'I spotted you coming over here. And I have a key.' Jesus Christ! How long had Cadigan lived in the Gatehouse? And he already had a key to Sampson?

Tom was holding the knife in our general direction, but he looked like a man who had had no experience menacing people with weapons of any kind. 'Lily's note said to ask Agatha Dorn. Well, I'm asking you. What did you do to her?' His voice was breaking. He may have been a troll, but he appeared genuinely to be distraught at his wife's death.

'Mr Cadigan,' said Ian. 'I think implicating Miss Dorn in your wife's death may have been a piece of misdirection. If you would sit down, I think I could explain it to you.'

Tom Cadigan adopted a mulish expression and remained standing as Ian rehearsed an abbreviated version of the chain of events we had just assembled between us: that Rick Fawn had been responsible for two murders, one victim's having been a friend of mine, and the other's having been Tom's wife Lily. The motive had been the hushing-up of the fact that Arise had condoned Tom's creation of the fake manuscript; something that, had it got out, would have scuppered Sir Ed's spotless reputation, Arise's hopes of acquiring the Neele, and much else besides. Furthermore, Ian added, unless we figured out a way to stop him, Tom, Agatha, and he, Ian, were surely next on the hit list.

'This is assuming we're right,' said Ian, 'that art-brute created the manuscript, and that art-brute is you.'

Tom Cadigan crumbled. 'Oh, Christ!' he said. 'Oh, Christ!' He sat down, put the knife on the table, and held his head in his hands. 'What can we do? What can we do? This guy is a psycho.'

That seemed a decent appraisal of the situation. But as Ian had spoken, a potential solution had formed itself in my head.

'You need to come clean,' I said.

'What?' said Tom.

'You heard me,' I said. 'The murders are all about keeping the secret that Ed Ratchett knew about *The Dog's Ball*. You need to own up. If you own up to it all, there won't be any secret left to keep, will there? Ian, do you have a pen and paper?' He toddled to his bag in the corner and returned with them. 'Write it out,' I said—'"I, Tom Cadigan—also known as art-brute, wrote the fake Gladden Green manuscript *The Dog's Ball* with the full knowledge and coöperation of Sir Edmund Ratchett, in order to better facilitate"—no, wait, that's a split infinitive—better make it just "to facilitate"—"to facilitate Arise's purchase of the Gatehouse Estate."' It was far from the most elegant sentence I had ever composed, but needs must, &c.

'Wait a minute,' said Tom Cadigan. 'Wait a minute. I'm not sure this is called for.'

'Tom!' I cried. 'We are preventing murders here!'

'No,' he said. 'There's got to be another way. I don't admit to anything you just said I did. I don't admit to any of it. I've got to go.'

He stood up and began to back towards the stairs, clearly preparing to make a dash for it, but Ian had realized what was going on more quickly than I and was already moving to block Tom's route to the exit, with Tom's knife in his hand. He looked much more comfortable with it than Cadigan had. Those muscular upper-class upbringings—they taught you to kill things and skin things as a matter of course, I supposed.

'I really think Agatha's is the best course of action for everyone concerned,' he said, pressing the blade into Tom's side. It was a very good job he was here. I would have made a complete hash of all this tough-guy business.

'All right,' said Tom. 'No, you're right. All right. Let's take it easy. I just had a few jitters, all right. You're talking about ruining my whole life here, remember?' He laughed in a way that was supposed to be ingratiating, but merely came across as sad.

He glanced to the left and right, gauging whether he was fast enough to spin away from Ian and make it to the stairs.

'You're much fatter nowadays than when you used to make those videos,' said Ian.

'Yeah, well,' Cadigan said. 'I've let myself go a bit, haven't I? Kids and all. They'll do it to you, won't they?' Ian handed Tom the biro.

'Just under the sentence, if you would?' Tom sighed, paused for a long moment, and slowly signed his name. 'Thank you so much,' said Ian. 'I'll call Mrs De Castina, tell her she can open up again.'

'Of course you couldn't prove any of it any other way,' said Tom with a hint of a smile. 'You have to give me that.'

'No, that is true,' said Ian.

'I don't know,' I said. 'If we compared the inks on the papers Murgatroyd had with all the pens in your flat, I wonder if we'd find a match?'

'Who?' said Tom in a newly urgent voice.

'My friend who was killed.'

'Her name was Murgatroyd?' said Tom.

'Yes, didn't I say? The first one Fawn killed. She was onto this before anyone. She stole a page of the *Dog's Ball* manuscript and another paper. I bet we could match them to something in your flat.'

Tom didn't answer. 'There's one thing about which I'm still confused,' I said to Ian. 'Why did you go and see Dimitra in Camden that day?'

'Right,' he said. 'You were there. I had decided to disappear, but I felt guilty. I wanted to tell someone I thought Arise might be killing people. I'd got as far as discovering that Dimitra was your Murgatroyd's girlfriend, and Oliver said he'd heard she had some kind of family connection to Arise—so I thought, well, she's as good a person as any. It was pretty cowardly of me I—' But Ian never finished his sentence. I span around; there was the steak knife sticking out of his shoulder and Tom Cadigan belting up the stairs.

'Ian!' I shouted as he fell down. The street door slammed shut. There was no point in following Cadigan. He'd disappear into the City crowd in seconds.

'F—!' said Ian, sitting down heavily.

'Are you OK?' I asked, terrified.

'Do I look OK?' he said. 'Everything was fine, and then he just went crazy. It's OK. I think it's OK. It's just oozing. Get my phone, would you? We need to dial 999. Ambulance as well as police, I suppose.'

'I can't call the police, Ian,' I said. 'I'm a murder suspect! I can't let them find me here!'

'You're as bad as Cadigan,' he said. 'But OK, OK, I see your point. Just—help me find something to put pressure on the wound. If we can get the bleeding under control, you can get out of here. Take my phone, call them when you're out of the way, and tell them where to find me.' That seemed like a sensible plan.

'Thanks,' I said. I hunted around for a bar towel and found one. 'OK,' I said, 'how do we do this,' and yanked the knife out of Ian's shoulder.

Ian howled in pain and doubled over. 'Jesus, Agatha! Jesus!' he said between gritted teeth. 'Did you never take a first-aid course? You never pull anything out of a wound!' I put the towel against Ian's shoulder and pressed, but it didn't seem to be having much of an effect. Blood was coming much faster now the knife was out. Ian's shirt, and the towel on top of it, were completely red in what seemed like just a few seconds.

'Agatha!' said Ian in a smaller voice.

'OK,' I panicked, 'OK, OK.' I ran back behind the bar to search for another towel. I filled a brandy balloon from one of the optics as well. I seemed to remember from somewhere that hard liquor came in handy in situations like this, but whether it was supposed to go on the wound or into the person I had forgotten.

When I got back, Ian was white and slumped on the table. Perhaps I shouldn't have wasted time with the brandy.

'Agatha,' gasped Ian. 'Put the towel on the wound. Fold it over. Press *hard*. *Hard*. You must have nicked the artery. I'm going to get worse really, really fast. Put my phone in your other hand. Dial 999. We need a doctor *right now.*'

I thought about it for longer than Ian would have liked. I couldn't be here when the emergency services arrived. I couldn't get arrested and end up in the system—I did not for a moment believe that everything would straighten itself if allowed to run its course.

Then I had an idea. There was a way we could get a doctor on the scene without having to call the ambulance. I released Ian's shoulder for just a moment and dialled a number that was longer than three digits.

32

After everything was cleared up, Heri and I were sitting companionably in his consulting room.

Rather gallantly for him, Heri had agreed to come and dig us out of Sampson with only a small amount of wheedling on my part. He was going, he said grumpily, to have to postpone an operation. But since he did not give two figs for his patients' schedules, this was more about his wounded self-importance than anything else.

When he arrived, Heri's view was that there was in fact no emergency. With my improved towel-holding skills, the bleeding had slowed quickly. Heri superciliously noted that victims of stabbings often faint or feel dizzy; it doesn't mean that they are about to die. He directed us to continue putting pressure on the wound with the tablecloth. I noticed he did not examine Ian too closely himself; he didn't want to get blood on his Turnbull & Asser shirt.

He rather liked the fact that I was wanted by the police, which appealed first, to his sense of adventure and second, to his sense that I was in some essential way reprehensible. Therefore it took little persuasion to convince him to take us to his consulting rooms on Harley Street to deal with Ian.

Once we were there, things seemed much less urgent. Ian consented not to telephone the police until I was out of the picture. Heri made me stay in the waiting room while he did whatever one does with stab wounds—cleaning it, stitching it up, I don't know. Perhaps something involving an intravenous drip? Eventually, however, Ian emerged under his own steam, still in his bloody shirt, pale and wobbly, but with a smile on his face.

'If I were you,' said Heri to Ian, 'I would get to A&E straight away. Make up whatever story you like, but with a deep stab wound like that, you can't be too careful.' I didn't think I had ever seen Heri's bedside manner in action before. He was positively gracious. I hardly recognized him.

Once he had gone, Heri suggested I stay for a drink, noting that he had both gin and water. I was flattered he remembered my tipple, even if I suspected he just wanted to grill me for stories on which he could dine out once my adventures became public knowledge.

'So tell me about this insanity you seem to have got yourself mixed up in,' he said. 'It sounds delicious.' He was on his third scotch by this time.

And so I laid it all out from start to finish. In the beginning, Murgatroyd must somehow have got a hint of Tom Cadigan's dubiousness and decided to find out what she could about this manuscript in whose discovery I was glorying. Why she didn't tell me then I didn't know—maybe she wanted to spare my feelings until she was sure. That explained her disappearing on me too. I supposed it did, anyway. Somehow, Arise got wind of what she was doing—maybe she confronted Tom Cadigan—maybe phoned him—that would explain how he had her number. And Sir Ed Ratchett must have realized that if Cadigan's shenanigans were exposed, that would hurt the company very badly—not only no more campus, maybe no more Arise! And so he must have dispatched his shadiest security bully to fix things up—did he know Fawn was going to kill Murgatroyd? It hardly mattered. Like Harry Lime in *The Third Man*, to someone like Sir Ed, ordinary people were just dots viewed from the top of a Ferris Wheel. And then I started poking around, and so did Lily Cadigan—she must have realized that her husband had as good as owned up to knowing Murgatroyd during my visit to Yorkshire—and at that point Fawn *was in blood stepped insofar*, &c. &c., he might as well just keep going.

Was Fraser Green in on it, I thought? I remembered his little smirk as he gave me my one per cent of the royalties. On its face, the *Dog's Ball* scandal was terrible for the Green brand. But everyone had spent the last year talking about Gladden Green one way or another. And he had made millions from *The Dog's Ball*, fake or not. If Fraser Green could have been brought on board, that would have been all to the good for Tom Cadigan. I wondered...

'Why do you think Cadogan did a runner?' said Heri. He was on his fourth whisky and getting loquacious. I had only had half my gin and water but felt tired half to death. The adrenaline of the day had worn off, and I suddenly wanted quite badly to go home.

'Who knows?' I said. 'He was a narcissist and a sociopath almost—maybe he just couldn't bear the thought of public disgrace?'

'Fascinating. It's like a dreadful film or something. I shall enjoy being related to the protagonist. And this fellow Fawn, he dressed up as your childhood terror, the Crooked Man, to do these murders? Why on earth would he do that, do you suppose?'

That did seem a bit odd, now that I thought about it. How would he have known? Well, Arise's tentacles reached into every corner of our lives, I supposed. One had no secrets from them. And it fit nicely with the Crooked Man's rôle in *The Dog's Ball*—muddying waters and so forth.

'Arise,' said Heri. 'There's a company that went further than I thought it would. I knew them in the early days. Well, Aristide Leonides, really. He was the money. But Ed Ratchett was the brains, and he worked like a dog. But they never were quite straight, were they?' He said it as if the early days of Arise was a subject on which one could expect everyone, even me, to be well informed. I hated it when people (i.e. Heri) did that. He went on: 'I did an IHR—that's an Inguinal Hernia Repair to a pleb like you—on Leonides, back when I still wielded the scalpel myself. Metaphorically of course. It's laparoscopic.'

I had spent all this time thinking about Arise over the last year or so, and I had entirely forgotten that the company was named for two people, not just one, so synonymous was it these days with Sir Ed's photogenic face and ubiquitous public presence. Was Aristide Leonides even still around? I wondered drowsily. He was dead, wasn't he? When had that happened?

'Nineteen ninety-seven,' said Heri, as if reading my thoughts, 'Aristide died.'

A horrid thought came into my head. *997 IHR, Aris–*. From the paper in Murgatroyd's house. IHR. What if it didn't stand for Ian Harcourt-Reilly? What if it stood for Inguinal Hernia Repair? Nothing to do with the Neele. Part of one of Heri's medical records. Why the page of *The Dog's Ball* then? Because Murgatroyd hadn't wanted to prove that the manuscript was a fake: she had wanted to prove that the same forger had written both things.

It was about Heri. Forgeries that Heri must have commissioned from Tom Cadogan way back when. Right about when Aristide Leonides had died.

Q: how did the Neele and *The Dog's Ball* tie in?

A: (I suddenly realized) There was no need for them to tie in at all. They didn't tie in. It was a mere fluke of circumstances that made it appear as if they did.

These thoughts drifted lazily around my head. I felt as if I were dreaming it, I was so tired. I could just let it all lie, I supposed. It would be so easy just to drift off. But I didn't. I had to say something.

'What year did you operate on Aristide Leonides, Heri?' I asked.

'Ninety-seven. Same year. Lord, the booze does turn me into a blabbermouth.' He was leaning on the back legs of his chair, tie undone, staring at the ceiling. 1997. The same year Heri bought me my flat. Wasn't it also the same year he was rumoured to be in some kind of trouble?

'Heri, did you know Tom Cadigan before the book launch?'

'I did, as a matter of fact. Wasn't his name then, though. Used to spell his name differently. Forger. But then you knew that. Did odd jobs for Aristide—amending financial records, that kind of thing. That's how he got in with that mob. That's how I met him as well.'

'Heri,' I asked. 'Did you *kill* Aristide Leonides?'

He settled his chair back on four legs and looked me in the eyes, suddenly as alert as a leopard. 'I was wondering when you'd catch on,' he said. 'I think I'll have another,' he said, reaching for the decanter. 'It's only coloured water, after all. You, by contrast, have a couple of temazepam mixed in with your stupid watery gin.' He stood and picked something up from the counter on the far side of the room, then walked towards me. 'But look, if you want the whole story, you can read it all right here.' He dropped in my lap a purple journal made for tweenage girls, with SECRETS BOOK embossed on the front. The lock had been wrenched off. I opened it. It was blank. Nothing was written on any of the pages. That termagant Murgatroyd had never written anything about me in there at all!

'Here,' said Heri, turning to the back of the book. There was a letter tucked between the last page and the back cover.

'These f—ing Dorns!' Murgatroyd had said to Dimitra. I had assumed she meant me and Clara. But she had nothing against Clara. She meant me and *Heri*.

I wanted to open the Secrets Book, but my hands didn't seem to want to work. Heri did it for me. 'Dear Ag,' I read. I tried to make it to the next line, but the words swam and span away from me, and then faded into darkness with the rest of the room.

33

I know that in the past I have rather luxuriated in the idea of foreboding. But over the last months, I have come to realize that there's something childish and self-indulgent about that kind of misery. There's a kind of Gothic sublime pleasure, which I have refused to acknowledge, in the notion that something terrible is always about to happen.

These actual thriller-type things that keep happening—they are not me at all. This B-movie stuff—well, I hardly know how to act. I don't have the etiquette down at all.

I think this as I wake up, again, unable to move.

Oh no. I can see the glint of the Crooked Man's eyes again in the darkness. This time, though, it's not that my limbs don't work. Rather, there is an unpleasant cutting sensation at my ankles and, especially, my wrists. I think I may be tied to a chair.

Also, I both must and cannot close my mouth. My jaw seems clamped tight. Not my lips, though. Something cold, hard, and painful is digging into my gums and pulling my lips back from my teeth.

The Crooked Man glides forward.

'It's called a dental gag. For oral surgery. American. It was very expensive, actually,' says the Crooked Man with Heri's voice.

Heri! I try to say, though I can't do it very well with my lips the way they are.

'It works on a ratchet. Ironically,' he says, and steps closer. I wanted to shout at him that this was not, in fact, ironic. 'That means it's very easy for me to make the aperture bigger—' He puts the gloved hand I remember from the episode with the tissues up somewhere near my mouth—'but impossible for you to make it smaller.' He squeezes some little dingus, the ratchet clicks, and the pain in my gums becomes worse. I think the flesh is about to tear.

'Were you attempting to say my name?' he asks. 'Yes. It's me. One is supposed to say "It is I", but I always think that sounds silly, don't you? No, I don't suppose you do, with your grammar fixation?'

He steps back, and fiddles around some more. A blue flame lights in the darkness. Its shape and sound immediately take me back to school lab benches and orange rubber tubing. A Bunsen burner. The flame lights the room a little. Familiar. I think we are still in the consulting room on Harley Street. Heri raises the horrible stump, the Crooked Man's calling card—and takes it off. His other hand, ungloved, emerges from the sleeve.

'Like the disguise?' he says. 'I wore it just for you.'

He picks up a little jar of something and waves it over the flame, like he's warming brandy. I expect him to go on with his spiel, but he does not. A tarry, waxy smell rises into the room, presumably from the little jar. It's familiar, mostly from childhood. Shoe polish. What does he want with shoe polish?

After a moment of heating the polish, he steps forward. Presumably it has attained whatever consistency he has desired. He walks forward until he reaches me. What horror is coming? Will it involve a scalpel? Whatever I think of in the couple of seconds before he acts, it bears no resemblance to what happens. Heri produces a paintbrush from his pocket, dips it in the polish, and begins to paint it onto my teeth. *Paint, paint, paint.*

Heri is silent while he paints. Unable to move my mouth as I am, I find myself lulled into a kind of trance by his performance.

'You must, I suppose, be wondering what this has to do with *that*,' he says, gesturing over his shoulder. The flame lights the room sufficiently well now, and my eyes have adjusted, such that I can make out the candy stripes of a birthday-balloon helium canister. 'Is there some kind of sedative in the polish? Is this how I managed to get the hood on your Murgatroyd, and that other one, Cadigan?' He looked at me as if I were going to prompt him, then remembered. 'Oh, right.

'Well, I regret to tell you that the answer is, nothing. It is simply that I once had a uniquely horrid dream in which I found myself unable to move, while a malevolent being painted my teeth with black shoe polish, and, since then, I have always fancied trying it in real life. On somebody else, I mean. Is it in fact uniquely horrid?' He waits as if for me to speak, again. 'Oh, *right*.'

The sight of the helium canister knocks me out of my trance. Is my brother—my brother is—going to kill me. My *brother* killed Murgatroyd and Lily Cadigan.

The shoe polish is oozing between my clenched teeth and into my mouth. I feel sick. I don't want to swallow it. God knows what's in it. But I can't spit it out, either. *Paint, paint*, goes Heri.

'I've always liked this sort of thing. Those boys at school who used to beat me up. But here I am, getting the last laugh. There's a nice circularity to all this—since you both were my first subject and will be my last. The obscene phone calls. The famous incidents with the razor blade in the apple. The bone in the choc ice. A few others I don't know if you even remember. There was a boy at school who sold Ecstasy. He had been one of my bullies, until I started paying him for drugs. I used to put a bit in the milk you drank before bed because I heard it caused night terrors. No idea if it worked or not. I think that was when it first struck me that medicine was my calling. Of course, the boy who sold it to me was tragically found to have taken a bad pill from his own supply and died.'

Now that I thought about it, I vaguely remember that cautionary tale from school. *Don't do drugs, kids*, they told us in a special assembly. *You'll end up like*—but remembering his name was a step beyond me.

I'm right here with you, the voice in the obscene calls used to say, *I'm in the room*. And so he had been.

'Then, later, I had to find new material. So a few of my groin clients would wake up to find themselves with testicular pain, or lame, or impotent, for instance—*Oh, what a terrible mishap*—*It is always a possibility that such a thing can happen with this kind of surgery, as we discussed*—*There are therapies, of course*. Not too many, though. One had a reputation to uphold.

'And occasionally I'd allow myself the luxury of a little murder on the table. Aristide Leonides in ninety-seven.

'Couldn't do too many like that. Shouldn't have done Leonides. Only because he used to laugh at me for being new money. And him a b—y Greek and a crook whose father owned a f—ing kebab van! Stupid of me, though. Deaths in theatre get scrutinized—coroners, post-mortems, all that sort of thing. Got Leonides's own little minion, Cadogan, to doctor the records. Still cost me a packet to hush it up with the family though And had to divest a lot more, too, in case they sued me. Had to buy you that f—ing flat that made you so big-headed. And his sister with debts out the wazoo—didn't cost me much to get her to sign an NDA.'

Having had little experience with psychopaths until now— or, at least, that was what I had believed—I would have been sceptical, if you had asked me, about murderers' supposed tendency to unburden themselves in detail before dispatching their final victim. However, here we were. As I said, I had no idea about the etiquette of situations like these. Of course, it had occurred to me that, since Heri was giving me the full history of his misdeeds, and since there was a canister of helium standing in the corner of the room, his plan likely did not involve my leaving the room alive.

'I apologize for boring you with all this,' he said, as if reading my thoughts. 'One frustrating thing about committing a series of wonderful crimes is having no one to revel in one's success with.' Was he ending the sentence with a preposition in order deliberately to annoy me, I wondered, or did he simply not care? 'But that's what family is for, I suppose.

'In any case, I hope you'll indulge me,' he continued. 'I imagine you'll want to know why I have ended up having to murder you as well. Despite everything, I respect you enough not to kill you merely on a whim. Maybe *respect* is a bit strong. I did enjoy your getting so excited about your little book project and not telling you it was a con. But, you know, blood thicker than water and all that. On which note, I must have told Tom Cadogan back in the day about your whole Crooked Man obsession. Very clever of him to put the character in his book for you. I imagine that would have made you even keener to believe in it.

'I did try to warn you off, you may remember, with that little midnight visit—that was a curare derivative I've been working with. Temporary paralysis. No one's seen anything like it.'

Heri is warming to his theme now. He's always been full of himself. I suppose, it turns out, because he is a sociopath. Who'd have thought? Well, hindsight's always twenty-twenty. But his bloviating gives me a second to think. I wiggle my hands a bit, and they collide with something hard. It's the bone-handled steak knife I pulled out of Ian's shoulder. I attempt to poke it towards the opening of my greatcoat pocket.

'But so, would you believe it, your sapphic friend Amy Murgatroyd begins an affair with none other than Leonides's estranged sister Dimitra and starts dredging the whole d—d thing up again. Gets herself all the way to Tom Cadogan. Easy enough to fake up a little suicide. Though I f—ed it up a bit, as you noticed. Gave her a little more of the curare than you had, shut her lungs down, then rigged her up with that suicide kit. Should have actually killed her with the f—ing helium, I'd have been home and dry. I can't tell you how many times I have kicked myself.'

Dimitra! Murgatroyd's perennially impoverished girlfriend was the billionaire Aristide Leonides's sister? That one was a surprise.

'Then you start digging into the whole thing! Breaking and entering!'

I remember the phone call from the Crooked Man. How on earth had Heri known? 'I cloned your phone,' he said. 'Which is scandalously simple. And an easy means of keeping tabs on someone.'

'And so *then*, thanks to your refusal to stop poking your b—y nose in, Cadogan's wife starts sniffing about as well. He's a b—y fool, can't tell a lie to save his life. Tries to call Murgatroyd on her mobile four months after she died, so I have to clear that up. Then I have to take care of the wife as well.'

The tip of the knife handle is almost at the edge of my pocket. My fingers stretch and stretch to get purchase on it.

'So by now these perfect crimes are getting less perfect by the minute. The second suicide is barely convincing at all. All in all, I think it's best if I disappear. It's getting a bit hairy, the murdering life. You need to disappear too, Sis. The difference is, I am going to disappear to—well, I'm thinking about the UAE—no extradition treaty, and lots of rich expats to pay for expensive doctors. But *you* are going to decide to end it all in despair as you realize your conspiracy with Tom Cadogan is going to come out—the flat you gave him in return for making you a celebrity, and so forth. Which is pretty plausible, frankly. I'll rub the shoe polish off before they find you.'

While he was doing this last bit, Heri was padding over to the suicide kit in the corner of the room. That gave me some time to work with the knife. I had a grip on the end of it now—the sharp end, unfortunately. I was going to have to transfer my grip to the handle without dropping the blooming thing on the floor, which was considerably easier said than done, especially since I had the sweaty hands of the mortally afraid, as well as the confirmed geek's utter lack of coördination.

Heri started heading back my way, lugging the cylinder and the hood. I was gratified to see that he looked extremely ungainly trying to move the helium canister. At least he couldn't do everything stylishly.

I made to turn the knife on its end, so I could hold the handle, and use the blade to cut what I hoped was a rope, or a cable tie, or something else cuttable that was holding my wrists. It felt as if knife was going to spin out of my hand and onto the floor, but I got it under control, and worked it with my fingers to get it into position behind my bonds, between my wrists.

'Now, here we go,' said Heri, who was once again right in my face. He undid the dental gag and put the suicide hood—more of a plastic bag really, over my head, then gathered it at my throat and held it with his forearm while he rolled out a length of gaffer tape, then wound it around my neck to hold the bag in place. How many breaths did I have left, did I suppose? I waited for panic to set in, at which point I would breathe in wildly, drop the knife, and the game would be all over. But, like a miracle, it held off.

Heri peered into my eyes. 'Are you afraid? I think you are. I think you are,' he said. 'Don't worry, we'll turn on the helium in a while. It's supposed to be quite pleasant.' I sawed at something with the knife. After a moment, a wet feeling on my hands told me I had cut into my own wrist. Well, at least the knife was sharp!

Heri turned around and twisted the valve on the canister. The bag, which had been tight against my face from the vacuum my breath had made, filled up again. I tried not to breathe in. I sawed again with the knife. My hands got no wetter, which I took to be a good sign. Then I did take a breath. I couldn't help myself. My stomach sank as my lungs realized they couldn't do anything with the gas I had just delivered to them. This was the moment at which one's life was supposed to flash before one's eyes. It didn't, though. It was just adrenaline, the darkness, the plastic bag on my head, and the knife in my hands.

'So,' said Heri. 'I'm going to make a cup of tea. I expect you'll be dead when I get back. Bye-bye, et cetera.' He turned away and walked a step.

Then he turned back. He looked at the floor under me, at what must have been a bit of a puddle by now.

'Are you—bleeding?' he said.

I wrenched my hands from behind my back. Before Heri could react, I ripped the hood off my head. He stood in front of me, gaping, rather appropriately, like an asphyxiating fish.

Heri, I want you to know that what I am about to do is completely out of character, I attempted to shout. It came out all high, from the helium. Heri stopped for a moment, then burst out laughing. Then I stabbed him in the side of the neck.

People don't die all that quickly, I know that. But my experience of Heri's dying was like when people have sex in old films: they go to kiss, it fades out, and when it fades back in it's all done and everyone's happy. Not remotely like my own efforts, incidentally. But I digress. After I stabbed Heri, everything also seemed to fade out around me, and when it faded back in, it was all over. He was lying on the floor and there was blood everywhere. Really a lot of it. Just loads. Everywhere. Not like Gladden would have one believe.

I had killed my own brother. Worse, I didn't seem to feel any particular way about it.

Shh, said Murgatroyd. *You're in shock. Of course you don't feel anything.*

Are you sure I'm not a sociopath? I asked.

Maybe a little bit, she said. *But I think you're redeemable.*

I was sitting with my legs still tied to the chair. I had got as far as getting the gag thing off completely and wiping my shoe-polishy mouth. I could have cut through the leg cable ties (it was cable ties), I supposed, but somehow I didn't have it in me. I didn't know how I was going to get from here to whatever was the next thing. I didn't know how I was going to do anything again. So I decided to continue having a bit of a sit-down.

There was a splintery thump on the consulting-room door and it burst open.

PC Dorothy sprang in, followed by a gaggle of *Sturmtruppen* with guns and those helmets with the oversized goggles. 'Agatha Dorn, you are under arrest on suspicion of the murders of Amy Murgatroyd and Lily Cadigan,' said Dorothy. She looked at her feet, which were in a puddle of blood, and followed the stream with her eyes across the room to Heri's corpse. 'And this man as well,' she added. 'You do not have to say anything, but it may harm your defence if you do not mention when questioned something which you later rely on in court. Anything you do say may be given in evidence.' I had always wanted to have someone say that to me. Although, in reality, the game isn't worth the candle.

34

For the second time in less than a year, I was a public figure.

How could I not have been, really? It became clear quite swiftly that I had murdered neither Murgatroyd nor Lily Cadigan. Biddy Cust was able to attest that I was chatting with her about *Bergerac* at the time Lily was killed. In addition, as luck would have it, I happened to have been in an All Bar One (why?), where my credit card number was still stored in the computer system, on the night of Murgatroyd's death. Less fortunately, I had in fact killed my brother and, to the untrained eye, it looked as if I had brought a sharp knife with me for the purpose.

Given the circumstances, it seemed clear enough I had acted in self-defence; there were still traces of temazepam in both my system and the glass, and they had after all found me secured to the chair with cable ties. However, it is not the job of the police but the courts, they informed me, to determine what constitutes *reasonable force* when it comes to claims of self-defence, and so I was charged with Heri's manslaughter. Even the expensive lawyer Ian procured for me couldn't stop that—although he did manage to get me released on bail.

From Palmers Green, I watched the saga play out. The police picked up Tom Cadigan without too much trouble and he, so rattled by the whole business that he had run out of front, confirmed the story Ian and I were telling about *The Dog's Ball*. He had attacked Ian and run only when he realized I had connected him with Murgatroyd, who was linked not with *The Dog's Ball* but with a much more serious crime.

You did it, said internal Murgatroyd. *You figured it all out.*

No thanks to you, I said. *You didn't tell me anything.*

How could I? she said. *I'm in your head. I'm proud of you, though.*

Well, that's something, I suppose, I said.

Sir Ed hung Rick Fawn out to dry, claiming he was a loose cannon who had acted entirely on his own, and even managed to put over the story that Arise had known nothing about the forgery until well after the fact. Remembering Sir Ed's turn as the Crooked Man on the occasion I met him, I found this highly unlikely. In any case, Arise succeeded in hanging on to the Neele. It is, I believe, now home to the London end of their legal department, so I'm sure Oliver feels quite at home. When additional investigation confirmed that Heri had been quite truthful regarding his criminal history, public sympathy for Sir Ed, whose beloved business partner had been cut down in his prime, increased still further.

I was much in demand with the fourth estate to tell my side of the lurid story, but I stayed in Murgatroyd's house with the curtains drawn, letting in only my solicitor and the people who delivered supplies.

I did venture out of the house to visit Clara, who was, the nurse Mabel Palmer told me, fading fast.

'I killed Heri, did you hear?' I said. I thought I'd open with the big news. Clara was lying in bed, under the covers.

'What?' mumbled Clara weakly and turned to the nurse. 'Who is this?'

'It's your daughter, Mrs Dorn,' she said.

Clara looked unsure, but seemed to acquiesce. 'Heri's doing very well for himself,' she said.

'Not any more,' I said. 'I stabbed him in the neck with a steak knife.'

Clara looked to Mabel Palmer again. 'Who is this person? Why is she saying these awful things?'

'It's your daughter Agatha,' said Mabel, looking pointedly at me. 'I'm not sure why she's saying these things though.' Mabel doubtless knew all about my stabbing Heri. I could just imagine her poring over the newspapers, breathlessly telling her cronies she knew the family. But she must have thought Clara deserved to be spared.

'Could I have a minute with her?' I said to Mabel. She looked unsure, but left the room.

I was about to go on where I had left off, give the old bag all the gory details. But something stopped me. She looked so pathetic, lying there. Somehow the cruelty didn't seem worth it. Instead I said, 'I think you find Agatha difficult, don't you?'

'Well,' said Clara, rallying a little, 'she *is* difficult. Always malcontent. Ever since she was a child. Making things up to get attention. And when she grew up. Nothing was ever good enough. Never made anything of herself. Chip on her shoulder. That's Agatha.'

I wanted to shout that I had never made those things up—Heri had terrorized me. But, from another point of view, Clara was right. I *was* a malcontent. Nancy had said something similar while I was staying with her. Things were never right with me. It was quite an astute observation—for a woman with dementia.

'Did you love Agatha?' I asked. 'When she was growing up?'

'What a question!' said Clara haltingly. 'I was busy. I was a widow with two children: one who got beaten on the playground every day, the other who made up stories. It was difficult. But I did my duty by them. I kept a roof over their heads and food on the table. I did my duty to my children. Love would have been extra. I didn't have time or energy for extra. But no one can accuse me of not having done right by them.'

'But you loved Heri,' I said.

'He was easy to love,' she said. 'In the beginning, he was a sad little boy and later he did so well for himself.'

'He was a psychopath,' I said.

'You must be thinking of someone else,' she said and closed her eyes.

I didn't know what to say to that, so I sat silently for a while. After a few moments, Clara's breathing got heavy; she was asleep.

'I killed my brother, Clara,' I said. 'I had to do it. He was going to kill me. He'd killed other people. At least three, probably more. He killed Murgatroyd—you realize that? Murgatroyd, the daughter you never had. But I killed him. I suppose I was hoping you could help me figure out how to feel about that.'

Clara let out a snore.

Although I had given my mobile number to very few people, it appeared to have got around a bit, most likely thanks either to Nancy or to Hattie Reedburn. The producer of *The Lost Green* restarted the project as a true crime documentary; I refused to coöperate. Nora Blackborow said she could get me a six-figure advance for a memoir. I found, however, that I didn't fancy doing anything like that at all.

One day, a small box arrived, wrapped in a tasteful candy-striped ribbon. Inside was a single whisky miniature and a note that read: 'Want to record some more pods?' I did not, but I phoned Nancy.

'Agatha,' she said, 'I didn't know if you'd call.'

'Well, here I am,' I said.

'Listen,' said Nancy, 'I hope you know I never really thought you were an alcoholic old hag. It was just—I was just going with the flow.'

'But I was an alcoholic old hag,' I said.

Nancy audibly smirked. 'You know what I mean. I just mean, I'm sorry. I'm really very sorry.'

'Thank you,' I said, finding that I meant it.

When I saw a newspaper, I found that I was often featured somewhere in it. Strangely, this left me cold. The media attention was good for one thing, though. Under normal circumstances, someone who had killed their brother might well have had to undergo the rigours of a criminal trial in order to determine whether or not they had really been justified in doing so. In my case, however, the court of public opinion had already so loudly—and, as it happened, correctly—declared my innocence that the Crown Prosecution Service did not want to risk the embarrassment of a courtroom. They dropped the charge.

Soon after, Clara died from complications related to her dementia, which was probably best all around. I don't think she had much of a sense of what had happened to either Heri or me. I did not attend her funeral, reasoning that I did not want to lead a pack of paparazzi to such an event, though I did a more diligent and punctual job of administering her affairs than I had with Murgatroyd. Having wanted entirely to destroy my roots there for most of my life, I also thereby inherited a second house in Palmers Green.

When the hullabaloo had died down, I sold both houses and paid Murgatroyd's debts, as well as my solicitor's bill. Having dispensed with the services of Clara's nurse, I found that there was actually a decent amount of money left over from the proceeds of the two Palmers Green properties and the Gatehouse flat. I kept a bit, to get myself back on my feet till I found a job, then I went to see Dimitra.

Gee-Haw looked the same as always. I averted my eyes from a display of penis-shaped pasta and turned to the till, where I found Dimitra. For a moment, she looked as if she were going to tell me off as usual, but then her features softened. She had read the newspapers. Maybe she thought I'd been through enough. We exchanged pleasantries for a moment, then she asked, 'But really, what can I do for you, Agatha?'

I wondered briefly what she could do for me. What did I want that Dimitra had? Did I want to know whether Murgatroyd had been in love with me, whatever that meant? Did I want some kind of absolution for the feelings that I seemed to have retained, in my repressed and selfish way, for Murgatroyd? Did I want Dimitra to forgive me for having solved the mystery of Murg's death? In the end, I didn't think Dimitra could give me any of those things.

'Dimitra, did Murgatroyd want to close down Gee-Haw?' I asked.

'I don't think she knew what she wanted, near the end,' she said, with unusual tenderness. 'Not telling me about the cancer. Leaving everything to you. I think she wanted to spare me the pain of her dying and everything that would go with it. Beyond that, I don't think she was thinking very logically.'

At the end of the meeting, I told Dimitra I was giving her the rest of Murg's estate, to pay off her creditors and keep the business going. I reasoned that she wanted the money more than I did.

Oh, and I should probably show you the letter Murgatroyd wrote to me, that she had concealed in the Secrets Book. The police gave it back to me, eventually. I imagine you're curious:

Dear Ag—

You're not to worry about me. I may have had a few cider and blacks, but it's the truth, all right? I can imagine what you're thinking right now—*if you must drink that swill, it's ciders and black, not cider and blacks!* The main reason I have waited until I am about to die to try any of this is that it doesn't really matter what happens to me at this point, does it?

But I wanted to write to you for two reasons. First, I'm (almost) definitely being paranoid, but I think it's just possible that something might happen to me before I can finish what I'm doing. The Colonel has put the wind up me a little bit. And second, I'm afraid that you are being made a fool of. Either that or—and I don't really think this for a minute—the darkest timeline!—that you are deliberately involved in all this mess somehow. But as I say I don't really think that for a moment.

I can't really think of the best way to tell this, so I will just tell it from the beginning and if it goes on too long, you can skip ahead to the good bits.

Now not long after I met Dimitra, I discovered that she was the sister of Aristide Leonides, the billionaire. The fucking billionaire, mind.

Rather like Biddy Cust, I have decided that my principled stand against bad language might in fact be a mere prejudice.

She never mentioned it, never. She went by the surname Leonard. Though she stayed close to Sir Ed, for some reason. But that's by the by.

I remembered the glimpse I had caught of the woman I had thought was Dimitra—rightly, it turns out—hugging Sir Ed at the Arise building.

She and her brother had fallen out, and he had written her out of his will. Would have been rather easier for me had he not, but there you go. But also, you may remember that Aristide Leonides died during a hernia operation performed by your brother Heri. As you know, I have never much liked Heri. I always had him down as a sadist. So it struck me as especially suspicious when I found out that Heri's practice had apparently paid Dimitra quite a lot of money to sign a non-disclosure agreement regarding the circumstances of her brother's death.

Dimitra had taken the money and let herself forget all about it. I wanted her to pick it up again, try to uncover evidence against Heri. She didn't want to do that. She had her money. She wasn't going to put that at risk, and she didn't see why I cared about it at all.

But she didn't know Heri like I did. Not that I really knew him—you two hardly socialized—but I had met him a few times. Do you remember when he came to dinner that time, right around when he was buying you the flat—which I now have terrible doubts about—but meaningless ones, meaningless I'm certain! And he sat there, as if he was talking about the weather or something—asking me, *What childhood trauma do you think caused you to become a queer, Amy?*—and at the same time he's cutting neat little slices off the tofu I made, and each time he would bring a slice up to his mouth, look at it like it had a bad smell, and put it down on the side of his plate. By the end of dinner he hasn't said one thing openly about the food, but he has a pile of neat little slices of tofu on one side of his plate.

I started digging around. There turn out to be medical malpractice chat boards on the Internet, and Heri's name came up a lot. There were men who claimed they woke up impotent after Heri worked on their hernias. More than one person who got what they call faecal fistulas—shit literally coming out of their skin! These are all complications that can happen with groin surgery, but there seemed to be an *awful lot* of them. And Heri was a really good surgeon, who shouldn't have been making these mistakes. Was he doing it deliberately? I didn't know. Paranoid, paranoid. But I just didn't *like* him, you know? He gave me the creeps.

That was as far as it was going to go. But then I got diagnosed. Three months to live, like I told you. And I thought, forget about Dimitra's NDA and her money. This is right and wrong here. And anyway, *I* didn't sign a non-disclosure agreement!

So here's what I did. I went to Heri's surgery. Sorry, his offices. If you're a fancy doctor, you don't call it a surgery. There was a big filing cabinet behind the receptionist's desk. I had no idea if it contained Leonides's records, but I thought it was worth a try. I noticed a pot of coffee in the corner. I asked the receptionist if I might have a cup, and when she pointed at the carafe, I asked if there was any way I might be able to have a fresh one. Surgeries as expensive as Heri's don't say no to that kind of request, so off she went to make it for me.

Although I hadn't really made a plan, it all turned out to be very easy. The filing cabinet was unlocked, and the file was there. So I stuffed it in my bag. It's incredible how few precautions people take, really. Then, back came the receptionist, and I drank my coffee and then, off I went to have myself diagnosed and to be told there was no evidence of a hernia. No one noticed I had pancreatic cancer, either, which makes me wonder about the value of private physicians. No sign of your brother anywhere in the place.

So now I had the file—the paperwork that Leonides had supposedly filled out. It was all a bit dodgy looking. There were consent forms, notes about consultations, all looking like they had been written with the same pen on the same paper.

Through the message boards, I was able to get hold of copies of Heri's business accounts, all illegally obtained, no doubt. Looking at the time around Leonides's death, I found a single payment of £5,000, which had been made a few days after the operation, to a man named Tom Cadogan.

He is a forger who lived in York, and was surely, *surely*, I felt certain, the man who fabricated the medical records. I thought, *If I can find this guy, the jig's up!* And as I continued looking, I discovered he had moved to Harrogate with a rather brazen new name.

Now, I am afraid, I have been cowardly. For if you have not guessed, Tom Cadogan is Tom Cadigan, who has recently turned up as custodian of the Gladden Green manuscript you have been working on.

I'm very afraid, you'll be able to guess, that the Green book is a fraud, written by Cadogan/Cadigan. Is Heri playing some nasty prank on you with this or something?? If I'm right, I'm so sorry. I'm going to see if I can pinch a scrap of the Green and get it compared with one of the papers from the file. See if the writing is the same. Or maybe he used the same pen, or something.

You'll tell me I ought to have told you this as soon as I found out, and I probably should. I could have spared you the humiliation, but I don't think I could have avoided that—it'd already gone too far. And besides, I had three reasons not to. First, I want to contact Cadigan. Maybe I can use the manuscript against him—not expose him as a forger if he goes to the police about Leonides, something like that? And second—there's still a chance the manuscript is genuine, and I don't want to ruin it for you. You've been so happy since this all started—happier than I've ever known you. All the attention, all the recognition. That's not very flattering to me, is it, now I think about it? But I don't want to rob you of it until I'm sure—because of that, I hope very much that I'm wrong.

And three—the one I hope isn't true! I hope, Ag, you didn't know about any of this?—I hope to god he wasn't buying you off somehow with that flat in the Gatehouse—he bought it you the year Leonides died, you know? I hope you don't. I hope to god you and him didn't deliberately cook up this fake novel with his old forging buddy for some stupid reason or other.

So there it is. My lurid imagination, eh?

But is it? I think it is, I think it is. The Colonel keeps saying there's someone hanging round the house. But I strongly suspect he's imagining it. I'm sure he loves the thought of derring-do. Also I'm not certain his eyes are what they used to be, honestly. But if he's right? He's not, but if he is?

So I'm half drunk and I'm writing this as an absurd little insurance policy. The consolation for me is that none of this will be a surprise unless I turn out to have been right in the worst way, and there really is someone out to get me. Just because you're paranoid doesn't mean they aren't after you, eh? As you'll realize when you find it, I've left this in the first place you'll look, if I know you!

Lots of love (No really. You need it),

MURG

That was that, then. No loose ends left to tie up. Except maybe one.

I had been sending out CVs for several months, and my slush fund was showing signs of running dry, when I got a phone call. It was an area code I didn't recognize—a sure sign of spam. But a minute or so later, the phone binged to say I had a voicemail. It was a voice I hadn't heard in a while: Ian. I called him back.

'Where the blazes are you phoning from?' I asked.

'Sunningdale. That's where we live now, remember?' *We* was the Neele—the new Neele, all metal and glass. The Steel Neele.

'How are you?' I asked. We caught up for a while. Ian was never one to cut to the chase. But after a bit, I asked him why he was calling me.

'Well, not to put too fine a point on it, I'd like you to come back and work at the archive.'

'Me?' I said. 'Am I not the one who destroyed your good name?'

'Well, true,' he said. 'But considering what we went through together, I thought I owed you something. Blood brothers, after an experience like that. Not that you're a brother. Blood siblings. Though you probably don't want to think about blood and siblings together, do you? Well, you know what I mean. And besides, there is a particular reason.'

I asked what it was, and Ian told me. He had been thinking. Tom Cadigan had sworn up and down that the only thing from Alexander Cust's papers he had forged was the novella itself. Everything else was genuine, including Cust's story about meeting Gladden and being given the unsellable manuscript, destined to remain forever a secret. Now we knew, of course, that the *Dog's Ball* we had seen was not the true one, and that, if Cadigan was to be believed, there was no manuscript in the box. That's a big if, but surely not even Cadigan would have destroyed something that could bring him as much money and fame as a *real* lost Green. But that didn't mean there wasn't one out there somewhere. And let's not forget, it was Cadigan's forgery of the Houdini autograph that created the myth of Cust as a crook and a liar. Take that away and, for all we knew, Cust was as honest as the day was long.

And Ian asked, then, if I would be interested in taking up my scholarly interest in Gladden Green where I had left off—and, time permitting, seeing if I couldn't manage to track down the true *Dog's Ball*. It was a project that I was one of the only people in the world qualified to undertake. When he put it like that, I didn't see how I could say no.

And besides, he said, Nancy had left the archive to pursue her media career full-time. The Steel Neele was much in need of a new curator of prose.

ACKNOWLEDGEMENTS

Quite a few people helped with matters great and small; here they are, in alphabetical order. Melissa Barton, Tommy Brown and the staff of Auburn University Special Collections, Darren from the Metropolitan Police, Amy Gentry, Jim Hilgartner, Allie Keith, Jordan Lees (the best agent), Louisa Macnair, Denzil May, Thomson McCorkle, Tom McDonald, Abby McGinn, Michael Meeuwis, Georgia Moseley, Kate Murray-Browne, Robin Pender, Harry Perrin, Zach Pippin, Daniel Seton and all at Pushkin, J. Cameron West and Alexis Wineman. The greatest thanks, of course, go to my wife, Elizabeth Hutcheon, for everything.